MW00510456

FROM CONFRONTATION
TO COVENANTAL PARTNERSHIP

From
CONFRONTATION
to COVENANTAL
PARTNERSHIP

Jews and Christians Reflect
on the Orthodox Rabbinic Statement
To Do the Will of Our Father in Heaven

Edited by
Jehoschua Ahrens, Irving Greenberg and Eugene Korn

Preface by
Karl-Hermann Blickle

Introductions by
Rabbi Shlomo Riskin, Cardinal Timothy Dolan
and Former Archbishop of Canterbury Rowan Williams

Urim Publications
Jerusalem • New York

From Confrontation to Covenantal Partnership:
Jews and Christians Reflect on the Orthodox Rabbinic Statement
To Do the Will of Our Father in Heaven
Edited by Rabbis Jehoschua Ahrens, Irving Greenberg
and Eugene Korn
Preface by Karl-Hermann Blickle
Introductions by Rabbi Shlomo Riskin, Cardinal Timothy Dolan
and Former Archbishop of Canterbury Rowan Williams
Language editor: Michelle Rosen-Oberman

Front cover image: "*Synagoga* and *Ecclesia* in Our Time" by artist
Joshua Koffman was commissioned by Saint Joseph's University in
Philadelphia to mark the fiftieth anniversary of the 1965 Second
Vatican Council declaration *Nostra Aetate* and the 1967 founding
of the university's Institute for Jewish-Catholic Relations.

Typeset by Ariel Walden
Printed in Israel
First Edition
ISBN 978-1-60280-411-1
Published by
Urim Publications
P.O. Box 52287, Jerusalem 9152102 Israel
www.UrimPublications.com

Contents

Contents

THE ORTHODOX RABBINIC
STATEMENT ON CHRISTIANITY

To Do the Will of Our Father in Heaven: Toward a Partnership between Jews and Christians

December 3, 2015

After nearly two millennia of mutual hostility and alienation, we Orthodox Rabbis and teachers of Torah who lead communities, institutions and seminaries in Israel, the United States and Europe recognize the historic opportunity now before us. We seek to do the will of Our Father in Heaven by accepting the hand offered to us by our Christian brothers and sisters. Jews and Christians must work together as partners to address the moral challenges of our era.

1. The Shoah ended 70 years ago. It was the warped climax to centuries of disrespect, oppression and rejection of Jews and the consequent enmity that developed between Jews and Christians. In retrospect it is clear that the failure to break through this contempt and engage in constructive dialogue for the good of humankind weakened resistance to evil forces of anti-Semitism that engulfed the world in murder and genocide.

2. We recognize that since the Second Vatican Council the official teachings of the Catholic Church about Judaism have changed fundamentally and irrevocably. The promulgation of *Nostra Aetate* fifty years ago started the process of reconciliation between our two communities. *Nostra Aetate* and the later official Church Doc-

uments it inspired unequivocally reject any form of anti-Semitism, affirm the eternal Covenant between God and the Jewish people, reject deicide and stress the unique relationship between Christians and Jews, who were called "our elder brothers" by Pope John Paul II and "our fathers in faith" by Pope Benedict XVI. On this basis, Catholics and other Christian officials started an honest dialogue with Jews that has grown during the last five decades. We appreciate the Church's affirmation of Israel's unique place in sacred history and the ultimate world redemption. Today Jews have experienced sincere love and respect from many Christians that have been expressed in many dialogue initiatives, meetings and conferences around the world.

3. As did Maimonides and Yehudah Halevi[1] we acknowledge that the emergence of Christianity in human history is neither an accident nor an error, but the willed divine outcome and gift to the nations. In separating Judaism and Christianity, God willed a separation between partners with significant theological differences, not a separation between enemies. Rabbi Jacob Emden wrote that "Jesus brought a double goodness to the world. On the one hand he strengthened the Torah of Moses majestically . . . and not one of our Sages spoke out more emphatically concerning the immutability of the Torah. On the other hand he removed idols from the nations and obligated them in the seven commandments of Noah so that they would not behave like animals of the field, and instilled them firmly with moral traits. . . . Christians are congregations that work for the sake of heaven who are destined to endure, whose intent is for the sake of heaven and whose reward will not be denied."[2] Rabbi Samson Raphael Hirsch taught us that Christians "have accepted the Jewish Bible of the Old Testament as a book of Divine revelation. They profess their belief in the God of Heaven and Earth as proclaimed in the Bible and they acknowledge the sovereignty of Divine Providence."[3] Now that the Catholic Church has acknowledged the eternal Covenant between God and Israel, we Jews can acknowledge the ongoing constructive validity of Christianity as our partner in world redemption, without any fear that this will be

exploited for missionary purposes. As stated by the Chief Rabbinate of Israel's Bilateral Commission with the Holy See under the leadership of Rabbi Shear Yashuv Cohen, "We are no longer enemies, but unequivocal partners in articulating the essential moral values for the survival and welfare of humanity."[4] Neither of us can achieve God's mission in this world alone.

4. Both Jews and Christians have a common covenantal mission to perfect the world under the sovereignty of the Almighty, so that all humanity will call on His name and abominations will be removed from the earth. We understand the hesitation of both sides to affirm this truth and we call on our communities to overcome these fears in order to establish a relationship of trust and respect. Rabbi Hirsch also taught that the Talmud puts Christians "with regard to the duties between man and man on exactly the same level as Jews. They have a claim to the benefit of all the duties not only of justice but also of active human brotherly love." In the past, relations between Christians and Jews were often seen through the adversarial relationship of Esau and Jacob, yet Rabbi Naftali Zvi Berliner (Netziv) already understood at the end of the 19th century that Jews and Christians are destined by God to be loving partners: "In the future when the children of Esau are moved by pure spirit to recognize the people of Israel and their virtues, then we will also be moved to recognize that Esau is our brother."[5]

5. We Jews and Christians have more in common than what divides us: the ethical monotheism of Abraham; the relationship with the One Creator of Heaven and Earth, Who loves and cares for all of us; Jewish Sacred Scriptures; a belief in a binding tradition; and the values of life, family, compassionate righteousness, justice, inalienable freedom, universal love and ultimate world peace. Rabbi Moses Rivkis (Be'er Hagoleh) confirms this and wrote that "the Sages made reference only to the idolator of their day who did not believe in the creation of the world, the Exodus, God's miraculous deeds and the divinely given law. In contrast, the people among whom we are scattered believe in all these essentials of religion."[6]

6. Our partnership in no way minimizes the ongoing differences between the two communities and two religions. We believe that God employs many messengers to reveal His truth, while we affirm the fundamental ethical obligations that all people have before God that Judaism has always taught through the universal Noahide covenant.

7. In imitating God, Jews and Christians must offer models of service, unconditional love and holiness. We are all created in God's Holy Image, and Jews and Christians will remain dedicated to the Covenant by playing an active role together in redeeming the world.

NOTES

1. Mishneh Torah, Laws of Kings 11:4 (uncensored edition); The Kuzari, section 4:22

2. *Seder Olam Rabbah* 35–37; *Sefer ha-Shimush* 15–17.

3. *Principles of Education*, "Talmudic Judaism and Society," 225–227.

4. Fourth meeting of the Bilateral Commission of the Chief Rabbinate of Israel and the Holy See's Commission for Religious Relations with Jewry, Grottaferrata, Italy (October 19, 2004).

5. Commentary on Genesis 33:4.

6. Gloss on *Shulhan Arukh, Hoshen Mishpat*, Section 425:5.

INITIAL SIGNATORIES (IN ALPHABETICAL ORDER):

Rabbi Jehoschua Ahrens (Germany)
Rabbi Marc Angel (United States)
Rabbi Isak Asiel (Chief Rabbi of Serbia)
Rav David Bigman (Israel)
Rabbi David Bollag (Switzerland)
Rabbi David Brodman (Israel)
Rabbi Nathan Lopes Cardozo (Israel)
Rav Yehudah Gilad (Israel)
Rabbi Alon Goshen-Gottstein (Israel)
Rabbi Irving Greenberg (United States)
Rabbi Marc Raphael Guedj (Switzerland)
Rabbi Eugene Korn (Israel)
Rabbi Daniel Landes (Israel)
Rabbi Steven Langnas (Germany)
Rabbi Benjamin Lau (Israel)
Rabbi Simon Livson (Chief Rabbi of Finland)
Rabbi Asher Lopatin (United States)
Rabbi Shlomo Riskin (Israel)
Rabbi David Rosen (Israel)
Rabbi Naftali Rothenberg (Israel)
Rabbi Hanan Schlesinger (Israel)
Rabbi Shmuel Sirat (France)
Rabbi Daniel Sperber (Israel)
Rabbi Jeremiah Wohlberg (United States)
Rabbi Alan Yuter (Israel)

SUBSEQUENT SIGNATORIES (IN ALPHABETICAL ORDER):

Rabbi Yitzhak Ajzner (Israel)
Rabbi Levi Alter (USA)
Rabbanit Nechama Goldman Barash (Israel)
Prof. Shraga Bar On (Israel)
Rabbi David Bauman (USA)
Rabbi Abraham Benhamu (Peru)
Dr. Adena Berkowitz (USA)
Rabbi Todd Berman (Israel)
Rabbi Michael Beyo (USA)
Rose Britton (USA)
Rabbi Michael Chernick (USA)
Rabbi Kolel DaDon (Chief Rabbi of Croatia)
Rabbi Barry Dollinger (USA)
Rabbi Josef Douziech (Canada)
Rabbi David Ellis (Canada)
Rabbanit Devorah Evron (Israel)
Rabbi Seth Farber (Israel)
Rabbi Miriam Sara Feigelson (Israel)
Rabbi Michael Feuer (Israel)
Rabbi David Freilech (Australia)
Rabbi Shaul Friberg (Germany)
Rabbi Daniel Geretz (USA)
Rabbi Ariel Goldberg (USA)
Rabbi Daniel Goodman (USA)
Rabbi Mark Gottlieb (USA)
Rabbi Mel Gottlieb (USA)
Rabbi Ben Greenberg (USA)
Rabbi Steve Greenberg (USA)
Rabbi David be Meir Hasson (Chile)
Rabbi Joel Hecker (USA)
Rabbi Herzl Hefter (Israel)
Rabbi Zvi Herberger (Norway/Estonia)
Rabbi Brad Hirschfeld (USA)
Rabbi Yeshayahu Hollander (Israel)
Rabbi Elie Holzer (Israel)
Rabba Batya Riskin Jacobs (Israel)
Rabbi David Jaffe (USA)
Rabbi David Kalb (USA)
Rabbi Shaya Kilimnick (USA)
Rabbi Reuven Kimelman (USA)
Rabbi Frederick Klein (USA)
Rabbi Joseph Kolakowski (USA)
Rabbi Doniel Kramer (USA)
Rabbi Aaron Leibowitz (Israel)
Rabbi Hayim Leiter (Israel)
Rabbi Yehoshua Looks (Israel)
Rabbi Ronen Lubitch (Israel)
Rabbi Ariel Mayse (USA)
Rabbi Jair Melchior (Chief Rabbi of Denmark)
Rabbi Alon Meltzer (Australia)
Rabbi Daniel Milner (USA)

Rabbi Ari Montanari (USA)
Rabbi Alain Nacache (Chief Rabbi of Luxembourg)
Rosh Kehillah Dina Najman (USA)
Rabbi Gabriel Negrin (Chief Rabbi of Greece)
Rabbi Yonatan Neril (Israel)
Rabbi Bryan Opert (S. Africa)
Rabbi David Rose (UK)
Rabbi Avram Rosenfeld (USA)
Rabbi Zeev Rubins (Germany)
Rabbi Elisha Salas (Portugal)
Dr. Shana Strauch Schick (Israel)
Rabbi Menachem Sebbag (Netherlands)

Rabbi Chaim Seidler-Feller (USA)
Dr. Faydra Shapiro (Israel)
Rabbi Daniel Sherbill (USA)
Rabbi Yair Silverman (Israel)
Rabbi Daniel Raphael Silverstein (USA)
Prof. Malka Simkovitch (USA)
Rabbi Zvi Solomons (UK)
Rabbi Nahum Twersky (USA)
Rabbi Mashada Vaivsaunu (Armenia)
Rabbi Avraham Walfish (Israel)
Rabbi Avraham Weiss (USA)
Rabbi Shmuel Yanklowitz (USA)
Dr. Dov S. Zakheim (USA)
Rabbi Lawrence Zierler (USA)

Preface
and
Introductions

Preface

On the Orthodox Rabbinic Statement on Christianity from the Perspective of the Stuttgart Lehrhaus Foundation for Interreligious Dialogue

KARL-HERMANN BLICKLE

From the perspective of the Stuttgart Lehrhaus Foundation, which has supported the publication of this book as well as from my own perspective as the Chairman of the Foundation, with decades of active engagement in interreligious, mostly Jewish – Christian dialogue, I wish to make three key remarks.

First, addressing the authors of the Statement, I wish to express my deepest gratitude to the Orthodox rabbis who wrote and signed *To Do The Will Of Our Father In Heaven,* not only in the name of our interreligious foundation, but also as a Protestant Christian. Like *Dabru Emet*, the Statement has particular historical relevance, since it is not just one person but a whole group of Orthodox rabbis who are taking a stance on Christianity – and doing so in a spirit of partnership and brotherliness. It is vitally important that the Statement comes from an inner Jewish Orthodox circle, since Orthodoxy is at the core of Judaism and argues from the depth of its tradition. As a Protestant Christian participating on a historical path with holders of Orthodox Jewish beliefs who incorporate Jewish tradition gives me enormous joy on interfaith monotheistic togetherness.

My second point addressed my sisters and brothers in Christian belief. The Jewish response: "accepting the hand offered to us by our

Christian brothers and sisters" (in the Statement's preface) calls for a Christian response in return. On January 8, 2017, an important conference on the Orthodox Rabbinic Statement on Christianity took place at the University of Jewish Studies in Heidelberg in cooperation with the Stuttgart Lehrhaus Foundation. On that day, the daily reading of the Moravian Church was a New Testament text, Matthew 4: 8–10, with a quotation by Jesus: "... for it is written (Deut. 6:13), 'Worship the Lord your God, and serve only him." This answer by Jesus to the devil tempting him was a quotation from the Torah, and as such it unambiguously shows that Jesus – as a Jew – was devoted to strict monotheism and never considered himself equal to God. If Orthodox Jews choose to walk a mutual path with us Christians, then we Christians should remember the Jewish-monotheistic roots of our own belief. For example, when we say "Lord" in a prayer service, we may not know, or perhaps leave open, whether we mean "Lord Jesus" or "Lord God." I believe we should follow the example of Jesus instead, who taught us in the "Our Father" prayer to exclusively pray to God the father, and therefore to consistently believe in and practice monotheism. In this we take up the "common covenantal mission to perfect the world under the sovereignty of the Almighty, so that all humanity will call on His name and abominations will be removed from the earth" (in paragraph 4 of the Statement). I am aware that my inner-Christian request for a "non-anti-Jewish Christology" is a far from easy position, but I believe that we Christians should pursue this in light of our Jewish roots and Jesus the Jew's belief in the ONE God of Israel.

My third remark on the Orthodox Rabbinic Statement concerns Muslims. Our Stuttgart Lehrhaus Foundation is dedicated to cooperation between the three Abrahamic religions: Judaism, Christianity and Islam. As much as I appreciate the Orthodox Rabbinic Statement on Christianity and accept it with great emotion, it is equally important that it should not be used against Islam, and not be instrumentalized as a Jewish-Christian alliance against Muslims. Our mission at the Foundation has to be a trialogue between Christian, Jews and Muslims, and the building of solidarity between all the Abrahamitic faiths, including the youngest. This is the most important legacy of our Foundation's Jewish co-founder Meinhard Mordechai Tenne, who was Honorary Chairman of the Jewish Community in Wuerttemberg (IRGW) and active member in the Central Council of Jews in Germany. Mordechai Tenne wholeheartedly supported the reformation of the Lehrhaus as a foundation, following the tradition of the former Jewish Study House in Stuttgart, founded in 1926 by Martin Buber, Otto Hirsch and Karl Adler. However he participated in the new Stuttgart Lehrhaus Foundation only on one condition: that Muslims would be involved as well, and that the Jewish-Christian dialogue in the Lehrhaus would be expanded to a Jewish-Christian-Muslim trialogue. He encouraged Foundation members, including my wife and me to open up to Islam.

We look forward to expanding the trialogue legacy of Meinhard Mordechai Tenne in the future.

A Jewish Introduction

Rabbi Shlomo Riskin

A decade ago, God put in my heart to establish the first Orthodox Jewish institution to religiously dialogue and cooperate with Christians – the Center for Jewish-Christian Understanding and Cooperation (CJCUC). It was no easy task. Many within Orthodox Judaism were not ready for an institutional response toward Christianity. The wounds of the past of what the Church did in the name of Jesus toward the members of the Synagogue prevented some from entering into a positive relationship with a Christian. Others felt that the remnant of Christians who stand with Israel and the Jewish people have a hidden ulterior motive to convert the Jews to Christianity. There are those who feel on principle that Judaism needs to keep its distance from other faith communities, while others sense that in a collective post-traumatic period after an event like the Holocaust, there is more to do in rehabilitating the Jewish community before entering into a dialogue with other faiths.

As the CJCUC advanced its relationships with Christian leaders and laity from traditional denominations as well as the non-denominational movements, we always made it a point to speak about the importance of the Jewish-Christian alliance to other Jews. Slowly, we saw a transformation from within Orthodox Jewry. What began with reactions of apprehension and suspicion changed as many Jews began to appreciate the theological advances and proactive support for Israel from the Christian community.

In May of 2015, there was a major gathering in Israel of rabbis, cardinals, and priests in Israel sponsored by the Neocatechumenal Way of the Catholic Church at the Domus Galilaeae International Center. Those in attendance included CJCUC's Academic Director Rabbi Dr. Eugene Korn, Rabbi David Rosen of the American Jewish Committee, Jewish theologian Rabbi Dr. Irving Greenberg, and my former rabbinical student Rabbi Jehoschua Ahrens. The seeds of drafting some type of positive statement on Christianity were planted. Over the next six months, various drafts of the Statement were written and by November it was finally taking shape. The final drafts were reviewed by CJCUC's Executive Director David Nekrutman and me.

On December 3, 2015, we published *To Do the Will of Our Father in Heaven: Toward a Partnership between Jews and Christians*, the first positive Orthodox rabbinical statement on Christianity. The Statement rests on the firm foundation of *Halakhah* (Orthodox Jewish law) and precedent. Beginning with 25 rabbinical signatories, more rabbis from around the world signed their names to it. In less than two weeks, we had over 60 rabbinical figures sign the Statement.

No one could have predicted the massive media attention to it. This could be attributed to the historic nature of such a document, combined with the 50th anniversary of official dialogue between the Catholic Church and the Jewish people. As you will learn in this book, another possible contributing factor for popular attention to the Statement was caused by distorted headlines such as "Orthodox Rabbis Bring Jesus Home for Christmas." Some agenda-driven Christians, overly enthusiastic and misunderstanding the Statement, thought rabbis had rejected Judaism and accepted Christianity in its place. Due to these headlines going viral, CJCUC then had to publish a clarification about the Statement. However, I believe the Statement had a divine timing to it and the people who came together to draft it were operating for the sake of Heaven.

When we combine the past rabbinic appreciation of Christianity with today's non-replacement Christian theologies toward Judaism, we find fresh possibilities for rethinking a Jewish relationship with

Christianity in pursuit of common biblical values. Of course, this new relationship requires that Christians respect the right of all Jewish peoples to exist as Jews with complete self-determination – free from any attempts of conversion to Christianity.

At the same time, Judaism must respect Christian faithfulness to their revelation, value their role in divine history, and acknowledge that Christians have entered a relationship with the God of Israel. In our pre-eschaton days, God has more than enough blessings to bestow upon all of His children.

In *A Tale of Two Cities*, Charles Dickens begins with "It was the best of times, it was the worst of times. . . ." Indeed, we as the Jewish people are living in "the best of times" by witnessing the confirmation of God's promise to Israel, the beginning of the sprouting of redemption, with our return to our national homeland. We are seeing the fulfillment of God's promises as stated in Deuteronomy 30:4–5: "Even if your exiles are at the ends of the earth, He will gather you and bring you back from there. The Lord your God will bring you into the land your fathers possessed, and you will take possession of it. He will cause you to prosper and multiply you more than He did your fathers."

We are also "living in the worst of times," because the world is being threatened by yet another global war, this time with the extremist enemy speaking in religious terms of jihad and the will of Allah. We are at the brink of redemption and at the precipice of world destruction. The rapprochement – mutual love and respect – between Jews and Christians could not have come at a more fateful and opportune period. If we can work together, join forces with moderate Islam, and provide a model for a peaceful world perfected under the Majesty of the God of Love, perhaps we can realize the prophetic dream of Zephaniah: "For then will I restore to the people a pure language, that they may all call upon the name of the Lord, to serve him with one accord" (3:9).

I wish to thank the original authors of the Statement, the rabbis who were courageous in signing it, and my staff for their instrumental role in promoting it. In addition, I wish to express my sincere gratitude to Karl-Hermann Blickle for underwriting this book. Karl is truly a servant of God and his friendship has enriched my life. Lastly, I wish to thank my dear student, Rabbi Jehoschua Ahrens, for his boldness in making this Statement become a reality. May this book become a springboard for more advanced relations between Jews and Christians.

A Catholic Introduction

CARDINAL TIMOTHY DOLAN

It is a privilege to write this introduction as a way of expressing my encouragement to the signatories of the 2015 Orthodox Rabbis' Statement, *To Do the Will of Our Father in Heaven* (*TDW*). My congratulations also extends to all the contributing authors in this book – Jewish and Christian scholars who have identified a new moment in the relationship between our two covenantal religions. Together, these thinkers intend to widen the conversation between Catholics and Orthodox Jews, and to build on the opportunity for further dialogue set in motion by *TDW*. As Archbishop of New York – home to the largest neighboring communities of Jews and Catholics in the U.S. – I am deeply gratified to share in their work and achievement.

From a Catholic standpoint, *TDW* must be viewed as a Jewish response to the call of the Second Vatican Council's declaration, *Nostra Aetate* (1965), inaugurating a new era in Jewish-Catholic relations. Rabbis since then have acknowledged how *Nostra Aetate* has opened their eyes to the fundamental and irreversible transformation of the Catholic Church's attitude toward Judaism and the Jewish people. *Nostra Aetate* moved Catholic teaching away from conflict with Judaism to an affirmation of God's enduring faithfulness to his covenant with Jews. Over the past half century, this development has inspired an even broader partnership between Jews and other Christians based on friendship, mutual learning and a shared commitment to *Tikkun Olam*, or the building up of a more just and peaceful world.

As Pope, the Bishop of Rome has a special role in fostering unity among all Christians. He teaches with a unique authority in concert with his predecessors and all his brother Bishops throughout the world. The providential developments we have seen in Jewish-Christian relations, then, further enhance my admiration for the five popes of the 20th century who carried forward the Council's mandate to increase understanding between Catholics and Jews. Each of these men has made a unique contribution to the work envisioned by *Nostra Aetate.*

In Pope Saint John XXIII (d. 1963), the Second Vatican Council was convoked and encouraged to become the forum for revolutionary reflections on the relationship of the Church with Jews. Pope St. Paul VI (d. 1978) then personally intervened to assure the Council's passage of *Nostra Aetate* against significant opposition. In the nearly thirty years that followed, Pope St. John Paul II linked the expression of heartfelt repentance to the message of *Nostra Aetate* with many moving, public apologies to the Jewish people for Christian mistreatment. Surely his stunning example of *teshuva* at both the Western Wall and Yad Vashem remains a memorable symbol of a desire for reconciliation and renewal.

The profound theological reflections of Pope Benedict XVI, made on his visits to Auschwitz, Jerusalem, and the great synagogue of Rome in the footsteps of John Paul II, demonstrate that a lasting change of heart has taken place in the papacy itself. In our own day, the warmth and friendship of our present Holy Father, Pope Francis, for his many Jewish colleagues and friends is acknowledged worldwide. Affirmed again and again by his own travels in the legacy of John Paul and Benedict, Pope Francis' unique love for the Jewish people springs from friendships cultivated over an entire lifetime from Argentina to Rome.

As a result, we can say with confidence that Jews and Catholics are today in a new situation, guided by a new appreciation of a shared hearing of the Word of God. The Catholic Church no longer sees Jews as the enemies of Jesus, but rather as members of the one family of Abraham and Moses into which Christians have been adopted. Such a rediscovery of St. Paul's teaching as found in his letter to the Romans chapters 9 to 11 has opened both communities to a healing of painful memories and a renewed desire to walk together on a path of partnership and mutual esteem. In this way, do we not fulfill our common mandate to do the will of the Heavenly Father?

In 2007 I accompanied rabbis and fellow bishops on a visit to Nazi death camps in Poland. What awaited us there was unforgettable: the all-too-real memory of the horrors inflicted on Jews as inmates, slave laborers and, ultimately, as victims of gas chambers and crematoria. Together, we learned how the Nazis diabolically exploited past expressions of anti-Semitism found within Christian preaching and catechesis. We saw how easily human beings can confuse a *Furher* with God, a *Reich* with a family, and a traitor with a neighbor. Nazi idolaters created a thousand hells whose names echo still today: Treblinka, Mauthausen, Dachau, Chelmno and Auschwitz. Silent, we stood in this darkness as Jews and Christians, only to weep and then embrace. It was then that I felt a deep gratitude toward the popes who had put the Catholic Church of our day on a sure path of reconciliation and had resolved to uproot every form of anti-Semitism that draws its poison from misreading Christian sources. Our common witness became a powerful assurance that "Never again!" had worked its way into our Catholic identity. No longer would complicity or apathy in the face of such a crime against Jews be sanctioned or tolerated.

From Poland we traveled on to Rome, arriving in the Eternal City shortly after the death of Pope St. John Paul II. Again, we wept and prayed, but now to console each other on the loss of one whose own passing had somehow bridged centuries of contempt and reminded us of how far we had traveled to become friends. John Paul's accomplishments were hard to number: establishing full diplomatic relations with the State of Israel; empowering the Pontifical Commission for Religious Relations with the Jews; visiting Jewish communities across the world; repeatedly expressing regret for Christian aggression against Jews; publicly confronting Catholics whose anti-Semitism had contributed to Jewish suffering, and praying over and again at the holy sites in Jerusalem. Surely these achievements put the lie to the error-filled theology that saw centuries of Jewish homelessness as punishment for a refusal to recognize Jesus as the *Mashiach* (messiah). John Paul II taught the Catholic faithful to embrace Jews as our elder brothers and sisters in the never-revoked covenant of Abraham. Now, when Catholics speak to Jews, they address members of their own family.

Over the past fifty-five years, the Catholic Church has vigorously pursued a process of reconciliation with Jews across nations and cultures. Driven by the horror and shame of the Holocaust, the Church has acted to remove the vestiges of anti-Judaism found within her teaching, her institutions and even her liturgy that may have helped set the stage for the Shoah. At the heart of this effort is dialogue: the continuous conversation between all segments of both communities when and wherever possible. Today, the U.S. is gratefully home to three formal dialogues between the USCCB and representatives of diverse rabbinic groups. These exchanges are essential for another reason: the mutual re-discovery of Jewish and Catholic identities, freed from centuries of oppression and victimization which disguised and distorted not only the religious "other," but the true "self" of each. John Paul II was clear that this process, which he termed "a purification of memory," would demand courage on both sides. It is everyone's hope that this effort will bring to an end a past of continuous rivalry and build, instead, a future of lasting friendship.

The Orthodox Rabbis' document, *To Do the Will of Our Heavenly Father,* then emerges as a remarkable and unexpected gift to the on-going dialogue between the two religions. As a statement from the heart, it acknowledges that the Catholic Church in particular may now be considered a true partner in the work of welcoming God's kingdom because it has demonstrated a profound and authentic *teshuvah,* or conversion of heart, that refuses to return to previous expressions of anti-Judaism. In light of this, *TDW* boldly affirms the dignity of Christian believers generally and expresses appreciation for Christianity and its contribution to humanity. It recognizes not only that Christianity is a divinely willed gift to the world, but also an instrument for carrying out God's plan of redemption for all people. This new perspective calls for and enables a providential partnership for pursuing the truth in love for one another and for the other members of the human family.

A central affirmation of *To Do the Will of the Father* is that both faiths are "unequivocal partners" in voicing "the essential moral values" needed "for the survival and welfare of humanity." Once very much apart, we now freely share our witness to God and human dignity so often at risk in the face of today's nihilism and relativism. Jew or Christian, we strive as fellow believers to strengthen humanity's trust in God, protecting it against the threat of moral anarchy. But the rabbis' statement reaches even further, showing how our shared moral voice rises from "a common covenantal mission to perfect the world under the sovereignty of the Almighty." Isn't this very idea also echoed in Pope Francis' repeated call to honor human fraternity and to deepen our care of the world's poor? As well, his compelling 2015 encyclical, *Laudato si* ("Praise be to You, My Lord"), reminds us that in Genesis we were made stewards, not profiteers of creation. Such a Jewish-Christian partnership, then, would enable us all to touch "the better angels of our nature" and to see the worth of every human being fashioned in the image and likeness of God. Because it is the Holy One of Israel who seeks us out, we must look to join God in the repair of the world and become together a light for all nations.

Orthodox Jews can undertake this mission with Catholics because both are committed to the word of God as found in Sacred Scripture. Both traditions know that what Jews call the "Oral Torah" and what Catholics refer to as "Sacred Tradition" are their respective lenses for seeing God's revelation come alive in thought and practice. Both are also committed to the Bible's ethical norms as authoritative guidelines for answering modernity's many unsettling questions. Both reflect upon the prophet Micah's (6:6) plea, "What does God ask of us?" in order to take their places in the divine plan at all times. Lastly, their leaders and scholars can offer us a sure and steady wisdom, ready to engage the world no matter its need.

As an exploration of our shared heritage, I welcome the reflections on *TDW* by the Jewish and Christian contributors to this important volume. My own hope is that other scholars, clergy and laity – especially among the young – will use this book as a basis for their own inquiries and on-going dialogues. May this effort inspire many more Christians and Jews to travel this providential path of mutual learning, so that all can grow in the faith to which they've been called. Let future generations then join together to become more effective channels of witness to all of humanity: "Each will help his fellow; to his brother he will say 'be strong.'" (Isaiah 41:6)

A Protestant Introduction

FORMER ARCHBISHOP OF CANTERBURY
ROWAN WILLIAMS

In the world of internal Christian conversation between the historic Christian confessions or denominations, you will sometimes hear discussion about whether the divisions between Christians are simply a disaster or are in some sense opportunities. When Catholics and Protestants separated at the Reformation, the results were violent and lastingly damaging – not only to the communities who suffered violence, but to the credibility of Christian faith itself. Yet some who now look back at this will say that both sides of the conflict represented an aspect, a dimension of Christian identity that needed to be understood more deeply than it had been before. Opposition between Christians was destructive, but it sharpened understanding of certain themes – and perhaps reminded all Christians in the long run of the great difficulty of encapsulating the whole of the divine mystery and the divine purpose in just one community or tradition. As the memory of violent confrontation recedes and Christians become freer to acknowledge to each other the hurt inflicted and seek some kind of forgiveness, the development of separated communities becomes an opportunity to see some things more clearly. Not that God directly "wills" the separation, let alone the violence; but the Almighty is able to use the results of human confusion, even the human eagerness to find and to demonize enemies, so as eventually to deepen our vision of the divine reality and the sense of our calling in response to the divine self-communication.

Reading the essays in this very remarkable book suggests that all this might be a remote but not completely artificial analogy to how Jewish-Christian relations could develop, if once we could let go of a straightforward "zero-sum" model of their encounter. The writers of the Statement *To Do the Will of Our Father in Heaven* proposed, notoriously and controversially, that the existence of Christianity might be more than merely an error – that (following Maimonides) the divine purpose could use and work with aspects of the narrative of Jesus and the growth of the Church to achieve what the Jewish people alone could not achieve. To put it another way, there might be a Jewish story of the divine purpose unfolding in history which included the story of the Church – even while identifying the Church's errors and failings in both doctrine and practice.

In the light of the consistent and horrendous cost to the Jewish people of the existence of the Christian Church across most of two millennia, this is a perspective of startling generosity. It certainly does not say that differences between Judaism and Christianity are superficial or insignificant; it would echo Maimonides' own belief that Christianity would have to change radically before any true convergence was possible. But it acknowledges some sense in which we can think of a diversity of vocation in the Almighty's dealings with humankind, a diversity in which no one person and no one community has to do everything, but all are summoned to seek to do the will of the Almighty as best they are able.

So these essays pose a question to both communities. Granted that both have an overarching story of the shape of God's healing purpose, how is it possible for Jews and Christians to tell their stories in such a way that – on the one hand – the "outsider," the Other, is acknowledged as having a legitimate place, and – on the other – that Other is not misrepresented or co-opted into a frame of reference that denies their integrity? Christians have routinely assumed that the Christian narrative simply relativizes if not abrogates the lived reality of Jewish experience: Jewish identity is, theologically, a thing of the past, and contemporary Jewish reflection and life play little if any part in how Christians make sense of Jewish reality now. Tropes and myths from that imagined past can be deployed against Jews today, against the state of Israel, against fantasies of Jewish political and economic influence and so on, but there is no real attention paid to how Jews think about themselves. But it is also true that, however understandably, Jewish attitudes often assume things about Christian thought and practice that bear no relation to what Christians themselves think they are doing or believing. Ultimately the issue is whether both communities are capable of a new level of attention to each other, not hurrying to an all-embracing theory of how everything might "come together," but learning more of how – for example, people actually, concretely, read Scripture, what certain devotional disciplines actually mean for practitioners, and, not least, how each community inherits images and narratives about the other that need to be brought to light and thought through afresh.

This is a hard but not hopeless task. There are small groups here and there (I think of one such in Manchester in the UK) that set for themselves the task of reading together classic texts of contemporary Christian and Jewish reflection, naming and exploring the points of deep tension and historic misunderstanding – not "negotiating" some sort of settlement, but simply opening up to illumination and challenge. The work of a Christian biblical scholar like W.D. Davies or a theologian like Katherine Sonderegger, the thinking of Jewish interpreters, philosophers and spiritual guides like Joseph Soloveitchik (much discussed in these pages), Shear Yashuv Cohen, Michael Wyschogrod and others – to study and absorb these in company, in a climate of trust and attentiveness, is a great gift for all those who have experienced it. There is an urgent need for this to be encouraged at local level – though for this to happen, much needs doing to make sure that such a group encounter will genuinely be a safe place, where myths and prejudices are confronted and set aside. This means that Christians have a special responsibility to examine some of their familiar vocabulary and to "hear" it with Jewish ears for a moment, because it has been Christians who have, since the first Christian century, been in the position of power and advantage and have refused to imagine how their language sounds to the Jewish neighbor.

As many of these essays argue, there remains a solid core of common history and language. The God of Hebrew Scripture is a God who heals the fractured creation by his own commitment to its ongoing life – centered uniquely in the commitment, the covenant, with Israel, of which the promise of the Land is a lasting sign. The Christian should not be disputing a word of this; but the Christian also claims that this covenanted divine presence is in turn uniquely active in the life of Jesus, in such a way that association with him allows non-Jews to enter a covenantal relation with God and to know God as Father, in the way that Jesus claims to know God – a claim not at odds with Jewish history but presented originally by Christians as the fullest possible realization of the covenantal relation between God and Israel. Within the territory marked out by these beliefs, there will be ongoing disagreements, sometimes very radical; but there is a language in which thoughtful disagreement is possible, and mutual learning can happen. If we can thus learn to tell our stories in a way that leaves room for the Other to be who they are, each community granting that they cannot yet see how God will bring both stories to fulfilment, something may be done to mend the appalling history generated by the original moment of separation and the arrogant Christian assumption that the Jewish story is over. The very fact of the Statement *To Do the Will of Our Father in Heaven* bears witness to the life and vigor of Orthodox thinking, still capable of fresh, powerful and illuminating insight; and for that we can together give thanks to the One Lord, the God of Abraham, Isaac and Jacob, who keeps his promise for ever and "in whose will is our peace."

I. Background and Implications of *To Do the Will of Our Father in Heaven*

To Do the Will of Our Father in Heaven
The Emergence of the Orthodox Rabbinic Statement to Christianity from a European Perspective

Jehoschua Ahrens

It came as quite a surprise to many when a group of leading Orthodox rabbis published the pioneering statement *To Do the Will of Our Father in Heaven* (henceforth *TDW*) at the end of 2015, which advocated a close partnership with Christians and so marked a historic reset of the relationship between the religions. In the following introductory essay, I will take a closer look at the context, origin, and reception of the Statement from a European perspective, and briefly describe current discussions and developments.

To better understand why Orthodox rabbis published the Statement at that time and in that form, it is necessary to look back at history. As described in the preface of the Statement, for a long time the relationship between Jews and Christians was characterized by hostility and alienation – mainly due to the hatred of Jews by the Christian majority. The Shoah marked the final, negative climax of centuries of contempt, oppression, and rejection of Jews, as mentioned in paragraph 1 of *TDW*. The Churches and Christians played their part in this. Theological anti-Judaism, such as demonizing the *Talmud*, accusations of host desecration, allegations of ritual murder, and alleged well poisonings, were used by the Churches whenever opportune for them. There was also irrational ethnic hatred towards Jews. Together, these formed the basis for modern racial anti-Semitism.[1]

THE LONG PATH TOWARDS DIALOGUE

At the time of the Enlightenment and emancipation, there was a glimmer of hope on the Jewish side that Jews and Christians could approach each other not only as citizens but also religiously, and could someday be equal partners. As examples, I would like to point to three rabbis:

• Rabbi Jacob Emden, *the* rabbinic authority in Germany and Europe in the 18th century, who *halakhically* valued Christianity very positively and even described Christians as brothers who work for the sake of heaven and whose reward would not be denied.[2]

• Rabbi David Zvi Hoffmann, who in the 19th century promoted unity between Jewish and "Christian fellow citizens" and sharply rejected the allegation that Christians were idol worshippers.[3]

• Rabbi Samson Raphael Hirsch, who also in the 19th century envisioned a symbiosis of German culture and Judaism, and placed Christians in all respects on a par with Jews, with a claim to "active human brotherly love."[4]

Hopes for a religious approach were disappointed, however. The Churches never positively responded to Jewish initiatives. On the

---

1. Johannes Heil, "Die Bürde der Geschichte: Stationen der langlebigen 'Lehre der Verachtung,'" in Ahrens et. al. (Ed.), *Hin zu einer Partnerschaft zwischen Juden und Christen: Die Erklärung orthodoxer Rabbiner zum Christentum* (Metropol Verlag, Berlin, 2017).

2. Cf. *Seder Olam Rabba* and *Sefer HaShimush*; cited in *TDW*.

3. Rabbi Dr. David Zvi Hoffmann, *Der Schulchan Aruch und die Rabbinen über das Verhältnis zu Andersgläubigen.*

4. Rabbi Samson Raphael Hirsch, Beziehungen des Talmud zum Judentum und zu der sozialen Stellung seiner Bekenner; Matthias Morgenstern, "Rabbi. S. R. Hirsch and his Perception of Germany and German Jewry," in Aschheim/Liska (Eds.), *The German-Jewish Experience Revisited* (de Gruyter, Berlin/Boston, 2015). Hirsch is also cited in *TDW*.

contrary, Liberal-Protestant circles within the Churches even intensified their rejection of Judaism in the 19th and early 20th centuries.[5] Unlike in the USA, Jewish initiatives for dialogue in Europe tended to come from Orthodox, not Liberal circles. Orthodoxy regarded Christianity as an equal, and wanted dialogue at eye level. Liberal rabbis like Ludwig Philippson viewed Judaism as a rational religion superior to the "mystic religion" of Christianity. It was Philippson's belief that the differences between Christianity and Judaism were too wide to permit dialogue.[6]

This continued until after the Shoah. In Europe, the early pioneers of dialogue on the Jewish side mainly came from the Orthodox traditional spectrum, and decisively paved the way for the institutionalization of dialogue. As examples, we can name the following: Selig Brodetsky (Professor of Mathematics and Chairman of the Board of Deputies of British Jews), Adolph G. Brotman (Secretary of the Board of Deputies of British Jews), Dr. Georg Guggenheim (Chairman of the Israelitischen Cultusgemeinde Zürich), Dr. Meyer A. Halevy (Rabbi of the Choral Synagogue Bucharest), Dr. Joseph H. Hertz (Chief Rabbi of the British Empire), Dr. Fabian Herkovits (Rabbi in Budapest), Dr. Maurice Jaffe (Rabbi of the British Army), Dr. Jacob Kaplan (Chief Rabbi of France), Dr. Alexandre Safran (Chief Rabbi of Romania, later of Geneva), Dr. Zwi Chaim Taubes (Chief Rabbi of Zurich), and Dr. Georges Vadnai (Secretary General of the Union Mondiale des Etudiants Juifs, later Chief Rabbi of Lausanne).

All the above participated in at least one of the first three international Christian-Jewish conferences 1946–1948. All expedited the foundation of the International Council of Christians and Jews and were either founding members of, or actively engaged in, lo-

---

5. W. Kinzig, *Harnack, Marcion und das Judentum* (Leipzig 2004: Evangelische Verlagsanstalt), 20; Hans Martin Kirn, "Schleiermachers Stellungnahme zur Judenemanzipation" in Barth et.al (Ed.) *Christentum und Judentum: Akten des Internationalen Kongresses der Schleiermacher-Gesellschaft in Halle, März 2009* (Berlin/Boston: de Gruyter, 2015), 204–205; Tal Uriel, *Christians and Jews in Germany: Religion, politics and ideology in the Second Reich 1870–1914* (Ithaca: Cornell Univ. Press 1975) 163f.

6. Ludwig Philippson, "Vergleichende Skizzen über Judentum und Christentum" in: *Gesammelte Abhandlungen: Band I,* (Leipzig 1911), 199–324.

cal or national Christian-Jewish associations or councils in Great Britain, France, Switzerland, Romania, or Hungary. Thus they did the groundwork for the dialogue we know today. Orthodox rabbis were particularly visionary about dialogue. For example, as early as during World War II, Rabbi Taubes wrote a leading essay supporting a trialogue between Jews, Christians, and Muslims. The Orthodox rabbis hoped that the catastrophe of the Shoah would lead to fast and enduring changes in the theology of the Churches concerning Judaism and Jews. But even though there were several successes, like the theses adopted at the Seelisberg Conference in 1947, and in spite of several engaged individuals or circles within the Churches, nothing much changed.

Even in Germany, the country of the perpetrators, the Churches failed to recognize any particular co-responsibility for the Shoah, nor did they find it necessary to change their theology. The well-known *Stuttgart Declaration of Guilt* of 1945 is only partly a real declaration of guilt, as it mentioned neither Jews nor the persecution of Jews. Furthermore, it was only written at the urging of the World Council of Churches.

The Statement, *A Message Concerning the Jewish Question*, issued by the Council of Brethren of the Evangelical Church in Germany in 1948 is even clearer:
1. That since the Son of God was born a Jew, the election and destiny of Israel found its fulfillment in him. [...]
2. That since Israel crucified the Messiah, it rejected its own election and its own destiny. [...]
3. That through Christ, and since Christ, the chosen people is no longer Israel but the Church [...]
5. That Israel under the judgement is the ceaseless confirmation of the truth, the reality of God's Word and God's constant warning to His Church. The fate of the Jews is a silent sermon, reminding us that God will not allow Himself to be mocked. It is a warning to us, and an admonition to the Jews to be converted to him, who is their sole hope of salvation."[7]

7. Matthew D. Hockenos, *A Church Divided: German Protestants Confront*

Even in the year of the foundation of the State of Israel, the Churches (not only Evangelical as illustrated above, but also the Catholic Church) maintained their theological triumphalism, supersessionism, mission to the Jews, and what may be worst of all, their view of suffering and persecution as God's punishment, self-inflicted by the Jews.

Understandably, the Jewish side was very wary about dialogue, until long after World War II. Rabbi Moshe Feinstein even explicitly forbad dialogue in a *responsum*. For him, even positive developments in the Churches were nothing other than new variations on old strategies. His colleague Rabbi Joseph B. Soloveitchik, in his famous 1960s article, "Confrontation," also advised against dialogue with Christians, although *halakhically* speaking, i.e., under religious law, he did not forbid it. On the contrary, he permitted very learned rabbis, whom he trusted to be able to represent Judaism in a dignified manner, to start theological dialogue with Christians. Rabbi Soloveitchik did not want dialogue as "public policy," particularly because he feared the so-called mission to the Jews. At that time, he was absolutely right. So soon after World War II and the Shoah, Judaism was weak and vulnerable, and the missionary efforts of the churches were viral. There was indeed a specific danger of being missionized, which was often an ulterior motive of Christian organizations.

Rabbi Soloveitchik, however, supported socio-political dialogue. Accordingly, the Modern Orthodox Rabbinical Council of America (RCA) stated in their often forgotten 1964 *Policy Statement On Ecumenicism and Interreligious Dialogue*: "We are pleased to note that in recent years there has evolved in our country as well as throughout the world a desire to seek better understanding and a mutual respect among the world's major faiths. The current threat of secularism and materialism and the modern atheistic negation of religion and religious values makes even more imperative a harmo-

the Nazi Past (Bloomington: Indiana University Press, 2004), Appendix 7: Message Concerning the Jewish Question (Council of Brethren of the Evangelical Church, Darmstadt, April 8, 1948), 195–197.

nious relationship among the faiths. . . ." Still, there was very limited dialogue from the Orthodox side, if any at all.

THE TURNING POINT: *NOSTRA AETATE*

Nostra Aetate, published in 1965, began a new dimension in dialogue from the Christian side. This is why we emphasized this Vatican Council declaration in paragraph 2 of our Statement. *Nostra Aetate* was a milestone in the development of dialogue and had an effect far beyond the Catholic Church, extending to other Christian Churches.[8]

At the Second Vatican Council, the Christian teaching referring to Judaism was corrected in a way that was downright revolutionary. This opened up entirely new opportunities. The Vatican confirmed its position once again in *Nostra Aetate's* 50th anniversary year with the document *The Gifts and the Calling of God are Irrevocable.*[9] From the Jewish point of view, the clear rejection of the so-called mission to the Jews was particularly important. "In concrete terms, this means that the Catholic Church neither conducts nor supports any specific institutional mission work directed towards Jews."[10]

The question within Jewish Orthodoxy was how to act appropriately in the anniversary year of *Nostra Aetate*. Particularly in Europe, discussion was taking place on whether to make a statement and if so, how. On April 20, 2015, 50 years after the promulgation of *Nostra Aetate*, an official delegation of the Conference of European Rabbis (CER), the European association of Orthodox rabbis, made the first ever visit to Pope Francis for an audience. The leaders of this

---

8. See, among others, Reinhold Boschki; Josef Wohlmuth (Ed.): *Nostra Aetate 4: Wendepunkt im Verhältnis von Kirche und Judentum – bleibende Herausforderung für die Theologie*, Paderborn 2015; Hans Hermann Henrix (Ed.), *Nostra Aetate – ein zukunftsweisender Konzilstext. Die Haltung der Kirche zum Judentum 40 Jahre danach*, Aachen 2006.

9. Found at http://www.vatican.va/roman_curia/pontifical_councils/chrstuni /relations-jews-docs/rc_pc_chrstuni_doc_20151210_ebraismo-nostra-aeta te_en.html

10. Ibid. 6:40.

delegation were CER Chairman Rabbi Pinchas Goldschmidt, Chief Rabbi of Moscow, and Rabbi Haim Korsia, Chief Rabbi of France. The latter also had a private audience with the Pope shortly after the delegation's visit. Both rabbis have a very positive attitude towards Jewish-Christian dialogue.

The importance and potential of this anniversary year was recognized by the CER, and some rabbis were urging for a declaration on *Nostra Aetate* and Christianity. Others, however, although they basically supported dialogue and valued the change in Church attitudes, thought that it was unnecessary to make an explicit statement. So at first there was no concerted position in Europe. Some hoped that the Chief Rabbinate of Israel, representing Orthodoxy in general, might make a comment. But it soon became clear that this was not going to happen.

It is important to point out that the events mentioned above should be understood as part of a general development towards intensified dialogue over the previous 10–15 years. Particularly in Europe and the USA, but above all in Israel, Christians were increasingly viewed as partners. In Israel, interreligious dialogue was falling into place, including institutionally in different groups and institutes. The first dialogue center in Israel, the Center for Jewish-Christian Understanding and Cooperation (CJCUC), was founded in 2008 by the Chief Rabbi of Efrat, Rabbi Shlomo Riskin. As early as 2011, the CJCUC published an Orthodox declaration on Christianity entitled *A Jewish Understanding of Christians and Christianity*,[11] but which unfortunately attracted little attention.

DECLARATION OF THE ORTHODOX RABBIS OF FRANCE[12]

The first declaration to be published in the anniversary year of 2015

11. CJCUC (2015), *A Jewish Understanding of Christians and Christianity* http://cjcuc.org/2011/05/24/cjcuc-statement-on-a-jewish-understanding-of-chr istians-and-christianity/
12. See: http://iccj.org/redaktion/upload_pdf/201609011603070.Declaration_ of_Upcoming_Jubilee_of_Brotherhood_(French%20Jewish%20Community).pdf

was a local one, in France. The *Declaration for the Upcoming Jubilee of Brotherhood: A New Jewish View of Jewish-Christian Relations* by Orthodox and non-Orthodox Jews was handed over to Cardinal André Vingt-Trois, Archbishop of Paris, and Pastor François Clavairoly, Chairman of the Protestant Federation of France, by Rabbi Haim Korsia, Chief Rabbi of France, on November 23, 2015. I wish to emphasize two central aspects of the new orientation within Jewish Orthodoxy:

• First, the positive, extensive and profound changes in the Churches initiated by *Nostra Aetate* are recognized, and it is now the duty of the Jewish side to more profoundly engage in dialogue. The changes are even seen as *teshuva* (repentance) and a precedent, for which great respect needs to be paid.

• Secondly, as the hostility between Christians and Jews has ended, they should work together as sisters and brothers. After all the conflict, it is finally time to strive together for a better world, and reach out to other religions too. In doing so, our different theologies must not be relativized. On the contrary, other religions and their values must be appreciated for what they are. Instead of aiming to convince others of our beliefs, we must strive to better understand those of others.

THE STATEMENT *TO DO THE WILL OF OUR FATHER IN HEAVEN*

At about the same time, the idea of an international Orthodox Jewish declaration came up in Israel in May 2015, at a Catholic-Jewish conference. Together with Rabbi Yitz Greenberg and Rabbi David Rosen, I was one of the initiators. There were four key reasons behind our proposal:

• First, we considered it a must to set out a clear and strong Jewish reaction to the 50th anniversary of *Nostra Aetate*. We had actually wanted a statement from the Israeli Chief Rabbinate, or at least the Chief Rabbinate's Commission with the Holy See, but unfortunately, it was clear that this was not going to happen.

• Secondly, there had been further improvements in relationships taking place in the past few years, partly due to fundamental changes such as the strict rejection of the so-called mission to the Jews.

• Thirdly, we wanted to react to some anti-Christian actions in Israel, and make it clear that a small, extremist minority was not behaving in line with Jewish values.

• Finally, we wanted to go a step further in dialogue from the Jewish side, and reiterate our position, especially regarding the theological state of Christianity.

I wrote the first draft of the Statement in close coordination with Rabbis Greenberg, Rosen, and others. This draft was expanded, corrected and changed by a small circle of other rabbis, including Rabbi Shlomo Riskin and Rabbi David Bollag, until we reached the final version of the text that we presented to the first signatories. After they had all accepted the wording, the text was published on the homepage of the CJCUC on December 3, 2015. It was not by chance that this was one week before *The Gifts and the Calling of God are Irrevocable* was published by the pontifical Commission for Religious Relations with the Jews. Although we did not know the details of this Vatican paper, we had a rough idea of some of its theses. The most important of these was the passage concerning the so-called mission to the Jews.

TDW has spread quickly and much to our delight, it has gained a lot of attention. This is certainly influenced by the fact that the signatories were or are renowned personalities, chief rabbis of different cities and countries, leaders of rabbinic seminaries and rabbinic associations, and other important rabbinic institutions. As of now, over 100 rabbis have signed the Statement, seven of whom are current or former chief rabbis of European countries. The signatories cover the entire spectrum from progressive "open Orthodox" to ultra-Orthodox.

The structure of our Statement is simple. The title of the document is particularly important: *To Do the Will of Our Father in Heaven*. It expresses our belief that dialogue – and therefore the partnership of humankind – is not just something positive, but actually God's will. Of course, claiming to know God's will is always quite presumptuous, but Rabbi Moses Rivkis (Be'er Hagoleh), Rabbi Jacob Emden, and others put it more or less like this in connection with Christianity. The preface names the consequence thereof: after a traumatic past, the objective now is to "work together as partners to address the moral challenges of our era." Moral challenges here refer to more than just social-political cooperation. In the sense of the Jewish concluding prayer (*Aleinu*), this is to be understood theologically as well, challenging us to mutually take responsibility for the whole world and to recognize God as the one God.

The first paragraph looks back to the unspeakable past. "The Shoah ended 70 years ago. It was the warped climax to centuries of disrespect, oppression, and rejection of Jews and the consequent enmity that developed between Jews and Christians." This points out that this conflict caused incredible damage, with human casualties as well as theological sacrifices. Instead of doing God's will and cooperating, Christians and Jews hostilely separated from one another. In religious matters, differences were stressed rather than what united us. Additionally, Christianity denied its Jewish roots.

With the publication of *Nostra Aetate*, however, that changed. On the occasion of the anniversary, one item of our Statement is dedicated to the Vatican Council's declaration. The revolutionary changes within the Catholic Church are recognized in the second paragraph: "*Nostra Aetate* and the later official Church documents it inspired unequivocally reject any form of anti-Semitism, affirm the eternal Covenant between God and the Jewish people, reject deicide and stress the unique relationship between Christians and Jews . . ." Although the focus is on the Catholic Church, in the same paragraph we also address "other Christian officials," as today "Jews have experienced sincere love and respect from many Christians that have been expressed in many dialogue initiatives, meetings, and conferences around the world." Concerning Protestant Churches, it was difficult for us to find any universal declaration as they are too heterogeneous in their views. Nevertheless, we included Protestant Christians in our Statement just the same.

Beginning with paragraph 3, the theological discussion deepens. As Orthodox rabbis, it was important to us that our position regarding Christianity's status is *halakhic*, i.e. flawless from a religious/ legal standpoint. In order to underpin our statements that "the emergence of Christianity in human history is neither an accident nor an error, but the willed divine outcome and gift to the nations," and that "God willed a separation between partners with significant theological differences, not a separation between enemies," great rabbinic authorities of different times are cited and named, such as Maimonides and Yehuda Halevi of medieval Spain, Rabbi Emden and Rabbi Hirsch of 18th and 19th century Germany, as well as Rabbi Shear Yashuv Cohen of modern Israel.

Incidentally, our declarations concerning Christianity and our positive points about the role of Jesus are not the most revolutionary aspect of our Statement. These have been accepted by rabbinic authorities since the Middle Ages, or at latest in modern times.[13] What is revolutionary is that a group of Orthodox rabbis has now openly and clearly verbalized and published these ideas for a wide audience.

There is one sentence in paragraph 3 that is especially important and requires a brief explanation, as it has been misunderstood in the past: "Now that the Catholic Church has acknowledged the eternal Covenant between God and Israel, we Jews can acknowledge the ongoing constructive validity of Christianity as our partner in world redemption, without any fear that this will be exploited for missionary purposes." This does not mean that we can now talk nicely about Christianity because the Churches are nice to us. What it means is that after decades of Christian re-orientation concerning Judaism, genuine dialogue between Judaism and Christianity is finally possible, in particular because now, after the abolition of the so-called mission to the Jews by the established churches, the eternal covenant between God and His people Israel has been set down officially, rather than just claimed.

---

13. Cf. among others Rabbi Dr. David Zvi Hoffman, *Der Schulchan Aruch und die Rabbinen über das Verhältnis zu Andersgläubigen,* and *Rabbi Samson Raphael Hirsch, Beziehungen des Talmud zum Judentum und zu der sozialen Stellung seiner Bekenner.*

It was this danger of a mission to the Jews that Rabbi Soloveit-chik, one of the greatest Jewish authorities of our times, pointed out in his famous article "Confrontation" in 1964.[14] This is why dialogue skeptics have always justifiably referred to Rabbi Soloveitchik. But we have now entered a new phase of dialogue, in which these fears have fortunately not come true and the mission to the Jews has been ended. This is why we can now classify Rabbi Soloveitchik's article as it was originally intended: a religious-philosophical consideration of its time, and not a *halakhically* binding statement about dialogue. This opens up new opportunities for working together and deeper mutual understanding – also theologically.

As briefly mentioned earlier, paragraph 4 is oriented towards *Aleinu* (the concluding prayer). The beginning of this section is an almost word-for-word citation of the Jewish liturgy, describing what must necessarily follow as a consequence from paragraph 3: "Both Jews and Christians have a common covenantal mission to perfect the world under the sovereignty of the Almighty, so that all humanity will call on His name and abominations will be removed from the earth." Jews and Christians are brothers and sisters, and both religions strive to make the world we live in a better place. So we should act together. We are about to experience the fulfillment of the vision of Rabbi Naftali Zvi Berliner, the Netziv, which is cited in paragraph 4.

Many Christians are unaware that a key passage of Torah con-cerning the Jewish-Christian relationship is the encounter of Esau and Jacob. The key scene in the story is the cordial greeting and the kiss by Esau.[15] There is a *Midrash*[16] and Rabbi Shimon Bar Yochai teaches that Esau sympathized with Jacob and therefore kissed him wholeheartedly. Rabbi Yannai contradicts this. Based on the Hebrew language his interpretation is that Esau bit instead of kissed. In Hebrew "and he kissed him" (*vayishakehu*) and "and

---

14. Joseph B. Soloveitchik, "Confrontation" in: *Tradition. A Journal of Ortho-dox Thought*, Vol. 6, No. 3 (1964), 5–28.

15. Genesis 33,4.

16. *Bereshit Rabba* 78,9.

he bit him" (*vayishachehu*) differ in the vocalization of one letter only. That is significant for the Jewish perception of Christianity, as in the Jewish tradition Esau often represents Christianity. So this comment is a polemic against Christianity, which is illustrated as aggressive and unforgiving. In the Middle Ages, especially taking into account the experiences of repression and persecution, this attitude was understandable. Furthermore, it was a reaction to the early anti-Jewish polemic of the Letter to the Romans (9:10–13) in which Esau represents Israel and Jacob represents Christianity, to which God's covenant would now pass. The Netziv reversed this interpretation of Esau and Jacob in the 19th century in one of his commentaries, and appealed for true partnership between Jews and Christians. From a Jewish point of view, this is a revolutionary reinterpretation. Of course, on the Jewish side as well, reorientation is not easy, particularly when taking the Shoah into account. Distrust in Christians generally and in the Churches in particular is understandable and often still deep. What is different now? We comprehend this: "We understand the hesitation of both sides to affirm this truth," and yet "we call on our communities to overcome these fears in order to establish a relationship of trust and respect." This is the only way to succeed in the future, and the only way for both sides to open up a new chapter and to benefit, as explained in paragraph 5: "We Jews and Christians have more in common than what divides us."

We are aware of the partly irreconcilable contradictions, as we say in paragraph 6: "Our partnership in no way minimizes the ongoing differences between the two communities and two religions." But we also believe that "God employs many messengers to reveal His truth." We reject relativism and any watered-down dialogue. Christians and Jews have their own beliefs and should not have to give up any of their truths or perceptions. All the same, there are enough paths we can tread together. From a Jewish point of view, what humankind shares is that it must "affirm the fundamental ethical obligations that all people have before God that Judaism has always taught through the universal Noahide covenant." Non-Jews do not have to become Jews to take part in the redemption; a monotheistic belief in one God is sufficient. According to a vision of Micah,[17] this kind of religious pluralism will include theological differences and will persist even in the Messianic Age. In these days:

> The mountain of the Lord's house shall be firmly established at the top of the mountains, [...] and peoples shall stream upon it. [...] And many nations shall go, and they shall say, 'Come, let us go up to the Lord's mount [...] and we will go in His paths,' for out of Zion shall the Torah come forth, and the word of the Lord from Jerusalem. [...] and they shall beat their swords into plowshares [...] nations shall not lift the sword against nation [...] anymore. And they shall dwell each man under his vine and under his fig tree, and no one shall make them move [...] For all peoples shall go, each one in the name of his god, but we will go in the name of the Lord, our God, forever and ever.

To meet our requirement to show how important our traditions and values are in a modern and often secular world, Jews and Christians must, as described in paragraph 7, "offer models of service, unconditional love, and holiness" and play "an active role together in redeeming the world." That is, deeds must follow words. To give examples would have been beyond the scope of the Statement, especially as activities can differ widely by region. Most important is that we do become active.

Our Statement has been received favorably in Christian circles. In Jewish circles, it was evaluated differentially, although mostly positively. In this regard, it is useful to know that the majority of (Orthodox) Jews tend to be indifferent to interreligious dialogue. Some (a minority) reject it fully or partly, and some (also a minority) support it and even want to intensify it. The group of those who are indifferent, however, is undergoing change and the dialogue movement is clearly gaining pace.

Regrettably, due to a misunderstanding (which does not need to be detailed here), there was criticism from the executive board of

17. Micha 4,1–5.

the Conference of European Rabbis (CER), which requested that their members not sign the Statement. In an email to members it stated: "Rabbis should not join and sign the position paper being circulated of late under the title 'To Do the Will of Our Father in Heaven' – the content of which is deemed not in accordance with the spirit of our tenets."[18]

In a personal discussion with Rabbi Pinchas Goldschmidt, Chairman of the CER, I was able to clarify their reservations, so that the above-mentioned request is no longer valid. In the same email of December 2015, the CER announced the publication of its own declaration in cooperation with the Rabbinical Council of America and the Chief Rabbinate of Israel. Originally, this document was to be published on January 17, 2016, on the occasion of Pope Francis' visit to the Great Synagogue of Rome, but due to delays it was only published in the summer 2017.

THE DECLARATION *BETWEEN JERUSALEM AND ROME*

On August 31, 2017, a delegation from the CER, the RCA (Rabbinical Council of America), and the Chief Rabbinate of Israel, handed over the declaration *Between Jerusalem and Rome* to Pope Francis. Although it had taken a long time to be delivered, some two years after the anniversary of *Nostra Aetate*, this declaration represents a quantum leap, since for the first time the most important rabbinical councils and institutions of Jewish Orthodoxy officially and formally commented on Christianity.

The idea for a declaration had been raised at a conference of the standing committee of the CER in November 2015, when they decided to set up a committee to draft it. This committee consisted of Rabbis Pinchas Goldschmidt (Chairman of the CER), Arie Folger (Committee Chairman), Yaakov Bleich, Riccardo Di Segni, Bruno

---

18. For critiques of *TDW* see David Bollag, "The Orthodox Rabbinic Statement on Christianity: Criticism and Policy, Theology and Psychology" in this book.

Fiszon, Jonathan Guttentag, René Gutman, Moché Lewin, Aryeh Ralbag, and Yihyeh Teboul. The CER was able to achieve the cooperation of the RCA, represented by Rabbis Shalom Baum (Chairman of the RCA), Mark Dratch, Yitzchok Adlerstein, David Berger, and Barry Kornblau, as well as the Chief Rabbinate of Israel, represented by Rabbis David Rosen and Oded Wiener.

The structure of *Between Jerusalem and Rome* is intriguingly similar to *TDW*. This is possibly not a coincidence, since I had provided Rabbi Arie Folger with our Statement, before it was officially published. Furthermore, one of the Rabbis in charge of the new declaration, Rabbi David Rosen, was one of the initiators of our Statement. This shows that there is a general consensus within Orthodoxy concerning Jewish-Christian dialogue. Of course, the content of *Between Jerusalem and Rome* is not as broad as *To Do the Will of Our Father in Heaven* and the language is more reserved. Differences are repeatedly stressed. This is very natural, however, as *Between Jerusalem and Rome* is a compromise paper representing the opinion of the vast majority of Orthodox rabbis and scholars.

We knew from the beginning that some of our positions in *TDW* do not represent majority opinion within Orthodoxy. We wanted to deliberately position ourselves like this, not least to start a deeper discussion about our attitude towards contemporary Christianity within Judaism – and particularly within Orthodoxy. In that, we succeeded.

As in our Statement, the preface of *Between Jerusalem and Rome* refers to the very difficult past in which "the Shoah constitutes the historical nadir of the relations between Jews and our non-Jewish neighbors." Nevertheless, developments over the past decades are mentioned and the changes within the Catholic Church are appreciated in detail, especially after *Nostra Aetate*, which is called a milestone. With *Nostra Aetate* the Churches "began a process of introspection that increasingly led to any hostility toward Jews being expurgated from Church doctrine, enabling trust and confidence to grow between our respective faith communities." Naturally, there are important differences between Christianity and Judaism: "The theological differences between Judaism and Christianity are profound." This wording is quite similar to our paragraph 6.

Similar to paragraph 3, this new declaration cites *halakhic* sources (partly the same ones) to confirm the special and positive status of Christianity. "Despite those profound differences, some of Judaism's highest authorities have asserted that Christians maintain a special status because they worship the Creator of Heaven and Earth Who liberated the people of Israel from Egyptian bondage and Who exercises providence over all creation." For this reason, similar to our paragraphs 5 and 7, the new declaration states: "Despite the irreconcilable theological differences, we Jews view Catholics as our partners, close allies, friends and brothers in our mutual quest for a better world blessed with peace, social justice and security. We understand our mission to be *a light unto the nations* to include contributing to humanity's appreciation for holiness, morality, and piety. As the Western world grows more and more secular, it abandons many of the moral values shared by Jews and Christians."

The new declaration ends with a vision that we profoundly agree with, which reminds us of our own final sentence:

> We seek to deepen our dialogue and partnership with the Church in order to foster our mutual understanding and to advance the goals outlined above. We seek to find additional ways that will enable us, together, to improve the world: to go in God's ways, feed the hungry and dress the naked, give joy to widows and orphans, refuge to the persecuted and the oppressed, and thus merit His blessings.

CONCLUSION

Christian-Jewish dialogue is now in a new phase. Jews and Christians, the Churches and Jewish communities are increasingly aware of the need to cooperate as people of religion and goodwill in order to serve and promote God and our shared values within our societies.

Within Jewish Orthodoxy, it is increasingly widely understood that Christian theology concerning Jews has fundamentally and irrevocably changed. Furthermore, more and more Orthodox Rabbis and leaders have become aware that the role of religion has changed enormously in our societies and our voice – and the voices of other religions as well – is often not heard anymore. This situation leads to questions, discussions, and to further engagement with other religions. It also shows that the original, skeptical position of Jewish Orthodoxy after World War II, as formulated by Rabbi Joseph Soloveitchik, is now slowly adapting to the new situation. The type and complexity of Rabbi Soloveitchik's position permits a margin of interpretation – and I am sure that this was the intention.[19] Moreover, Rabbi Soloveitchik said (inter alia in *On Interface Relationship* in 1967),[20] that a dialogue between rabbis and Catholic priests must always be theological, and led from a theological perspective, since rabbis and priests are not social scientists but theologians.

The new Jewish Orthodox declaration is a big leap forward. As Bishop Neymeyr, Chairman of the Sub-Commission for Relations with Judaism of the German Bishop's Conference said, it was remarkable that "also from a Jewish point of view the Christian-Jewish relationship is a special one, precisely for theological reasons."[21]

19. See also Andreas Verhülsdonk: "Rabbi Joseph B. Soloveitchik or What Jews and Christians Could and Should Talk with One Another About" in this book; Eugene Korn: "The Man of Faith and Religious Dialogue: Revisiting 'Confrontation' After Forty Years," in: *Modern Judaism*, Vol. 25, No. 3 (Oct., 2005), 290–315 (also at: https://www.bc.edu/content/dam/files/research_sites/cjl/texts/center/conferences/soloveitchik/Korn_23Nov03.htm

20. Reprint: Joseph B. Soloveitchik: "On Interfaith Relationships" in: *Confrontation and Other Essays*, New Milford / Jerusalem, 2015, 85–114.

21. http://www.katholisch.de/aktuelles/aktuelle-artikel/neymeyr-lobt-judische-antwort-auf-nostra-aetate (accessed 16.10.2017).

To Do the Will of Our Father in Heaven – The Necessary Next Steps

Irving 'Yitz' Greenberg

The Orthodox Rabbinic Statement on Christianity, *To Do the Will of Our Father in Heaven: Toward a Partnership between Jews and Christians*, (henceforth *TDW*) should be welcomed as an important and constructive step in Jewish-Christian relations. Admittedly, the Statement expresses a minority viewpoint. The official Orthodox establishment statement[1] (which reportedly was speeded up and somewhat strengthened due to the publication of the Orthodox Rabbinic Statement on Christianity) is considerably more guarded in its address to the Christian faith. It is best described as *pareve*.[2] Still, both statements show that there is change even in the religious sector that is most traditional and unchanging. Among the Jewish religious leaders who are most influenced by memories of past history and the tradition of contempt between the two faiths,

1. *Between Jerusalem and Rome: Reflections on 50 Years of Nostra Aetate* issued by the Conference of European Rabbis, the Rabbinical Council of America and the Chief Rabbinate of Israel, Vatican, August 31, 2017. (http://files.constantc ontact.com/6f28f4f9001/7ba1a585-80c5-4ddb-b7ea-b2b36fbc8853.pdf).

2. In *Kashrut*, that which is neither milk nor meat is labeled *pareve*. This statement focuses on the improvements of Christian teachings about Judaism and the sincerity of these changes. It hardly addresses the validity of Christianity as a religion in its own right. Unlike *TDW*, it does not use terms such as "the ongoing constructive validity of Christianity ..." or that "Christians remain dedicated to the Covenant ..." *TDW*, article 3, 7.

the cumulative effect of the Christian dramatic turn to affirmation instead of past denial is evoking a positive rethinking of attitudes and rulings.

Although the Jewish liberal denominations, especially in America, have already incorporated many of these positive attitudes to Christianity, there is added value in making progress among the Orthodox. The Orthodox denomination is small but disproportionately influential in Jewish religious life – especially because it is dominant in Israel, where it is the established religion of the Jewish state. The Orthodox have been most resistant to substantive dialogue with Christians. This is a reflection of the ongoing influence of Rabbi Joseph B. Soloveitchik's essay "Confrontation." Soloveitchik argues the incommensurability of different religions' faith affirmations. He also impugns the integrity of interfaith attitude changes that grow out of dialogue.[3]

This important internal document, *TDW*, disagrees and cites past positive rethinking by Orthodox luminaries to support its own upholding of Christianity's religious authenticity and moral contribution to the world. The Statement will open the door to further interfaith conversation, joint learning, and cooperation between Orthodox Jews and Christians. This model of coming together is needed in the face of religions clashing around the world, and being used to justify violence and persecution. Moreover, continuing the quarrels of the past raises the danger of religion's irrelevance, as wide swaths of humanity reach for freedom of opinion and peaceful cooperation in many aspects of politics and culture for the sake of life advancement and universal dignity. The Statement deserves further attention (as in this book) in the hope that more Orthodox

---

3. Joseph B. Soloveitchik, "Confrontation," *Tradition*, vol. 6 (1969) 5–29. Soloveitchik was also suspicious that the Church still had unresolved missionizing goals. On his thinking, see Eugene Korn ["The Man of Faith and Religious Dialogue: Revisiting '*Confrontation*,'" *Modern Judaism* 25:3 (October 2005), 290–315], and his comments in his article in this volume. See also my contention that Soloveitchik left the door more open to dialogue than the Orthodox establishment has chosen to acknowledge or pursue. Irving Greenberg, *For the Sake of Heaven and Earth: The New Evolution of Judaism and Christianity* (Philadelphia, Jewish Publication Society of America, 2004), 12–17.

rabbis will sign on and the process of reconciliation and mutual understanding between Judaism and Christianity will speed up.

Nevertheless, my fondest wish for *TDW* is that it become for Orthodox Jews what *Nostra Aetate* became for Catholics. The Catholic document was momentous in its time (although it fell short of the full revolution in transforming attitudes toward Judaism that was needed). However, the document became more and more important, historically, as a series of further statements that it initiated, went beyond it.

The Orthodox signatories of *TDW* credit the Second Vatican Council for initiating the developments that eventually triggered their response. They state that the promulgation of *Nostra Aetate* fifty years ago "started the process of reconciliation between our two communities."[4] The later official Church teachings make clear that the official Catholic teachings about Judaism have changed "fundamentally and irrevocably." This includes repudiating anti-Semitism and the deicide charge, the affirmation of the eternal covenant between God and the Jewish people, focus on the unique relationship between Christians and Jews, and upholding Israel's unique place in sacred history and ultimate world redemption.[5]

The rabbis state that "now that the Catholic Church has acknowledged the eternal Covenant between God and Israel, we Jews can acknowledge the ongoing constructive validity of Christianity as our partner in world redemption, without any fear that this will be exploited for missionizing purposes."[6] It is important to understand this phrase. The affirmation of Christianity as the "willed divine outcome [of the divine plan for world redemption] and gift to the nations" is not a *quid pro quo* for the Church's recognition of Judaism. The Orthodox rabbi signatories share Rabbi Soloveitchik's view that religious teachings and classifications should not be traded as chits or exchanged as favors.[7] As *TDW* says, today's Jews and Christians

---

4. *TDW*, article 2.
5. Ibid.
6. Ibid., article 3.
7. Soloveitchik feared that the minority in particular, feeling inferior or subordinate, will be influenced by such theologically unworthy motives and betray

are trying to do the will of God and be faithful to a calling to be covenantal partners in *Tikkun Olam*. Relief from mistreatment or desire to find favor in the other's eyes are not worthy factors and would only distort authentic religious commitments. Rather, the rabbis are saying that as long as Christianity persecuted and spread hatred of Jews, then Jews were in defensive mode. There was no margin to step back and see Christianity objectively as a religion making a major contribution to spreading the values of human dignity and the commandment to love one's neighbor as one's self.

As long as Christianity insisted that it had superseded Judaism and it was proper, indeed necessary, to convert the Jews, then Jews could not see the positive in Christians role in teaching the nations about God – since that teaching was manifestly false and harmful to Judaism. Furthermore, acknowledging Christianity's value could be distorted and exploited to convince Jews to accept Christianity as a superior form of serving God. *Nostra Aetate* and the changed policies enabled Jews to see Christianity through the lens of its contribution to the nations, instead of the lens of its bad treatment and theological defamation of Jews.

One of the great teachings of the Torah is how it guides humans to see the world other than from the inescapable centerpoint of one's own body and location. The Torah teaches its students to see the world in all its wonder and infinity, *from the divine perspective*, as a creation. It is a cosmic, miraculous experience that is not about the individual human "me." Job, in the end, comes to see the magnificence of the cosmos and all its creatures. He then realizes that his personal tragic, heartbreaking experience is not the big picture truth about existence. In like manner, Jewry, released from the burden of crushing persecution and cultural slander, comes to see the scope of Christianity and the religious/moral contribution that it has made to the world.[8]

---

principles. Soloveitchik states that "... to trade favors [with Christianity] pertaining to fundamental matters of faith ... would be nothing but a betrayal of our great tradition and heritage." Ibid. 25.
    8. See Job, chapters 38 and ff, especially ch. 42:1–6.

One might add that when Jews are not worrying that they will be excluded and "disappeared," they can consider that other faiths – including Christianity – can play a positive role in advancing God's kingdom on earth. Thus *TDW* affirms that "neither of us can achieve God's mission in this world alone."[9] This statement hints that Judaism and Christianity represent major initiatives by God to bring this world to God and to the state of redemption that both religions call "the kingdom of God." Both need to cooperate and help each other, because neither alone can accomplish the fulfillment of this divine mission.

The broader implication is not openly and fully acknowledged in *TDW* because not enough Orthodox rabbis have reached this conclusion. Also, many were not willing to speak so openly and take the political risk of going so far ahead, in the face of Orthodox community consensus, which lags behind. The establishment, and probably the bulk of the lay Modern Orthodox community, is ready for tolerance and respectful language toward Christianity. It is not yet ready to affirm Christianity as a religion in its own right, acting as God's agent and in direct relationship with God as a covenantal community. Hopefully, full acknowledgement will appear in one of the future documents that I suggest will be the outgrowth of this one.

Why do I believe that future Orthodox statements will articulate Christianity's independent role and covenantal connection with God? It appears to me that *TDW* shifts the assessment/observation point: that Christianity is to be seen through the lens of *Nostra Aetate* and the Catholic Church's behavior during this last half-century. This is a wise and just response. But once we remove the lens of the almost 2,000 years of Christian supersessionism and persecution, which up to now (appropriately) shaped our view of that faith, we should look at Christianity within a broader framework, starting from the period when it came into being within Judaism and then moved out. What was the "original intent" of the Maker of heaven and earth? If the misinterpretation of Torah (i.e. that it was

9. *TDW*, article 3.

"outdated" and left behind) and mistreatment of Jews are no longer determinative of our assessment of Christianity, we should ask ourselves what was the intention behind the divinely "willed outcome" that this faith be born and become "a gift to the nations."[10]

In a forthcoming book,[11] I describe that period when Rabbinic Judaism crystallized. For a millennium and more, Jewry had lived as partners in the Sinai covenant. (I call this Stage 1 of the covenant in which God is a more controlling and dominant partner.) Now that Jewry had internalized and deepened their understanding of God and the covenant, as expressed in the rabbis' teachings, God self-limited again. God became more "hidden" – less controlling in history. God was less experienced as a high-voltage presence with which humans cannot come into direct contact without being obliterated.[12] God came closer and appeared as *Shechinah*, met everywhere in life. God self-limited in order to call the Israelites to a higher level of authority and responsibility for the outcome of the covenant. The rabbis explain that the sins that brought about the destruction of the Second Temple were all about human misbehavior: civil war, extremism, hot-headed revolt against Rome, feckless communal leadership and "baseless hatred." This is unlike the First Temple, which was destroyed by God's will because the Israelites betrayed God and lusted after idolatry.[13]

With the divine *tzimtzum* (self-limitation), the age of heavenly revelation and of prophecy (i.e. direct messages from God), as well as visible miracles, ends.[14] Now humans study the past records of revelation and interpret the events of their lifetime, and apply their insights to determine what God wants of humans now. This is the Oral Torah, which is the continuation of the Sinai revelation

10. *TDW*, article 3.

11. Irving Greenberg, *The Triumph of Life*, a Narrative Theology of Judaism (forthcoming).

12. Compare Exodus 33:12–23 and Samuel 6:6–9.

13. Yoma 9B. Compare the sins of the Israelites as depicted in the prophets with the rabbinic treatment of the destruction of the Second Temple in Gittin 55B-57B.

14. Baba Batra 12A.

and reveals God's word in the age of divine hiddenness. The rabbis make *Talmud Torah* (the study of Torah) a central observance for all Jews, so they can understand and internalize religious values as well as detect the hidden presence of *Shechinah* everywhere. Rabbinic Judaism is made possible by the divine *tzimtzum*. Religious life is the expression of a new level of partnership between God and Israel. This is a second stage renewal of the covenant. The vision of ultimate redemption is untouched, but there is a much greater autonomy and fuller responsibility of the human partner to achieve the desired outcome. As the rabbis put it, the acceptance of Purim – the hidden miracle of Exodus from death and destruction[15] – constitutes nothing less than a renewal and new acceptance of the Sinai covenant by Israel.[16] This time (i.e. at this stage) God is more hidden and less controlling, and, as the Purim story itself illustrates, the humans are more active in getting the results.

In my book, I argue that the God of Israel is the Lord of all humanity and loves all the nations. It would not be appropriate, and it is incompatible with infinite divine love, to leave the rest of humanity uncovenanted, while the people of Israel enter into a second stage of relationship. Then this is the moment when God offers the covenant to the nations. As with the Jews earlier, the entry point offer is at Stage 1 where the Lord acts like a parent to a child and is more directive and controlling. Such an offer to bring considerably more people to God is an important, if partial, fulfillment of the promise that Abraham's people would be a source of blessing for all the families of the earth.

Elsewhere I have argued that Christianity had to start within Judaism. Where else did the full covenantal vision exist in a living community? But Christianity had to grow into its new autonomous

---

15. *Kiymu v'kiblu hayehudim aleyhem v'al zar'am* – "the Jews ordained and took upon themselves and their descendants" (Esther 9:27.) *Kiymu mah sheh kiblu kvar* – the Jews ordained what they had already taken upon themselves (at Sinai) – Babylonian Talmud Shabbat 88A. See the treatment of these stories in Jeffrey Rubenstein, *Talmudic Stories: Narrative, Art, Composition and Culture* (Baltimore, Johns Hopkins University Press, 1999), 139–169.

16. Shabbat 88A.

existence – if you will, be somewhat de-Judaized and articulated in Hellenistic terms – in order to be absorbed by the Gentiles. By becoming distinctive, demographically and theologically, Christianity reached the Gentiles more successfully, even as it ensured that the continuing particularist Jewish lifestyle and witness would not be overwhelmed by its offspring.[17] Thus the parallel birth of rabbinic Judaism and Christianity represents an overflow of the infinite and varied divine love toward Jewry and toward all the nations.

This becomes crystal clear when we look at the central affirmations of both faiths, and our minds are not clouded by the lamentable history of the conflicted relationship. As I wrote: in their core teachings, the two religions are one. They share a central theological trope.

This world is a creation of God (who sustains it). The *telos* of human history is that creation is moving toward redemption (God's ideal of creation fully realized.) In this final state called God's kingdom, life will fully triumph over death. This movement will be facilitated by a covenantal partnership of God and humanity. In short: from creation to redemption through covenant. Furthermore, both communities have a common central goal – to be the avant-garde of humanity to bring the kingdom . . .[18]

In other words, Christianity represents the offer of entry into the covenant of Sinai to the Gentiles. This can constitute an equivalent offer, even though there are fundamental differences and even contradictions between the two faiths. The core of both remains the same, although many details of the covenant are modified to speak

17. See three earlier attempts to spell out the process of birth, maturation of birth mother (=Biblical and halfway Rabbinic Judaism) and child (=Christianity) and the continuing path of both faiths: Irving Greenberg, "Toward an Organic Model of the Relationship [between Judaism and Christianity]"; idem. "Covenantal Pluralism"; idem, "Judaism and Christianity: Covenants of Redemption." All three have been reprinted in Greenberg, *For the Sake of Heaven and Earth: The New Encounter between Judaism and Christianity*, Philadelphia, Jewish Publication Society, 2004, 145–161, 185–197, 213–234, respectively.

18. Irving Greenberg, "From Enemy to Partner: Toward the Realization of a Partnership between Judaism and Christianity" in Pim Valkerberg and Anthony Cirelli, editors, *Nostra Aetate: Celebrating Fifty Years of the Catholic Church's Dialogue with Jews and Muslims* (Catholic University of American Press, 2016), 18–178.

to the nations in their language and religious concepts. A primary difference is that the Christian New Covenant is offered in the biblical mode – with revelation, visible miracles, relative human passivity all part of the narrative – while Rabbinic Judaism constitutes renewal of the covenant with changed roles for the partners and a higher level of human responsibility and risk. Thus the guarantee that if one obeys God, one will gain victory, is no longer operative.

There has been discussion in the literature whether through the lens of post-*Nostra Aetate* understanding, Judaism and Christianity constitute one covenant or two. I would argue that the congruence of the core message of both faiths reflect the fact that we are dealing with one covenant, but it is being renewed with a divine *tzimtzum* to the Jews in Stage 2 forms and expectations, while being offered to the Gentiles in Stage 1 forms and expectations. Moreover, the de-Judaization and Hellenization – as well as the inclusion of departures from Jewish tradition, such as Jesus being part of the Godhead and the Trinity itself – ensure that the faith communities perforce will separate. Thus the offer to the Gentiles, which gestates within Judaism, is neither killed by the mother religion's spiritual immune system, nor will the mother faith be taken over by the multiplication of disciples of the new faith.[19] Once the two faiths separate, they operate as two parallel covenantal communities. Since a covenant is not a disembodied set of ideas but a committed love relationship with God, each covenant is distinctive and embodied in a different community. The history of antagonism and persecution as well as the further development of such clashing ideas as trinity and monotheism drove the two religions further apart. However, this generation has gained sufficient perspective to recognize the deeper truth. All the further developments in history do not change the fact that both communities are pursuing the same covenant of redemption and working for the same final outcome of *Tikkun Olam*.[20]

---

19. See the argument in "From Enemy to Partner," op-cit. 179–188, 192 ff.

20. I am aware that Christianity considerably spiritualized the kingdom of God and the concept definition of redemption in actual history. Nevertheless, I contend that Christianity never totally repudiated holistic redemption (i.e. incorporating material/political/carnal existence as well) and/or it is in the process of

The *TDW* has it right when it says: "God willed a separation between partners with significant theological differences, not a separation between enemies."[21] The side by side career of the two would allow the fuller exploration and realization of the dialectical elements of the tradition, such as individual/community, universal/particular, material redemption/spiritual redemption, biological family/intentional community, law/spirit, grace/good works, etc.[22] In all these cases we are not dealing with binaries. Rather each element is a dialectical compound. The two poles should be held together for maximum spiritual effectiveness. But the balance in each case may differ for each religion or community, depending on history, tradition, and experience. Had there been constructive interactions between Judaism and Christianity throughout the millennia, each tradition could have continually adjusted its dynamic balance on these components by learning from the other where it has gone too far in one direction, and where it could reshape the balance to increase spiritual impact and efficacy.

However neither side could imagine a world in which the divine outreach and revelation (*ruah ha-kodesh*) operates in pluralist frameworks. Instead, the separation led to rejection, enmity, and denigration of the other. Instead of balancing and correcting each other, the need to differentiate and to claim superiority led to inner distortions of each faith. To justify its Messianic claim in a world that was still unredeemed, politically and economically, Christianity moved away from the biblical vision of a holistic redemption of body and soul – and spiritualized redemption. This often led to abandoning the world to Mammon and Caesar, instead of letting religion be a force for justice and equity in distribution. In denigrating Judaism, the voice of the Hebrew prophets was less heard. This turned the Christian religion towards greater emphasis on ritual and worship of God instead of clinging to the prophets' message. The prophetic voice insisted that God had had more than enough

---

reaffirming this dimension as part of total redemption.
    21. *TDW*, article 3.
    22. "From Enemy to Partner," 199.

of sacrifices and Temple visits, but desperately wanted humans to do justice and relieve the oppressed.[23] Furthermore, the conviction that Christianity possessed the one, unitary truth that invalidated the other, earlier covenant, led to a common conviction and policy towards all believers. Any deviation inside the religion could/should be treated as false, heretical and subject to persecution and even violent suppression. The path to the Inquisition and hundreds of years of religious wars was paved by turning against Judaism – the original covenant – so totally and harshly.

Judaism too paid a heavy price for its inability to see Christianity as a positive phenomenon from which one could learn, and by which one could rebalance conflicting claims. Thus a tendency towards *halakhic* behaviorism became dominant in part in response to Christian polemical emphasis on the Gospels, spirit and love. Judaism developed a contempt for Gentiles and wrote off the political/economic world dominated by Christians. Judaism's inner worldview often shrank to a tribal ethic. The vision of a creation redeemed for all humanity was forgotten (or spiritualized and left for divine action to achieve). An in-group morality spread – not to save gentile lives on Shabbat, not to feel obligated to be just in dealing with Gentiles, and so on – and became normalized.[24]

What then would it mean to see the two faiths as partners intended by God to work together and strengthen each other until the end of days? I believe that this was the implied question in *TDW's* most inspired moment. *TDW* says: "We Jews and Christians have a common covenantal mission to perfect the world under the sovereignty of the Almighty, so that all humanity will call on His name and abominations will be removed from the earth."[25] On the one hand, both faiths would be reminded that the overarching goal of God is *Tikkun Olam*, not victory and supremacy for a particular faith. This would lead to a reprioritizing of each religion to advance

---

23. See Isaiah 1:11–17, Jeremiah 7, among hundreds of references.

24. For an extended treatment of the distortions in both faiths, see "From Enemy to Partner," op cit.184–189.

25. *TDW*, article 4.

the cause of repairing the world. This includes welcoming the remarkable development of human power and actually encouraging its practitioners to act as God's agents in completing creation. At the same time, religion should seek to guide the exercise of power toward life enhancement. Both faiths would teach the sense of covenantal partnership and apply it to place life-preserving limits on the exercise of power.

A second effect would be a sense that each religion has a stake in the success of the other. Instead of pointing to (or generating stereotypical) areas of superiority to the other faith, one would look for the areas of excellence of the other and seek to adopt or learn from it how to improve one's own performance. If there is a perceived weakness in the other, then one could lovingly reprove the other, or simply try to advise and guide the other to better performance. This would lead each religion to seek out more opportunities to learn together and learn from each other. Alongside this identification with upgrading the other would be the realization that malpractice by any one faith casts a shadow on all, and on the credibility of the religious world view in general. "You are my witnesses, says the Lord" (Isaiah 43:10). When the witnesses lie or spread destructive testimony, then the very presence of and respect for God is weakened. This is especially true in an era when God is totally hidden – and for many people the connection to the divine comes only through the intermediation of witnesses.

Another effect is the realization that completion of creation, even on this planet alone, is manifestly beyond the capacity of any one faith. We should look at the other not as rivals but as desperately needed allies and wanted helpers. The sense of partnership can pave the way for joint projects to help humanity and to enable development through the world.

Another expression of partnership is to care for the other. Both Jews and Christians face persecution and threats of violence in various areas of the world. The two must practice solidarity – stand together, speak up for each other in danger, condemn violence and those who mistreat Jews and/or Christians.

Both faiths need to jointly speak to Islam and help it through a period of crisis and frustration. In many Muslim societies, extremism has surged and suppression of internal diversity has grown apace. Moderates are widely intimidated by the coercion of the authorities or by the violence of the jihadists. Jews and Christians together can witness that the way of peace and pluralism is far more satisfying and life enriching. Both can show that past deep enmities and memories of cruel persecution can be overcome through empathy and new understanding. Developments in both faiths prove that giving up claims of exclusive possession of absolute truth can lead to a more loving and respectful relationship with God and with fellow human beings. Both can testify that the confession of past sins and repentance in actual policies have led to healthier internal spiritual lives. Islamic moderates need strengthening and encouragement. They can draw on these two "outside" groups, especially since this witness is intensified and made more impactful by the unprecedented level of partnership.

Finally, when both faiths reach the level of genuine feelings of partnership, they may be able to appreciate the other's religious life in its distinctiveness. Their statements will not praise the other for possessing our values or for advancing our truths. They will be open to the possibility that God's love and the common cause of *Tikkun Olam* may lead to a distinctive revelation and unique relationship and interactions with God in the other community. This will be perceived not as diminishing my covenant or life with God. Rather the other's existence illustrates that God's infinite love overflows any and all human receptacles. This leads to a feeling of gratitude and love that the blessings showered on me and my covenantal community supplement and complement the blessings showered on the other. All will feel greater gratitude and love for the Lord whose "love is [boundless and] extended to all of God's creatures." (Psalms 145:10). To reach this level of insight is truly to fulfill the prophet's call to "walk humbly with your God."[26] I hope that some future Orthodox rabbis' *TDW* will reach that level of humility and non-triumphalist love of God and neighbor.

26. Micah 6,6.

From Confrontation to Covenant: The Emerging Orthodox Theology of Christianity

Eugene Korn

On October 28, 1965, the world changed. On that day the overwhelming majority of the world's Roman Catholic bishops approved *Nostra Aetate* at the Second Vatican Council. The elevation of *Nostra Aetate* as official Church doctrine represented a Copernican revolution in Catholic theology regarding the Jewish people and Judaism. *Nostra Aetate* repudiated the Church's long standing "teaching of contempt," whose hallmarks over the centuries were the Church's unrelenting attempt to convert Jews, its encouragement of Jewish persecution, humiliation and discrimination, its insistence that God's "old" covenant with the Jewish people was nullified and that after the emergence of Christianity, Judaism was consigned to decrepitude. After almost 1,900 years of conflict, *Nostra Aetate* proclaimed that the Church's theological duel to the death with the Jewish people had ended.[1] Further, it also acknowledged that the

---

1. The Catholic theologian Sister Mary Boys has dubbed post-*Nostra Aetate* teachings on Jews and Judaism as the "the six R's": (1) the repudiation of anti-Semitism, (2) the rejection of the charge of deicide, (3) repentance after the Shoah, (4) review of teaching about Jews and Judaism, (5) recognition of Israel, and (6) rethinking of proselytizing Jews. *Has God Only One Blessing?* (Paulist Press: New York, 2000) 247–266.

historical and theological roots of the Church lay in Judaism and that Christian self-understanding could be fully realized only by entering into honest dialogue with Jews and their faith.

It was the shock of the Holocaust in the heart of Christian culture that forced Christianity into this radical theological reassessment. Something in Christendom had gone horribly wrong, and after deep introspection the Church came to understand that its traditional theological anti-Judaism had metastasized into virulent anti-Semitism and played a substantive role in the Final Solution.

With few exceptions – most notably the prophetic Rabbi Abraham Heschel – Jews initially reacted with caution to *Nostra Aetate*. The wounds of Christian persecution were still raw in the Jewish body, and the Jewish soul could not easily shake the belief that "Esau (the Church) would always hate Jacob (the Jewish people)."

It took 35 years for American Jewry to issue a public response to this new turn in Christianity. The first Jewish statement was *Dabru Emet*, appearing in 2000. Tellingly, it was composed not by rabbis but by a group of prominent Jewish academics, and signed primarily by scholars who interacted with their Christian university colleagues rather than with the clerical authorities of Christianity.

Because *Dabru Emet* advocated a more sympathetic attitude toward Christianity and Christians, very few Orthodox Jews signed that declaration. As the community most attuned to Jewish history – and thus the terrible Jewish historical experience with the Church – Orthodoxy was slowest to respond. Orthodox rabbis were also the Jews most committed to traditional Jewish theology, which had always been under ferocious attack by Christianity's *Adversus Judaeos* teachings. Thus even 35 years after *Nostra Aetate* and numerous post-conciliar Church documents proclaiming the Church's desire for better and more honest relations with the Jewish people, Orthodox Jews still manifested a deep suspicion of Christian motives. During the Second Vatican Council, Modern Orthodoxy's leader, Rabbi Joseph B. Soloveitchik, refused the Vatican invitation to be an observer and interlocutor at the council's deliberations, fearful of being used for Christian anti-Jewish purposes. The attitude he expressed in his influential essay, "Confrontation," remained the

Orthodox norm throughout the second half of the 20th century: "We certainly have not been authorized by our history ... to even hint to another faith community that we are mentally ready to revise [our] historical attitudes."

"Confrontation" was written in 1963 before *Nostra Aetate* and the Church's sweeping theological changes,[2] but its arguments and guidelines continue to have enormous sway in Orthodox circles throughout the world. Yet there *has* been perceptible movement among Orthodox rabbinic leadership toward Christianity since "Confrontation." In this essay I will examine Orthodox attitudinal changes toward Christianity over the last 53 years by comparing "Confrontation," and two more recent Orthodox documents on the topic, *Between Jerusalem and Rome* (2017) and *To Do the Will of Our Father in Heaven* (2015).

I. THE MEANING AND IMPACT OF "CONFRONTATION"[3]

The very title "Confrontation" reveals the traditional Jewish adversarial posture regarding Christianity. In his essay Rabbi Soloveitchik used the biblical narrative of Esau's visceral ongoing hatred of Jacob to characterize the Church's relationship with the Jewish people. The essay had a dual purpose: It functioned as the author's *apologia* for rejecting the Vatican invitation to participate in the Second Vatican Council's deliberations on relations with the Jewish people, and more generally, it laid down public policy guidelines[4] for Orthodox

2. "Confrontation" was first delivered at the 1964 Mid-Winter Conference of the Rabbinic Council of America (RCA) and published later that year as an article in the spring edition of *Tradition*, the official journal of the RCA. It thus preceded *Nostra Aetate* by almost two years.

3. For a systematic analysis of "Confrontation" see my "The Man of Faith and Religious Dialogue: Revisiting 'Confrontation,'" *Modern Judaism* 25:3 (October 2005), 290–315.

4. "Confrontation" was designed to lay out *public*, i.e. communal, policy only since the Orthodox leaders Michael Wyschogrod, David Hartman, Walter Wurzburger and Irving Greenberg told me that R. Soloveitchik saw no problem with them participating as individuals in theological dialogue with Church officials.

participation in future interfaith dialogues that R. Soloveitchik correctly understood would be offered by the Church.

The guidelines were crystallized in the Rabbinical Council of
America's (RCA) statement of February 3–5, 1964 stating that Jewish-Christian cooperation be confined to "universal problems" that
are "economic, social, scientific and ethical." Stressing that faith is
a unique, private and intimate experience for each community, it
asserted the RCA's opposition to dialogue in areas of "faith, religious
law, doctrine and ritual." To ensure this nuanced position was not
misconstrued, it concluded:

> To repeat, we are ready to discuss universal religious problems.
> We will resist any attempt to debate our private individual
> (faith) commitment.

"Confrontation" thus gave license to Jewish-Catholic dialogue on
non-theological topics ("universal problems"), but counselled Jews
to shun any dialogue around matters of faith and theology. By con-
fining Jewish-Christian dialogue to universal problems, R. Soloveitchik rendered Judaism immune to Christian theological attack.

Terming the latter such discussion "debate" was no accident. The
listed proscribed topics were the very subjects of medieval disputations in which the Church coerced Jews to participate when the
Church was at its height of domination. Reading "Confrontation,"
one senses R. Soloveitchik's defensive strategy stemming from belief
that the Church was permanently doctrinally constrained to under-
mine Judaism. He evinces a palpable fear that the proposed modern
interfaith dialogue would have the same nefarious objectives as the
medieval disputations, namely to demonstrate the truth of Christianity, expose Jewish error, prove that Jesus was the messiah and
establish that Jewish ceremonial laws were obsolete after Christianity. The essay's mood is one of resentment, with suspicion pervading
nearly every passage:

> ... non-Jewish society has confronted us throughout the ages
> in a mood of defiance, as if we were part of the subhuman

objective order separated by an abyss from the human, as if we had no capacity for thinking logically, loving passionately, yearning deeply, aspiring and hoping.... Heaven knows that we never encouraged the cruel relationship which the world displayed toward us.

and,

We shall resent any attempt on the part of the community of the many to engage us in a peculiar encounter in which our confronter will command us to take a position beneath him while placing himself not alongside of but above us. A democratic confrontation certainly does not demand that we submit to an attitude of self-righteousness taken by the community of the many which, while debating whether or not to "absolve" the community of the few of some mythical guilt, completely ignores its own historical responsibility for the suffering and martyrdom so frequently recorded in the annals of the history of the few, the weak, and the persecuted.

and again,

... any intimation, overt or covert, on the part of the community of the many that it is expected of the community of the few that it shed its uniqueness and cease existing because it has fulfilled its mission by paving the way for the community of the many, must be rejected as undemocratic and contravening the very idea of religious freedom.

Nor was this suspicion unwarranted in 1964. How could the Church be expected to change its age-old self-proclaimed eternal truth regarding Christianity's supersession of Judaism in God's Christological plan for history?

As we have seen, "Confrontation" couched its understanding of Jewish-Christian dialogue in a secular "democratic" frame of reference, with its derivative principles of equality and religious freedom for all. It thus studiously avoided expressing any theological or even *halakhic* comment about Christianity and Christians. Indeed, to do so would have violated its own guideline of opposing theological discourse with another faith. As the only official Orthodox statement of response to the Second Vatican Council, the impact of "Confrontation" spread far and wide, providing Orthodox leaders in American, Europe and Israel with the justification for declining Christian invitations to religious dialogue. Some even mistakenly understood "Confrontation" as constituting a binding *halakhic* opinion against interfaith religious dialogue, an interpretation which succeeded in strengthening Orthodox resistance to almost all interfaith discussion. Interestingly, while the Orthodox community accepted the "resistance" of "Confrontation" to theological dialogue, it largely ignored R. Soloveitchik's counsel for better interfaith understanding and communication on cultural, ethical, social, scientific and political issues, which he termed "desirable and even essential."

II. *BETWEEN JERUSALEM AND ROME* (2017)

Between Jerusalem and Rome: The Shared Universal and the Respected Particular – Reflections on 50 Years of Nostra Aetate was officially published in February 2017 in the name of the Conference or European Rabbis (CER), the Rabbinical Council of America (RCA), and it was later endorsed by the Chief Rabbinate of Israel. Its major contribution lay not in any new substantive claims, but in the positive tone of its rabbinic authors toward the Catholic Church.

The document bears the obvious influence of "Confrontation" and its policy guidelines laid down 53 years prior. This was to be expected since a majority of the RCA rabbis consider R. Soloveitchik their spiritual and *halakhic* authority. It even repeats R. Soloveitchik's norms for interfaith interaction, citing that the Israeli Rabbinate "carefully avoids matters pertaining to fundamentals of faith, but addresses a broad spectrum of social and scientific challenges" [i.e. non-theological issues] and it reiterates almost *verbatim* R. Soloveitchik's insistence that "doctrinal differences cannot be debated or negotiated" and that "religious experience is private" and "can only be truly understood within the framework of its own faith community." The 2017 document speaks at some length about Judaism's particular theology and election, and of Judaism's role in divine history, but studiously refrains from making any theological assertions about Christianity or hinting at any new theological relationship between Jews and Christians or their respective faiths.

Yet it is clear that most of Rabbi Soloveitchik's deep skepticism and cautiousness about the Church is absent in the 2017 document. Its rabbinical authors express a new trust – however guarded – toward the Roman Catholic Church, earned by the Church's statements and actions since the Second Vatican Council. In the 53 years since "Confrontation," the Church has shown its consistent good faith by publishing six major official documents about Jews and Judaism,[5] by establishing diplomatic relations with the State of Israel, through the visits to Israel of the last three popes (John Paul II, Benedict XVI and Francis) and its repeated categorical condemnations of anti-Semitism, each of which are mentioned in the Statement. This rabbinical statement explicitly acknowledges the "transformation" in Catholic teachings about Jews and Judaism, recognizing them as "sincere and increasingly profound." No doubt that the December 2015 Vatican document, *The Gifts and the Calling of God are Irrevocable*, with its explicit disavowal of any institutional Church effort to convert Jews, played a role in winning the trust of these rabbis.

Finally, this increased acceptance of current benevolent Church motives toward Jews and Judaism led the authors of *Between Jerusalem and Rome* to suggest specific areas of mutual cooperation, namely the defeat of radical Islam, the excision of anti-Semitism from liturgy and doctrine, the protection of the family and the end to active Christian mission toward Jews – again all social, political and moral, without venturing close to anything touching on the-

---

5. *Nostra Aetate* (1965); *Guidelines and Suggestions for Implementing Nostra Aetate* (1975), *Notes on the Correct Way to Present Jews and Judaism* (1985), *We Remember: A Reflection on the Shoah* (1998), *The Jewish People and their Sacred Scriptures* (2001), and *The Gifts of God are Irrevocable* (2015).

ology. While little active coordination or implementation between Church and Orthodox officials toward these specific objectives has been realized thus far, their articulation represents an advance over "Confrontation," which alluded to Jewish-Christian cooperation only in the most generic – and therefore ineffective – sense.

III. TO DO THE WILL OF OUR FATHER IN HEAVEN (2015)

If "Confrontation" was about survival, *To Do the Will of Our Father in Heaven* is about the covenantal dream of redemption. As indicated, R. Soloveitchik adopted a cultural strategy to "the community of the many" in his essay. His approach to the Church as an outside antagonist led him to resort to a secular matrix with neutral democratic principles from which he could insist on equal respect and dignity within interfaith dialogue. He thus implicitly counseled Jews in their relations with Christians and their "confrontation" with the Church to utilize the same conceptual framework as relations with any gentiles with whom Jews may be able to achieve peaceful relations.

As the name of the 2015 document indicates, *To Do the Will of Our Father in Heaven* approaches dialogue from a more integrated religious perspective, asking "Can Orthodox Jews relate to contemporary Christians on *religious* grounds?" and "Does Christianity fit into Jewish covenantal history and our people's divine mandate to become a holy people with a mission to the world?" In other words, the Statement strives to allow believing Orthodox Jews to see the Image of God in the face of religious Christians and find the God of Israel present in the historical reality of Christianity.

For the authors of *To Do the Will of Our Father in Heaven* there are no "secular orders,"[6] no naked public square, no "universal is-

---

6. Rabbi Soloveitchik asserted that ethical, social and political issues were part of "secular orders" – a term he uses repeatedly in "Confrontation" – and therefore interfaith dialogue could proceed in those areas without invoking theology. Realizing the problematics of such dualism, he back-peddled in footnote 8: "The term 'secular orders' is used here in accordance with its popular semantics.

sues" devoid of holiness and divine commandments, nor any enduring history stripped of God's presence. The rabbis of *To Do the Will
of Our Father in Heaven* insisted on approaching Christianity as
proud and confident Jews who relate to the world with Jewish covenantal responsibility. When interfaith dialogue moved from a secular cultural context and to a Jewish theological *Weltanschauung,* the
Jewish response to *Nostra Aetate* ceased to be a "trading of favors."
It represents, more appropriately, an authentic religious response to
Christians, one that is grounded in the natural human longing for
partnership and a worthy spiritual search for reaffirmation of living
out Jewish covenantal aspirations. If indeed the Church no longer
threatens Judaism nor engages in a hostile confrontation with the
Jewish people, religious Jews need not be defensive about seeking
spiritual partnership with Christians.

To Do the Will of Our Father in Heaven has as its axiomatic background the Torah's challenge to Abraham and his progeny to accept
a covenantal mission: "Be a blessing; through you all the families of
the earth shall be blessed." (Genesis 12:2–3) As Abraham's descendants, then, Jews have inherited a covenantal responsibility to the
world. By virtue of God's promise to Abraham, Jews are charged
with making God's presence known to the gentile nations and
bringing the message of divine moral law to humanity. This is our
covenantal *telos* and destiny – the *raison d'etre* for Jewish religious
existence. As Rabbi Naftali Zvi Yehudah Berliner taught, the people
of Israel was created for the world, not the world for Israel.[7]

Building on this covenantal responsibility, paragraph three in *To
Do the Will of Our Father in Heaven* seemed to break new ground in
rabbinic thought by stating: "We acknowledge that the emergence
of Christianity in human history is neither an accident nor an error,
but the willed divine outcome and gift to the nations." Christianity

For the man of faith, this term is a misnomer. God claims the whole, not a part
of man, and whatever He established as an order within the scheme of creation
is sacred." Yet without maintaining this distinction, the approach of "Confrontation" to interfaith dialogue is incoherent.

7. Commentary on the Pentateuch, *Ha-emek Davar*, Introduction to the
Book of Exodus.

as a historical phenomenon – as opposed to all tenets of Christian theology – is neither error nor accident, but plays a beneficial role in God's plan for sacred history.

It is this statement that proved to be the one that many Orthodox traditionalists found most difficult to accept. For this reason it is important to explain its rabbinic and theological background. Is it truly unprecedented in rabbinic literature? Upon analysis we can see that it is but the logical conclusion of a number of previous rabbinic claims about Christianity. The statement says explicitly what is implicit in the rabbinic writings of Maimonides and a number of modern authorities like Rabbis Moshe Rivkis, Jacob Emden, and Samson Raphael Hirsch and Elijah Benamozegh.[8]

As the greatest *halakhic* authority in Jewish history, Maimonides understood the Christian beliefs in the trinity and the incarnation to be profound theological errors, contrary to the correct belief about the One Universal God of Heaven and Earth. Yet, paradoxically, intellectual honesty forced him to admit the positive spiritual role Christianity has played in history: Here are his words:

> Human beings do not have the power to understand the thoughts of the Creator of the universe.... All these things that Jesus the Christian (and of Mohammad after him) were only to prepare the way for the messiah, and to repair the entire world to serve God in unison.... How so? The entire world is already filled with thoughts of the messiah, thoughts of Torah, and thoughts of divine commandments. These ideas have spread to the farthest islands and to many gentile nations [because of Christianity].[9]

Maimonides' admission is reaffirmed by Rabbi Jacob Emden in the 19th century:

8. For the full gamut of rabbinic opinion regarding Christianity see my "Rethinking Christianity: Rabbinic Positions and Possibilities" in *Jewish Theology and World Religions*, 189–215. (Littman Library of Jewish Civilization, 2012).
   9. Mishneh Torah (henceforth *MT*), Laws of Kings 11:4 (uncensored edition).

The goal of [Christians and Muslims] is to promote Godliness among the nations ... to make known that there is a Ruler in heaven and earth, Who governs and monitors and rewards and punishes.... We should consider Christians and Moslems as instruments for the fulfillment of the prophecy that the knowledge of God will one day spread throughout the earth. Whereas the nations before them worshipped idols, denied God's existence, and thus did not recognize God's power or retribution, the rise of Christianity and Islam served to spread among the nations, to the furthest ends of the earth, the knowledge that there is One God who rules the world.[10]

And as *To Do the Will of Our Father in Heaven* notes, R. Emden elsewhere adds that Christianity "eradicated *avodah zarah* (pagan idolatry), removed idols [from the nations] and obligated them in the seven *mitzvot* of Noah."

These are only two examples of rabbinic authorities who acknowledge that Christianity has aided the realization of *the Jewish religious mission* by spreading to the farthest corners of the earth fundamental Jewish religious tenets and Judaism's understanding of divine morality. Interestingly these spiritual tasks are the very ones that rabbinic tradition identified as Abraham's covenantal mission.[11] Jews can, therefore, see Christianity as part of God's plan for human history and Christians as their partners in realizing God's great covenantal dream for Abraham and his descendants.[12] If Jews are *zerah Avraham* (Abraham's biological descendants), non-supersessionist Christians may be understood as *benei Abraham* – members of Abraham's spiritual family who are also committed to fulfilling

---

10. *Commentary on Ethics of the Fathers* 4:11.

11. See commentaries of Isaac Abarbanel and Menachem Recanati on Genesis 12:2; Yehudah Leib Alter (*Sefat Emet*), *Sukkot* 5664; Maimonides, *MT*, Laws of Idolatry 1:13, Laws of Sacrifices 19:16, Guide of the Perplexed III:29 and Book of Commandments, positive commandment 3.

12. For a full explication of Christians and the Abrahamic covenant, see Eugene Korn "The People Israel, Christianity and the Covenantal Responsibility to History," in *Covenant and Hope* (Eerdmans, 2012).

the Abrahamic covenant – although as indicated many traditional Jews were hesitant to "share" Abraham's covenant with Christians both for historical reasons and due to Christianity's penchant for supersessionist claims against Judaism. Yet while some principles of Christian theology remain fundamentally incorrect and off-limits for Jews, there is no gainsaying the fact that Christianity has worked for world redemption in accordance with the Bible's covenantal vision.

As these rabbinical authorities imply, believing Christians are closer to Jews and Judaism than are other Noahides, such as Buddhists, Taoists and other Asian worshippers. Christians and Jews share belief in *creatio ex nihilo*, in Jewish Scriptures, in the Exodus from Egypt, revelation at Sinai and in the divine commandments. And both Jewish and Christian ethics are founded on the Bible's insistence that human beings are created in the Image of God. And as a universal evangelical religion, Christianity is well suited to spread these beliefs to the nations of the earth.[13] If so, shall faithful Jews not see non-threatening Christians as partners in their holy covenant? Should we not draw closer to them in doing our noble spiritual work – particularly when both secularism and materialism wait for believing Jews and Christians alike around nearly every corner of modern experience?

The intense historical Christian enmity towards Jews did not allow most Jews of the past to understand Christians and Christianity in cooperative and covenantal terms. Yet the modern Church's rejection of both anti-Semitism and anti-Judaism together with its transformation from competitor to ally now demands profound psychological and theological shifts from religious Jews. Given the

13. Rabbi Benamozegh claimed that as a universal religion it is Christianity that is "perfectly suited" to spread the Noahide commandments and fundamentals of correct theology more effectively than particularistic Judaism. He insists that Judaism and Christianity are "spiritual sisters" who should unite to work for their great common covenantal destinies. (*Israel and Humanity*, 51–52) The contemporary rabbinical scholar (and signatory to *To Do the Will of Our Father in Heaven*), R. Shlomo Riskin, similarly claims that "Christianity took up the original Abrahamic universal mission when diaspora Judaism could not." *Covenant and Hope*, 127–128.

weight of the past, no doubt these shifts are difficult for many Orthodox Jews. However the unprecedented Christian reality before us today with its new vast potential to effectively realize Jewish covenantal responsibilities makes these shifts spiritually imperative.

While the Statement's language of covenantal partnership and its nuanced acknowledgement of Christianity's theological legitimacy seem *nova* for Orthodox discourse, in reality they are the logical extensions of rabbinic precedents and hence justified within rabbinic tradition. And the near miraculous changed reality of Jewish-Christian amity allows Jews to safely build this theology of Christianity.

The new partnership is a further step in the historical fulfillment of God's challenge to Abraham and the divine plan for world redemption. As *To Do the Will of Our Father in Heaven* correctly declares, neither the Jewish people nor the Church can achieve this redemption alone.

IV. CONCLUSION

To Do the Will of Our Father in Heaven is a forward looking and outward looking document. While respecting the harsh Jewish past and deep scars of persecution, it acknowledges the new present and its great potential to create a better future for Jews, Judaism and the world. Realizing that Christianity is no longer the physical or spiritual enemy of the Jewish people and the God of Israel, its sights are set on God's covenantal mission for Jews to be a blessing to all of God's creation by influencing the nations of the earth and to be a priestly nation who brings God's blessing to humanity and human culture.

Despite our long history of persecution and anti-Semitism at the hands of Christians, Orthodox Jews are not free to give up on the covenantal responsibility for world redemption. Are believing Jews today strong enough to take a leap of faith out of insular Jewish life and recommit themselves to engaging the world? Will we have the courage to try to spread God's Name, to actively cooperate with Christians in our holy work, and to see this partnership as God's will and a giant step toward fulfilling the sacred biblical dream of providing blessing to all the families of the earth?

The rabbis of *To Do The Will of Our Father in Heaven* took this leap because they see the hand of God in history and believe that Jews are indeed blessed to live in the miraculous new era of Jewish-Christian cooperation and understanding.

Reflections on the Recent Orthodox Jewish Statements on Jewish-Catholic Relations

David Rosen

At the beginning of 1994, I chaired an unprecedented international Jewish-Christian leadership conference in Jerusalem titled *"Religious Leadership in Secular Society"* which was attended by hundreds of participants from some eighty countries. Consisting mainly of concurrent panels on a spectrum of contemporary challenges in the social and scientific fields, speakers at the conference opening and closing plenaries included Cardinal Joseph Ratzinger, Cardinal Carlo Maria Martini, the Archbishop of Canterbury George Carey, Chief Rabbi Rene Samuel Sirat, and Rabbi Irving (Yitz) Greenberg.

However those official Israel rabbinic leaders who had originally promised their participation, pulled out under a juggernaut of pressure coming primarily from within the *haredi* but also religious nationalist quarters. Condemnations of the conference and prohibitions against participation were issued (which happily many Israeli rabbis ignored) and intense pressure put on me personally to withdraw and even cancel the whole event.

This hostility within Orthodox Jewish quarters towards engagement with the Christian world was of course rooted in theological opposition, but above all reflected the result of the overwhelming negative historical Jewish experience of Christianity.

Modern outreach to Christianity was naturally pioneered and led by the liberal Jewish movements which sought greater integration into gentile society. The fact that Orthodoxy widely viewed these new Jewish streams as a threat to the preservation of traditional Judaism, only added to the latter's suspicion of this new outreach and fear that it might encourage abandonment of age-old commitments.

The Shoah was in many ways a turning point in Christian-Jewish relations that led to a reappraisal of past attitudes. But for many Jews especially within the Orthodox Jewish community, the fact that it took place in ostensibly Christian lands perpetrated by baptized Christians, was seen as proof of the unredeemable hostility of Christianity towards Jews and Judaism that had been experienced down the ages.

Accordingly for some, the Shoah itself only made the idea of engagement with Christianity more of an anathema. A proponent of such opposition was the Orthodox rabbi and philosopher Eliezer Berkowitz – himself a refugee from Nazism. He describes the world after the Shoah as a post-Christian world and sees Christian ecumenism as reflecting Christendom's loss of power.

Christians are only now interested in the freedom of religion, he declares, because they are interested in the freedom of Christians. He perceives Christian civilization and Christianity as morally bankrupt especially after the Shoah; and Jewish engagement with Christianity as accordingly lacking in self-respect. His position therefore is that the Christian world needs to demonstrate far more consistently and thoroughly over generations that it has repented and purified itself of its sins against Jewry before any Jewish-Christian cooperation let alone dialogue can be contemplated.

While Berkowitz's view is articulated harshly, it is not eccentric in Orthodox Jewish circles and is probably normative within *haredi* ultra-Orthodoxy if not beyond. Indeed, as *haredi* society reflects a reactionary withdrawal from the modern world and is thus isolationist by definition, the impact of the tragic historical experience under Christendom and its trauma is all the more prevalent (even unconsciously). However even among Orthodox religious nationalist circles, such a derogatory view of Christianity is still quite prevalent.

Nevertheless, the Shoah did serve as a major impulse for many Jews to reach out to Christian counterparts, precisely in order to protect their communities from such terrible consequences of bigotry and prejudice. Indeed for many it became the main purpose of the dialogue.

The philosopher Emil Fackenheim was ordained as a German Reform rabbi but in his later life identified increasingly with Orthodoxy. He was interned by the Nazis in Sachsenhausen concentration camp, but escaped to Britain from where he was sent for internment in a camp in Canada until he was released. He spent most of his life in Toronto before retiring to Jerusalem.

For him the primary moral imperative for Jews that flows from the tragedy of the Shoah is the obligation to survive and to deny Hitler a "posthumous victory"; and accordingly the fundamental obligation that the Shoah demands of Christians, is to recognize and support the integrity and vitality of the Jewish People. Indeed he sees this as essential for the salvation of Christianity itself. Jewish-Christian engagement therefore is necessary to ensure the future of Jewry in which Christianity has a fundamental stake and responsibility (even if denied for most of its history) especially in relation to the security and flourishing of the State of Israel.

Such motivation to enlist Christian support for the protection of Jewish communities and the State of Israel has served as a major impulse among an increasing number of Orthodox groups who in recent decades have welcomed Christian engagement with Jews and Judaism.

Rabbi Joseph B. Soloveitchik, a major figure in American Jewish Orthodoxy in the second half of the 20th century, presented something of a middle ground position between the poles of full engagement with the Christian world and those who eschewed it altogether.

In a famous article written in the early 1960s (Tradition, Vol.6, No.2), while advocating cooperation with Christians on matters of shared social and ethical concern and advocacy, he suggested that any theological dialogue that relates to the "inner life" of faith affirmation is inappropriate, if not actually unfeasible. Because the

Jewish community must always be mindful of the mystery of the uniqueness of its being, he suggested that it should avoid exposing the inner life of its faith to interreligious dialogue.

There has been much debate, commentary and critique on Soloveitchik's position, his motives and goals; and whether his comments were absolute or relative to time, place and person, especially as he himself apparently *did* participate in theological discussions with Christians. Nevertheless, an official position of maintaining a distinction between theological dialogue (to be avoided) and shared consultations and collaboration on social and ethical matters (viewed as desirable), has been held by most of mainstream Orthodox Jewry in the US and has had impact in Israel and further abroad.

In the 1970s, in response to the developments following the promulgation of *Nostra Aetate* by the Catholic Church, an umbrella body was established as the official Jewish interlocutor for the Holy See's newly established Commission for Religious Relations with the Jewish People. This council included all the major international and American Jewish organizations that had communicated with the Vatican during the Second Vatican Ecumenical Council and also included the Synagogue Council of America embracing all three major denominations of American Jewry, Reform, Conservative and Orthodox. However precisely because of the above mentioned distinction that Soloveitchik made between theological dialogue and other kinds of interreligious relations, this body was given the name, the "International Jewish Committee for Interreligious *Consultations*," and not "dialogue," in order to include the American Orthodox rabbinic and lay bodies.

In the modern era, institutional Orthodoxy in the Diaspora had generally appreciated the value of good relations with the Christian world and was cognizant of the significant changes that had taken place within it after the Shoah and in particular after *Nostra Aetate*. However in Israel, the fact that Jews are not required as a matter of course to take relations with non-Jewish society into consideration, served to widely maintain the traditional view of Christianity as hostile and to be shunned.

In addition, attitudes towards the State of Israel were seen within the Jewish community as a reflection of attitudes towards the Jewish people as a whole. The fact that the Vatican did not have diplomatic relations with Israel was also seen as "proof" by the skeptics within the Jewish community that negative prejudice still prevailed within the Christian world.

Thus the establishment of diplomatic relations between the Holy See and the State of Israel at the end of 1993 (of which I was privileged to have been one of the negotiators), was viewed as much more than a secular diplomatic achievement. But it was that which it facilitated that had a far wider effect upon Jewish society.

John Paul II's papacy was remarkable for Catholic-Jewish relations in many ways, taking the revolution ushered in by St. John XXIII to new heights. Moreover Karol Wojtyla's understanding of the power of contemporary media and the potential of dramatic gestures played a key part in this process, firstly his visit to the Great Synagogue in Rome in 1986.

But even more significant for Jewry was the establishment of full relations between the Vatican and Israel, which facilitated his historic state visit as part of his pilgrimage to the Holy Land in the year 2000, and the impact was dramatic.

The Christian presence in Israel is barely two per cent of the population. It is true that more Israelis today meet Christians than ever before through foreign workers – especially Philippino care givers. Nevertheless, there has been minimal awareness of the latter's Christian identity. And when Israelis travel abroad, they generally meet non-Jews as non-Jews, not as modern Christians. Accordingly for most Israeli Jews – especially among the more religiously observant – the image of Christianity has overwhelmingly been taken from the tragic past.

However to see the most visible head of the Christian world – as the vast majority did on television when John Paul II visited the country – paying his respects to Israel's highest state and religious officials; to see him at Yad Vashem in tearful solidarity with Jewish suffering; to learn of how he had saved Jews as a novice and then as a prelate instructed Catholic families who had saved Jewish children and brought them up as Catholic, to return them to their natural

Jewish parents; to see the Pope at the Western Wall honoring Jewish tradition and placing there the text of his prayer asking Divine forgiveness for the sins committed by Christians down the ages against Jews (part of the liturgy of repentance that he had conducted weeks earlier at St. Peter's); were stunning revelations for much of Israeli society.

Another significant outcome of that pilgrimage came from the Pope's meeting with the Chief Rabbis of Israel and members of the Chief Rabbinate Council. At that meeting John Paul II proposed the establishment of a permanent bilateral commission for dialogue between the Chief Rabbinate of Israel and the Holy See's Commission for Religious Relations with Jewry.

Even though this was surely something the Chief Rabbinate of Israel had never contemplated, this commission was established in 2002 – the first ever formal bilateral framework for dialogue between Orthodox Judaism with the Holy See. It meets annually, alternating between Rome and Jerusalem, holding consultations on themes relating to the teachings of the two traditions on a spectrum of social and scientific issues.

The impact upon the rabbis involved who had not been engaged in such endeavors previously has been substantial. Moreover they are influential in their own communities, and thus their own reappraisals of the relationship between Jewry and the Churches that have ensued from these meetings and relationships, have even wider ramifications.

Following the success of this bilateral commission, a similar one was established between the Chief Rabbis of Israel and the Archbishop of Canterbury to advance Jewish-Anglican dialogue and relations. Nevertheless until 2017, official Jewish statements acknowledging the transformation that had taken place within the Christian world had only come from the liberal streams of Judaism.

Most notable of these was the 2002 declaration titled *Dabru Emet* (Speak the Truth.) Formulated by Reform and Conservative scholars and rabbis, it affirmed both fundamental shared beliefs and values as well as what it called "the humanly irreconcilable difference between Jews and Christians (that) will not be settled until

God redeems the entire world as promised in Scripture." In addition to rejecting the idea that Nazism was an outcome of Christianity, it called on Jews and Christians to work together for justice and peace. Signed by almost two hundred and fifty rabbis and scholars, other than for a handful of Orthodox rabbis, they were entirely from the non-Orthodox Jewish world.

Thus the Statement *To Do the Will of Our Father in Heaven* issued by Orthodox rabbis in December 2015 was momentous, reflecting the significant changes within the Orthodox Jewish world in recent decades.

Indeed, it was acknowledged as such by Cardinal Kurt Koch, President of the Holy See's Commission for Religious Relations with Jewry, at the press conference for the release of his commission's document on the occasion of the 50th anniversary of *Nostra Aetate*, "The gifts and the calling of God are irrevocable."

In addition, *To Do the Will of Our Father in Heaven* galvanized the formulation of an official statement on Jewish-Christian relations from the three main institutional Orthodox bodies on three continents – the Chief Rabbinate of Israel, the Rabbinical Council of America, and the Conference of European Rabbis. Titled *Between Jerusalem and Rome* it was presented to Pope Francis at the end of August 2017.

It too expresses appreciation for the blessed transformation in the Church's approach towards Jews, Judaism and Israel; and affirms the partnership and mutual responsibility of the two faith communities to provide a religio-ethical vision and example for contemporary society.

In this regard, *To Do the Will of Our Father in Heaven* specifically quotes the Statement issued at the Chief Rabbinate/Vatican Bilateral Commission meeting held at Grottaferrata in 2004, that "we are no longer enemies, but unequivocal partners in articulating the essential moral values for the survival and welfare of humanity." But it also goes further in describing this sacred task as "a common covenantal mission."

Negative attitudes towards Christianity do still persist within the Orthodox Jewish community for the above mentioned reasons.

Moreover for as long as anti-Semitism continues to rear its ugly head; and for as long as Israel's physical and political survival and wellbeing are threatened (or at least perceived as threatened), these fears will often prevent an openness to recognizing let alone embracing the new reality of Christian-Jewish relations (even if sometimes they serve to provide the very contrary impulse, seeking to enlist Christian support and protection.)

Nevertheless, *To Do the Will of Our Father in Heaven* highlights a new era of increasing Orthodox Jewish engagement with the Christian world, indicating a growing appreciation of the dramatic change that has taken place within Christianity in relation to Jewry, Judaism and Israel; of the strategic importance of this relationship for the Jewish People and the Jewish state; and even of the theological as well as moral imperatives for deepening this mutual relationship to work together for the establishment of the Kingdom of Heaven on Earth.

The Orthodox Rabbinic Statement on Christianity: Criticism and Policy, Theology and Psychology

David Bollag

Each religion develops its own theology and ideology, and each religion views and defines itself as part of the divine plan for the world. The emergence, existence, and development, as well as the moral values, obligations, and goals of each religion are considered part of the divine plan.

Other religions are generally not regarded as part of the divine plan. The independent existence of other religions is therefore often not considered to be of any importance.

Sometimes, they are even regarded as an obstacle to the fulfillment of the divine plan, which may then lead to the conclusion that they must cease to exist.

In this respect, the Orthodox Rabbinic Statement on Christianity seeks to bring about a radical change.

THE STATEMENT

When Rabbi Jehoschua Ahrens showed me one of the first drafts of the Statement, I realized that Maimonides' important and seminal comments on Christianity (and Islam) were not referenced. I therefore suggested including these comments. This article focuses on Maimonides' comments, showing how the critiques and politics, theology and psychology of the Statement directly refer to Maimonides.

Paragraph 3 of the Statement begins as follows: "As did Maimonides . . . , we acknowledge that the emergence of Christianity in human history is neither an accident nor an error, but the willed divine outcome and gift to the nations." Maimonides was the first Jewish philosopher to integrate the emergence and existence of Christianity into his Jewish theology and *Weltanschauung*. He was the first Jewish theologian to consider and describe Christianity as part of the divine plan for the whole world.

The Statement refers to a passage in Mishneh Torah, Maimonides' Code of Laws: "Ultimately, all the deeds of Jesus of Nazareth . . . will only serve to prepare the way for *Mashiach's* coming and the improvement of the entire world [*Tikkun Olam*], motivating the nations to serve God together." (Mishneh Torah, *Hilkhot Melakhim* – Laws of the Kings, XI, 4)

Clearly, directly, and unambiguously, Maimonides expresses here his conviction that from his Jewish point of view, Christianity is no mere operational glitch in world history, but the deliberate and intended result of divine providence, planning, and steering of humankind's history. For Maimonides, Christianity is part of his Jewish theology and *Weltanschauung*.

It is important that 50 years after *Nostra Aetate*, Maimonides' words are pronounced loudly and clearly by the Jewish side.

CRITIQUES

Shortly after the publication of the Statement, Professor David Berger examined it thoroughly and carefully. In his article "Vatican II at 50," published on tabletmag.com. Berger, a Modern-Orthodox Rabbi and Professor of Jewish History at Yeshiva University, tracks the history of the impact of the Vatican document *Nostra Aetate*. In this context, he evaluates the Orthodox Rabbinic Statement on Christianity.

Regarding the Statement, Berger claims that "much of it is unexceptionable, even admirable." At the same time, however, he believes "nonetheless, elements of this declaration are decidedly problematic." Berger criticizes the Statement for not having fully presented Maimonides' statements and hence misrepresenting their meaning:

> The authors know very well that … Maimonides saw the divine plan in the establishment of Christianity as preparation for universal recognition of the truth of Judaism and the rejection of those religions. There is something disingenuous about citing only half the position.

Berger's critique is based on the text passage that immediately follows the above-cited passage in Mishneh Torah. There, Maimonides describes how Christianity and Islam have led to the dissemination of the values and commandments of the Torah, and of the Messianic expectation into wide parts of the world. Maimonides writes that although these two religions interpret the commandments of the Torah in a totally different way than Judaism, when "the true Messianic king will arise … they will all return and realize that their ancestors endowed them with a false heritage and their prophets and ancestors caused them to err." (Mishneh Torah, ibid.)

At first glance, Berger's critique seems fully justified, pointing to a serious mistake in the Statement. In my opinion, however, when we carefully analyze both his critique and Maimonides' phrasing, we will discover that the Statement is in no way inconsistent with Maimonides' statements.

Up to now, we have referred to Maimonides' statements in Chapter XI of Hilkhot Melakhim – Laws of the Kings. In the following chapter, Maimonides writes that in Messianic times all peoples "will all return to the true faith and no longer steal or destroy" (ibid. XII, 1). He by no means states that other peoples or religions will convert to Judaism. They will – finally – not persecute, oppress, or murder the Jews anymore. They will fully accept the moral values of the Torah. But Maimonides does not at all say that other religions will adopt and practice the ritual commandments of Judaism.

When Maimonides writes that other religions "will all return and realize that their ancestors endowed them with a false heritage and their prophets and ancestors caused them to err," he does not mean that they will abandon their own religions. Christians will remain Christians. They will not convert to Judaism but will continue to adhere to Christianity.

The false heritage, however, that is mentioned here refers to Christian theology, namely to the Trinity. In this respect, Maimonides indeed considers it indispensable that Christianity undergoes a change. Christianity must find its way to becoming a "Religion of Truth," an absolute monotheism.

In my eyes we thus refute Berger's critique and show that the Statement is fully consistent with Maimonides' statements. I communicated my arguments to the defense of our Statement to Prof. Berger, and this is what he answered: "When I wrote that the Rambam [Maimonides] saw the role of Christianity and Islam as preparation for universal recognition of the truth of Judaism and the rejection of those religions, I did not mean that Christians and Muslims would become Jews or practice Judaism.... However, Christians and Muslims will recognize that the theological doctrines of Judaism are true." (E-mail of December 28, 2015)

This is exactly how the Statement perceives Maimonides' words: "[A]ll the deeds of Jesus of Nazareth ... will only serve to prepare the way for *Mashiach's* coming and the improvement of the entire world, motivating the nations to serve God together. "Serve the one and only, entirely abstract and indivisible God.

The Statement, therefore, rightly calls Christianity a "willed divine outcome." Christianity is – even for us Jews – a preparation for the whole world, a *Tikkun Olam* to be serving God together.

POLITICS

The Orthodox Rabbinic Statement is primarily a theological document that seeks to re-define the relationship between Judaism and

Christianity. Yet as the Statement relates to religio-political issues as well, and as theology and politics of religion are often very closely connected, it is hardly surprising that immediately after the publication of the Statement, an inner-Jewish political debate arose.

A few days after the publication of the Orthodox Rabbinic Statement, the Conference of European Rabbis (CER) sent the following notification to their members:

"Rabbis should not join and sign the position paper being circulated of late under the title 'To Do the Will of Our Father in Heaven' – the content of which is deemed not in accordance with the spirit of our tenets."

At the same time the notification promised that the CER will shortly be publishing a clear and appropriate position and response, which was eventually made public in 2017 as *Between Jerusalem and Rome, Reflections of 50 Years of Nostra Aetate*.

It is important to reflect on the question as to why the CER believes that the Orthodox Rabbinic Statement is "not in accordance with the spirit of our tenets," why their members should therefore not sign the Statement, and why the CER felt compelled to try to write its own statement.

I assume that the explanation is directly related to the above-cited passage of Maimonides' Mishneh Torah mentioned in the Statement. It seems that the Conference of European Rabbis is neither capable nor willing to agree to a full recognition of the independent right of Christianity to exist, and to the idea that Christianity is also part of the divine plan for our world. They seem to think that considering Christianity to be part of a Jewish theology and *Weltanschauung* cannot be consistent with the tenets of Judaism.

Inner-Jewish theological and religio-political discussions of this kind sometimes arise. The question whether Judaism is willing to accept Christianity as a religion provokes severe disputes time and again. For this reason, some years ago Rabbi Dr. Jonathan Sacks, then Chief Rabbi of the UK and Commonwealth, was forced to change some passages in his book *The Dignity of Difference*.

In the first edition of his book (2002), in his comprehensive analysis of the relationships between different religions, Rabbi Sacks de-scribed the position of Judaism in these words: "Judaism . . . believes in one God but not in one religion." (52 f.)

After fierce criticism from ultra-Orthodox circles, Rabbi Sacks felt forced to revise his statement, so that in his second edition (2003) it reads: "Judaism . . . believes in one God but not in one ex-clusive path to salvation." (52)

Rabbi Sacks was forced to retract his statement that Judaism is willing to recognize only one God but is nevertheless ready to ac-cept the existence of several religions concurrently. Rabbi Sacks had to make a similar change in another passage of his book. In the first edition it read: "In the course of history, God has spoken to mankind in many languages: through Judaism to Jews, Christianity to Chris-tians, Islam to Muslims." (55) In the second edition, it now reads: "As Jews we believe that God has made a covenant with a singular people, but that does not exclude the possibility of other peoples, cultures and faiths finding their own relationship with God." (55)

While in the first edition Rabbi Sacks clearly states that Judaism recognizes that God has chosen Christianity to address Christians, in the second edition he has to avoid mentioning Christianity, let alone attributing to it a role in God's plan for the world.

Even in Judaism, significant changes will have to occur until all circles will be willing and able to view Christianity as an indepen-dent religion and part of a divine plan. The Orthodox Rabbinic Statement on Christianity wants to contribute to the process and bring about these changes.

THEOLOGY

The primarily theological question being discussed here – i.e. whether from a Jewish point of view other religions have a right to exist, willed by God, and whether they are part of a divine plan – was probably discussed as early as biblical times. A careful comparison between two very famous biblical passages lets us assume that this question caused disagreements already then.

We find passages in the books of the prophets Isaiah and Micah that are very similar: Isaiah chapter 2, verses 2–4; and Micah, chapter 4, verses 1–5. To a large extent, the verses are identical. Both prophets describe the days of the final redemption. In these days "the mountain of the Lord's house shall be established at the top of the mountains ... and peoples shall stream upon it. And many nations shall come, and they shall say: 'Come, let us go up to the mountain of the Lord ... and we will walk in His paths, for out of Zion shall the Torah come forth, and the word of the Lord from Jerusalem.... And they shall beat their swords into plowshares ... and no nation shall lift the sword against another nation anymore." To this extent, both prophets' texts are the same.

Yet while the prophecy of Isaiah ends here, Micah's continues:

> And they shall dwell each man under his vine and under his fig tree, and no one shall make them afraid.... For all nations shall walk, each one in the name of his god, but we will walk in the name of the Lord, our God, forever and ever.

Isaiah and Micah agree that in the days of the final redemption – in the Messianic Age – all nations will stream to Jerusalem in order to serve God and learn how to walk in His paths. All nations and religions will recognize God and accept His values, which He has revealed in the Torah. Isaiah and Micah also agree that there will be no more war between the nations. But unlike Isaiah and in contradistinction to him, Micah adds that even though all nations will recognize God and will "walk in His paths," there will still be theological-religious differences between the other nations and Israel. "All nations shall walk, each one in the name of his god."

Isaiah appears not to agree with that opinion, but Micah predicts that even in the days of the final redemption of mankind, the differences between religions will not completely disappear. Of course, all nations will serve the one and only God. They will not, however, all belong to the same religion. Jews will remain Jews, and Christians will remain Christians. Each religion is part of the divine plan for the world, each religion has its right to exist, even in the Messianic Age.

According to Micah, the Messianic Age distinguishes itself from our days not by all human beings belonging to the same religion, but by all of humankind living in peace. God's prophesied goal for us human beings is, therefore, to find a way to peacefully live with one another, despite all the differences between various religions.

PSYCHOLOGY AND PSYCHOANALYSIS

The Orthodox Rabbinic Statement addresses the relationship between religions. It thus relates to and focuses on a primarily theological issue. Nevertheless, it is appropriate – if not necessary – to take possible psychological factors into account. For the question whether a religion is capable and ready to fully accept the right of other religions to exist seems to be directly influenced by psychological factors.

The relationship of different religions to one another has a lot in common with the relationship between individuals. Two, or more, individuals or – respectively – religions meet, each with their own identity, *Weltanschauung*, needs, and goals. And here the question arises how each one views and relates to the other.

Regarding the relationship between different individuals, we can observe that the greater the confidence of an individual and the more firm his inner conviction, the more he will be able and willing to fully accept the existence of another individual, even though this other individual may be very different from himself, with a different *Weltanschauung* and personality, thinking and feeling in a different way. But the greater a person's own insecurity and the more doubts he has about himself, the more he will experience another person as a danger and threat, and will be afraid of him.

Regarding the relationships between religions, it is very similar. The greater the confidence of a religion and the more it is convinced that it represents something legitimate, the more it will be able and willing to accept the existence of another religion – even though the other religion advances a different *Weltanschauung*. However, the greater the insecurities and doubts of a religion, the more it will experience the existence of other religions as a danger and threat to its own legitimacy and existence, will be afraid of them, and may even want to antagonize them.

We Orthodox rabbis who have signed the Statement feel secure enough in our Judaism to be able to fully accept the existence of Christianity – and Islam – and to view them as part of the divine plan for mankind. The existence of Christianity is in our opinion neither a threat for us nor a danger to our Judaism, but is part of the divine plan for this world.

Finally, I want to take another psychological step, a step to Freud's theory of psychoanalysis. Freud analyzes and divides the human psyche into different parts (he calls them: id, ego, and super-ego), and examines their relationship to one another. Freud's theory is thus based on the assumption that there are different parts within man that have very different needs, forces, and goals. One of the most important purposes of psychoanalysis is to enable man to learn about these different parts of his psyche, to understand the interactions between them, and to bring them into a healthy balance and relationship. One basic condition for this is for man to be able to accept these different parts, not to negate them, and not to fight or suppress them. A healthy, balanced relationship between the different parts of the human psyche can only be achieved when all the parts are accepted, and when the purpose of all the parts are understood and integrated.

It seems that the relationship between different religions can be compared to the theory of psychoanalysis; i.e. not only the relationship between individuals, but also the relationship between the different parts within one individual can be compared to the relationship between religions. Just as it is necessary for the psyche to accept each of its different parts in order to be able to bring them into a healthy, peaceful, and balanced relationship with one another; and just as it is necessary to recognize that for this purpose every part is essential, serves a purpose, and therefore has a right to exist. In the same way we, as mankind, have to recognize that different religions have their legitimacy and their purpose, in order to lead all human beings to a healthy and peaceful relationship with one another.

To Do the Will of Our Father in Heaven, therefore, accepts the full right of Christianity to exist, views it as part of a divine plan, and thus calls it "the willed divine outcome and gift to the nations."

A Response to *To Do the Will of Our Father in Heaven*

MARCIE LENK

In a community that claims fealty to an unchanging tradition, change is afoot. In the past few years, three different Orthodox Jewish bodies have issued statements about Christianity that show respect and a desire for collaboration between Jewish and Christian communities. These official statements come at a time of growing enthusiasm among some Orthodox Jews to work with Christians to further their shared political and spiritual values in the USA and Israel. *To Do the Will of Our Father in Heaven* is certainly positive in tone, but it is so lacking in practical proposals that I worry that it fails to move Jewish-Christian relations forward, leaving readers with little sense of the complexity and work necessary in the field.

Any positive statement about Christianity endorsed by Orthodox Jewish leaders is significant. For half a century, the words of Rabbi Moshe Feinstein, as reflected in his responsa, and Rabbi Joseph Soloveitchik, expressed in "Confrontation," have continued to direct the ideas and actions of Orthodox Jews regarding Christians and Christianity. For Rabbi Feinstein, Christianity was idolatry, and Christians engaged Jews in dialogue for the sole purpose of converting these Jews to Christianity. Rabbi Soloveitchik did not trust the intentions of Christians in their desire for Jewish dialogue partners. Many have acknowledged that "Confrontation" was a lecture that was later written as an article, and never written in the language or form of a *halakhic* responsum. Still, a certain interpretation of "Confrontation" has continued to guide policy in American Jewish Orthodoxy until today: partnership with Christians on matters of social and political need is acceptable; discussion of theology is forbidden.

The writers and signatories of *To Do the Will of Our Father in Heaven: Toward a Partnership between Jews and Christians* moved on to say something new. Written 50 years after the Catholic *Nostra Aetate*, and 51 years after "Confrontation," the Statement points to Christians as fellow monotheists, and goes two steps further than did Rabbi Soloveitchik. The written statements by the Catholic Church and the experience of Jewish representatives in dialogue with representatives of the Church have led to an acceptance that "the official teachings of the Catholic Church about Judaism have changed fundamentality and irrevocably."

Rabbi Moshe Feinstein rejected all interfaith dialogue, and Rabbi Soloveitchik accepted limited cooperation, with a clear distrust of what he labeled "the community of the many" which, he feared, would continue its efforts to devour "the community of the few." The writers of the Statement *To Do the Will of Our Father in Heaven*, "call on our communities to overcome ... fears in order to establish a relationship of trust and respect." Furthermore, the Statement selects positive assertions about Christianity by rabbis from Maimonides to Rabbi Jacob Emden to Rabbi Shear Yashuv Cohen, to portray a positive place for Christianity in Jewish theology. The idea here is to move beyond Jews' well-founded fears of physical and spiritual destruction at the hands of Christians (as emphasized by the reference to the Shoah at the very beginning of *To Do the Will of Our Father in Heaven*) and to trust the theological and policy changes in the Church. The writers portray Christianity as part of God's plan for the world; a significant change, to be sure, from the historical images of Christians as idolaters and murderers of Jews.

The writers "seek to do the will of Our Father in Heaven by accepting the hand offered to us by our Christian brothers and sisters." But the Statement leaves me with many questions. What is the vision of "trust and respect" that the authors and signatories have in mind? If the goal is to encourage Orthodox Jews to work with Christians on communal or political projects, that work is already being done, and indeed, Rabbi Soloveitchik supported this type of activity more than half a century ago. There are references in this document to *Nostra Aetate* and all the positive work of "honest dialogue," "affirmation of Israel's unique place in sacred history and the ultimate world redemption," and Jewish experience of "sincere love and respect from many Christians." Is this a call for Jews to return the "sincere love and respect"? If so, how should Jews get there?

Paragraph 4 seems to point towards the new vision. It begins with a statement that may be seen as radical, benign and overly simplistic. "Both Jews and Christians have a common covenantal mission to perfect the world under the sovereignty of the Almighty, so that all humanity will call on His name and abominations will be removed from the earth." Clearly, the authors of the Statement hoped to convince other Orthodox Jews that there is a traditional basis for Jews to see the work of Christians in the world as part of God's plan (paragraph 3). The language of "covenantal mission" might seem sufficiently open-ended to allow Jews and Christians to read in their own sense of covenantal mission. Would all Christians agree with this statement? Does it matter to the writers and signers of *To Do the Will of Our Father in Heaven* that many Christians still believe that the Jewish covenant with God has been replaced by Christianity? While the Catholic Commission for Religious Relations with the Jews and a number of mainline Protestant theologians and committees have explicitly rejected any further evangelization to Jews, many Christians of other denominations continue to believe in and teach the replacement theology that by definition denigrates Judaism. Would such Christians respect Jews as sharing a covenantal mission? What about Christians and Jews who espouse an inward-looking theology, not connected to any sense of perfecting the world? Do they have nothing to gain by understanding one another?

The publication of *Nostra Aetate* was followed up by committees, statements, and actions that showed that the Catholic Church was sincere about the changes it intended. Even so, there is more work to be done to ensure that Catholics around the world learn about and accept these changes.[1] What changes in Jewish theology and practice are envisioned by the writers of this new rabbinic statement? For example, the Catholic Church encouraged Christians to learn more about Judaism from Jews. Would these Orthodox rabbis be at all interested in, or go so far as to encourage Jews to learn about Christianity from Christians, or even from Jews? Would they recommend that courses on Christian theology become part of the curriculum of Jewish schools? Or would they consider such study taboo and dangerous for Jews even now? Is it possible to "trust and respect" another group while insisting on ignorance of the basic texts, doctrines and practices of that group?

It is time for Jews to learn about Christianity, just as so many Christian seminaries have courses on and encourage the study of Judaism. Jewish schools have long included the history of Christian anti-Judaism in Jewish history courses. But Christians and Christianity have also been inspirations and forces for good in the world. Would it really endanger Jewish identity if we taught our students why so many people in the world are Christian? The books of the New Testament, and particularly the Gospels, were written in order to convince people to become part of the faith group that came to be known as Christians, and Jews have historically feared reading these books when they experienced pressure to become Christian. If the writers and signatories of *To Do the Will of Our Father in Heaven* mean what they say about trusting the "love and respect" that Jews have experienced "from many Christians" in this age, perhaps it is time to get over our fears and seek to read and understand some of the basic books of Christianity.

In this time of unprecedented freedom for Jews to be Jews, when there is more robust Jewish education than ever before, need we continue to fear that if we read about Jesus we will become so enamored that we will convert to Christianity? Jews continue to face

---

1. Jewish-Christian relations are emphasized in some Catholic seminaries, but ignored in many others, and even the brief statement of *Nostra Aetate* is not known to most Catholics in the pews.

challenges in many parts of the world, but the recent increase in anti-Semitism does not come from the organized Christian world. As a Jewish scholar of Early Christianity I maintain that serious study of the New Testament does lead to a change in attitude, but not one that should be seen as endangering Jews or Judaism. I have learned to deeply respect (and respectfully question and even criticize) Christian texts and ideas. Opening our minds often does lead to change, but we need not fear that change. While some Orthodox Jews have engaged with Christian leaders, encouraging them to learn about Judaism, particularly Judaism in its "authentic" (Orthodox) forms, I have seen no evidence of Orthodox Jewish engagement with Christian texts, ideas or history.

The first part of the Statement seems to refer to Catholics. This makes sense to a degree, as the Statement was meant to respond to the fiftieth anniversary of *Nostra Aetate's* publication. This 1965 proclamation by the Catholic Church was indeed revolutionary, and the Catholic Church has led the way to improved relations with the Jewish people by following up on *Nostra Aetate* in subsequent work, policies, statements, and actions, including the spectacular declaration in the Vatican's 2015 document *The Gifts and the Calling of God are Irrevocable* that there should not be a mission directed towards Jews, since God's covenant with the Jewish people still stands for them.[2] But *To Do the Will of Our Father in Heaven* claims to be about "a partnership between Jews and Christians" without explicitly referencing the fact that there are many different kinds of Christians. Roman Catholicism may be the biggest Christian denomination, but it does not represent the hundreds of millions of Christians who are Orthodox, Protestant, and beyond. Christian denominations have different authoritative hierarchies, practices, and theologies, each of which has ramifications for Jewish-Christian relations.

Was the lack of specificity moving forward intentional? There are

---

2. See part 6 "The Church's Mandate to Evangelize in Relation to Judaism" in *The Gifts and the Calling of God are Irrevocable (Rom 11:29) A Reflection on Theological Questions Pertaining to Catholic-Jewish Relations on the Occasion of the 50th Anniversary of Nostra Aetate" (No. 4).*

rabbis who have formed coalitions with Christian leaders in order to work towards conservative policies in the USA, as well as to support settlements in the West Bank and other right-wing causes in Israel. As written, the Statement provides cover for such partnerships. It does not suggest that Jews have anything to learn from Christians, or any need for Jews to learn about Christianity – neither of which would be necessary if the idea was to accept Christian material and political support. It is strange, however, to refer to popes and Catholic statements if the idea was to form such coalitions as I have suggested. While Catholic leaders have long agitated against legalized abortion in the USA, most of the Christians who have been partnering with conservative-leaning Jews have been Evangelical, and even a subcategory of Evangelical, i.e., Christian Zionist. For these Christians, statements by the Catholic Church have no authority.

Indeed, the 2015 Vatican statement that there should no longer be a Christian mission directed towards Jews for the purpose of evangelization has been seen by Evangelical Christians as nothing short of heretical, denying the "Great Commission" of Jesus (Matthew 28:19). While many Christians see evangelizing as an expression of love – sharing what is most precious with the world, Jews have often experienced these efforts as more of a bludgeon. The Vatican commissions that have worked on issues of Jewish-Christian relations have understood, since at least as far back as the Second Vatican Council, that this is a fundamental issue for Jews. In the correspondence between Rabbi Abraham Joshua Heschel and Cardinal Bea in 1962, Heschel insisted that the Church must agree, among other things, "that Jews be recognized as Jews … and that the council recognize the integrity and continuing value of Jews and Judaism." While the final form of *Nostra Aetate* did not include such a statement, half a century later the Commission for Religious Relations with the Jews insisted: "The Catholic Church neither conducts nor supports any specific institutional mission work directed towards Jews." The Commission's 2015 statement does not have the theological authority of a Church council like the Second Vatican Council, although it is a statement commissioned by the Vatican and posted on the Vatican website. At the very least, it represents work on Jewish-Christian relations approved by the Vatican, and at most, it sets out aspirational theology and practices for the Catholic Church as a whole. The facts that few Catholics in the pews know about the Statement, and that only a few Catholic seminaries spend much time on issues of Jewish-Christian relations, mean that few Jews or Catholics know that there has been a change. Still, the work of this Vatican Commission is available for those interested and concerned, and it has in fact led to improved relations with many Jewish leaders.

Many mainline Christian denominations have passed resolutions calling for respect for Jews and Judaism, including sensitivity when it comes to evangelical missions to Jews.[3] By contrast, Evangelical Christianity, more of a movement than a denomination, is radically decentralized in its structure. While some Evangelical communities identify with denominations, others see themselves as independent. With no clear authoritative hierarchy, there are no popes or bishops who speak for Evangelical Christians as a whole. Little theological work has been done in Evangelical seminaries to counter replacement theology, with its implication that Jewish faith has long been surpassed by Jesus and the faith of his followers. Expressions of faith in Jesus as Christ, as well as the urgency to bring unbelievers to faith, are central to Evangelical identity. For many Evangelical Christians, the mission to evangelize among Jews remains in place.[4] Some Christian Zionist organizations instruct employees and participants in their Holy Land excursions to refrain from evangelizing Jews in Israel so as not to offend, but Christian Zionist leaders such as Pastor John Hagee have been severely critiqued for trying to work out a coherent theology that respects Jewish faith without Jesus.[5]

---

3. Franklin Sherman, ed. *Bridges: Documents of the Christian-Jewish Dialogue*, 2 vols. (Paulist Press, 2011, 2014); Dialogika Resources (Council of Centers on Jewish-Christian Relations): https://www.ccjr.us/dialogika-resources/documents-and-statements/

4. http://www.worldevangelicals.org/tc/statements/willowbank-statement.htm

5. Faydra Shapiro, *Christian Zionism: Navigating the Jewish-Christin Border* (Eugene, OR: Cascade, 2015), 126–133.

Many Jews seem comfortable ignoring theology and ideology, which might be seen as a wedge between Jews and Evangelical Christians, as they find partnership in the Christian Zionist political views of many Evangelical Christians. The history of the support that Christian followers of premillennial dispensationalism expressed for Zionists from Theodore Herzl and Chaim Weizmann through Benjamin Netanyahu has been well documented.[6] More recent are collaborations between Orthodox Jews and Evangelical Christians. This is more than a case of realpolitik. There are claims on both sides of these relationships to be fulfilling God's will in the world. Both sides speak of realizing the words of the biblical prophets through Christian support of the State of Israel and the Jewish people. However, these partnerships necessarily ignore much Christian theology, emphasizing only those interpretations of the Hebrew Bible that are shared. They also ignore other Jewish interpretations of these same biblical prophecies, as well as other Jewish ideals. For example, many expressions of Jewish-Christian understanding between Orthodox Jews and Evangelical Christians demonize Muslims, despite the long history of a positive relationships between Jews and Muslims. Additionally, many Jews (including Orthodox Jews) do not share the extreme nationalism expressed by the Orthodox Jews who partner with Christian Zionist Evangelical groups. Should we necessarily celebrate the shared vision of a Greater Israel?[7] If one believes that such a vision is dangerous for any hope for peace and democracy in a future State of Israel, in what way is the relationship with Christian Zionists good for the Jewish people?

Third, I wonder why there is a need to begin the Orthodox statement with a reference to the Shoah. There is no doubt that the history of Christian anti-Judaism contributed significantly to Nazi anti-Semitism, and the history of Christian rejection and op-

6. Victoria Clark, *Allies for Armageddon: The Rise of Christian Zionism* (New Haven: Yale, 2007); Shalom Goldman, *Zeal for Zion: Christians, Jews, and the Idea of the Promised Land* (Chapel Hill: UNC Press, 209).

7. On a shared vision of Christian Zionists and Orthodox Jews to rebuild the Temple in Jerusalem, see Gershom Gorenberg, *The End of Days: Fundamentalism and the Struggle for the Temple Mount* (NY: Oxford, 2000).

pression of Jews must be part of any honest dialogue between Jews and Christians. Still, when the State of Israel now has one of the strongest militaries in the world, and when Jews are freer and more successful around the globe than could ever have been imagined a few generations ago, why not begin the Statement with an acknowledgement of Jewish strength and responsibility?

The single paragraph on this topic in *To Do the Will of Our Father in Heaven* is significantly less than the five full pages allotted to the rehearsal of Jewish suffering in the Orthodox Union's *Between Jerusalem and Rome*, yet I am troubled by the rhetorical move of beginning with the "lachrymose history" of Jewish suffering at the hands of Christians. By contrast, the *Declaration for the Upcoming Jubilee of Brotherhood* written by French Jewish leaders refers to this history only in the sixth paragraph (out of nine paragraphs in the full Statement). There is a sense that the authors of *To Do the Will of Our Father in Heaven* are trying to express their American Orthodox Jewish *bona fides*, which begin with expressions of Jewish fragility. There is irony in the fact that the French rabbis, living on the European soil of the Shoah, in a community that remembers and continues to see evidence of anti-Semitism, express greater confidence in the possibilities of Jewish-Christian relations than do Orthodox rabbis in North America and Israel.

Orthodox Judaism is by its very nature a conservative movement, making overt changes slowly over time. I am glad to see that there has been recognition of the fact that there are Christians who are now trusted partners. I hope to see this respect expressed through increased study by Jews of Christianity generally, as well as better understanding of the diverse approaches taken by different Christian denominations to Jews, Judaism and Israel. Only with such respect and understanding can we work through our disagreements and thus truly join together to pursue common goals with our Christian brothers and sisters.

II. The Statement and Jewish–Christian Relations

Reflections on the Orthodox Rabbinic Statement on Christianity

Abraham Skorka

Several verses from the Torah and rabbinical commentaries have bothered me since the very moment that I learned about them. The first of these is Balaam's vision of the people of Israel as described in Numbers 23:9: "I see them from the cliff tops; I watch them from the hills. It is a people that dwells alone; and not counting itself among the nations." The second is Rashi's commentary on Genesis 33:4, which describes the embrace and kiss of Esau and Jacob. The *midrash*[1] quoted by the great exegete puts in doubt the sincerity of Esau and the exceptional nature of his behavior because – as Rabbi Shimon bar Yohai taught: "It is a known rule that Esau hates Jacob." The third text that has troubled me is the *midrash*[2] that explains the change in the name Mount Horeb to Mount Sinai after God's revelation there to *Bnei Israel*. What's disturbing is that hatred (*sinah* in Hebrew) of the nations toward Israel appears at the very moment when Israel receives the Torah.

Thus begins a persistent history of anti-Semitism that Edward Flannery, among many others, describes in his well-known book, *The Anguish of the Jews: Twenty-Three Centuries of Antisemitism.* The *midrash* speaks from a reality of hostility that its rabbinic au-

1. *Sifri Bemidbar, Parashat Beha'alotkha, Piska* 69.
2. *Bavli Shabbat* 89a.

thor could not realize would culminate during the Shoah – the extermination of the people that received the Torah at Sinai/Horeb.

The minimal dialogue between Israel and the nations that occurred over these twenty-three centuries could be seen as the consequence of the reality of living alone, as Balaam's oracle foreshadowed. The particularity of Israel's faith, and the nations' response to it, deprived Jews of a deep spiritual interaction with other people. In Yehezkel Kaufmann's perspective, the faith of Israel was unique in human history. In the foreword of his monumental *Toldot HaEmunah HaIsraelit*,[3] Kaufmann says:

> The faith of Israel is taken here as an original creation of the people of Israel. This creation is absolutely different from everything that the human spirit created throughout the pagan world. Israelite monotheism has no roots in the whole pagan world. Moreover, Israelite monotheism wasn't born as a "theological idea" conceived and developed by individuals or schools; it is neither an idea expressed in this nor that text, in this or that literary layer, but is a basic idea of a national culture expressed in all the manifestations of the entire Israelite creation since its beginning.[4]

Beyond the accuracy of Kaufmann's hypothesis, it is very clear that in the times of the Second Temple the Jews were looked on as a strange people in the eyes of Greeks, Romans, and other pagan peoples. Kaufmann built up his vision of the history, essence and life of the people of Israel under the influence of the biblical and rabbinical self-understanding of Israel, which is made explicit, among other examples, in the biblical sentence: "And who is like your people Israel – a unique nation on earth?"[5] (2 Samuel 7:23; 1 Chronicles 17:21), and is interpreted by the Talmudic sages as referring to the

---

3. *Hotza'at Bialik, Yerushalaim* – Devir, Tel Aviv, fourth edition, 5720.
4. *Hakdamah*, 6–7. Translated by the author.
5. New International Version (NIV).

singularity of Israel among the world's peoples,[6] which is the view that Jews have had of themselves since their very beginning.

According to the words of Haman the Agagite to his King Ahasuerus (Esther 3:8), in the Persian empire of those days the Jews were clearly a singular people among the nations:

> There is a certain people dispersed among the peoples in all the provinces of your kingdom who keep themselves separate. Their customs are different from those of all other people, and they do not obey the king's laws; it is not in the king's best interest to tolerate them.[7]

The Jewish faith, especially as it developed after the generation of the eighth-century BCE prophets Isaiah, Hosea, Amos, and Micah, was strange in the pagan world view. Only after the second century BCE, when in Judea the development of Pharisasm took place, did certain philosophical schools in the Mediterranean basin such as Stoicism have certain commonalities with Judaism. But as Isaiah Berlin has affirmed, the Jews had a totally different cultural model dominating, "a totally different set of ideas, which would have been unintelligible to the Greeks."[8]

Only the development of Christianity and Islam changed Jewish reality among the nations. These two religions brought about a deep cultural transformation in Europe and much of Asia. European culture was defined as Judeo-Christian, and Islam recognized its Jewish and Christian roots. But Jews lived scattered throughout countries in which the different Christian denominations and Islamic schools controlled civil power, and in many cases sought to demonstrate the truth or superiority of their faith by compelling the conversion or subordination of the Jews. As a minority among the nations the Jews were the regular scapegoats for various social plagues. Religion was a primary social force in Christendom, and

6. *Berakhot* 6a; *Hagigah* 3b.
7. New International Version (NIV).
8. *The Roots of Romanticism*, Chatto & Windus, London, 1999, 3.

faced with Jewish rejection of their claims about Christ on the one side, and Islamic military might on the other, medieval Christians exerted control over Jews through persecution, expulsions, mass murders, inquisitions, and *autos da fé*, etc. They confined Jews into apartheid neighborhoods, which acquired a special, degrading name: ghettos.

Nevertheless, there were many documents in different European countries recognizing the rights of Jews, and there were periods when Jews prospered and developed their culture in extraordinary ways. Two outstanding examples are the Golden Age in Spain (12th century) and the spiritual insights and knowledge acquired by the Jewish communities in Eastern Europe in the two centuries before the Shoah.[9] It is possible to find texts in medieval rabbinic literature that reflect peaceful coexistence between Jews and Christians. Despite the ubiquitous graven images in churches, there were nonetheless *halakhic* authorities who did not consider Christians to be idolaters.[10]

The great social, political and cultural changes that unfolded in the Europe of the 18th century had an important impact on the continent's Jewish communities. The Enlightenment movement and its humanistic ideals, the fights for *liberté, égalité, fraternité*, and the rights given to Jews in central European countries under Napoleon, created a new reality for European Jews in which a Jewish Enlightenment movement took place and such important movements as Hasidisim, Mitnagdim, and more recently Zionism emerged. There

9. Abraham Joshua Heschel, *The Earth is the Lord's. The Inner World of the Jew in East Europe*, Meridian Books and the Jewish Publication Society of America, 1963, Cleveland and New York.

10. Especially in the glosses of Rabbi Menahem Ha-Meiri in his commentary to the Talmud Bet HaBehirah to Bava Kama 37b; 113b; Gittin 62a; Pesahim 21b; Yoma 84b; Bava Metzi'a 27a; *Avodah Zarah* 2a; 6b; 15b; 20a; 22a; 26; 57a; etc. It is interesting to quote here Harav Kook's opinion about the Meiri's position on the theme in Igrot Ha-Rayah, 89: "The essence is in accordance to the opinion of the Meiri, that all the peoples that are limited in their behaviour between an individual and his neighbour by norms of morality and society are already considered as *gerim toshavim* [gentiles that took upon themselves the Noahide Laws] in all the human responsibilities." In responsa literature, also, the opinion that Christianity is not a pagan cult is found.

is a great bibliography on Hasidism and Mitnagdim, their history and spiritual impact,[11] and Yehezkel Kaufmann's second volume of his *Golah VeNekhar*,[12] which he finished writing in 1929, masterfully describes the sociological evolution of European Jewry and the crossroads at which it stood at that time.

Nevertheless, anti-Semitism persisted as a devastating attitude in many countries, and the great humanistic ideas of the Enlightenment did not take root deeply enough in many parts of the so-called Western world. Christian Churches did not react adequately to the terrible crisis that arose in the dark moments before the Second World War. Jacques Maritain delivered an historic (even prophetic) speech on the dire situation of the Jews in Europe, urging Christian action on behalf of their Jewish neighbors,[13] but his efforts, as well as those of many others, were not successful among either the religious leaders or the political rulers of that time.

The Second World War and the Shoah marked a turning point in history. On the one hand, it reflected the bankruptcy of European Christian culture, and on the other, the shallowness of humanistic ideology. It is usually estimated that eighty million people were killed in this war or by related diseases and famine. Six million of them were Jews, annihilated in a systematic, industrialized manner in a crime with characteristics never seen before in human history. A peculiar and abhorrent crime, a genocide that "has a distinctive feature" that distinguishes it from all the others, in the words of the current Pope Francis,[14] and as explained by Élisabeth Roudinesco.[15]

---

11. See for instance: http://www.academia.edu/Documents/in/Hasidim_and _Mitnagdim

12. The third edition of the text was used, Ed, Dvir, Tel Aviv, 5722, 1962.

13. *Les Juifs parmi les nations: conférence faite par M. Jacques Maritain sous les auspices des "Groupes Chrétienté" au Théâtre des Ambassadeurs, le samedi 5 février 1938*. Paris, *Les Éditions du Cerf (29, boulevard de La Tour-Maubourg)*, 1938. (31 août.) The conference was translated into Spanish by Ediciones Sur in Buenos Aires, and published as a booklet on July 4, 1938.

14. Jorge Mario Bergoglio, Abraham Skorka, *On Heaven and Earth*, IMAGE, New York, 2013, 178.

15. *A vueltas con la cuestión judía*, ANAGRAMA; Barcelona, 2011, in the chapter: "*El Genocidio, entre la memoria y la Negación*" (163–212). Original in French: *Retour sur la question juive*, Éditions Albin Michel, Paris, 2009.

A great part of the Jewish people felt immediately after the Shoah that a turning point had come upon them because of the huge tragedy they had suffered. European Jewry, with its history of 2000 years on the continent, was devastated. The establishment of the State of Israel was not the direct consequence of the Shoah, but the materialization of a process that had begun in the nineteenth century. It was an answer to the trauma suffered and a manifestation of the Jewish decision to continue enduring in human history. Zionist leaders understood that the Jews could not continue being a people "that dwells alone; and not counting itself among the nations." The modern state established as one of its most important aims to be the nation of the Jews among, and together with, the other nations.

Both Christians and Jews throughout the world understood that another spiritual dimension, which had been denigrated and depreciated during the war, must be saved. It required an immediate and dramatic answer to why it survived. Nazism's ultimate aim was the total destruction of Jewish and Christian culture, replaced by a renewed pagan culture that was based on a racist distortion of Darwinism, a false reading of Nietzsche's ideas, and demented theories based on hate, prejudice, and absurdity.

There were people who understood even before *Nostra Aetate*,[16] that the saying that Esau hates Jacob had to be changed if Jews and Christians were to live in ways based on biblical values. Rabbi Abraham Joshua Heschel explained the importance of a change of attitude in relations between Jews and Christians because of the spiritual challenges in the modern, post-war world in his magisterial essay *No Religion Is an Island*.[17] The challenge was not merely to find ways to achieve a mutual toleration that permits us to live in peace together. The new challenge was to build a deep dialogical reality to

16. South America, for several reasons, was a place in which Jewish-Christian dialogue was significantly enhanced immediately after the promulgation of *Nostra Aetate* and has since advanced beyond it. See for instance: Abraham Skorka, *El diálogo judeo-católico a cincuenta años de Nostra Aetate. Una perspectiva latinoamericana*. El Olivo XXXVIII, 79–80 (2014), 33–44.

17. Union Seminary Quarterly Review, Vol. XXI No. 2 Part I, Jan. 1966.

demonstrate that the spiritual bankruptcy of European culture was a circumstantial phenomenon and not a perennial verdict.

Nostra Aetate was the Catholic answer to the Shoah. It inspired Pope John Paul II to ask forgiveness from God for the sins committed by the Church against the Jewish people,[18] to visit the Great Synagogue in Rome, to establish full diplomatic relationships between the Vatican and Israel, and to visit Israel and leave a special prayer of penitence and commitment in the *Kotel*.

Similarly, in many Churches throughout the world, the message of *Nostra Aetate* was very seriously considered. In Argentina, among the new generation of priests were several who developed a profound commitment to the concepts and ideas of the Second Vatican Council: Jorge Mejía, Rafael Brown, Estanislao Karlic, and the current Pope Francis among them.

The Catholic Church wondered if there would ever be a Jewish response to *Nostra Aetate* and subsequent documents and actions. There were many greetings, individual dramatic gestures, but very few formal declarations. The Christian persecutions of the past, previous theologies with hostile views on the Jews, and the ashes of Auschwitz, Maidanek, Treblinka, and so many others for which centuries of Christian teaching bore some responsibility, prevented a proper Jewish answer for a long time. Who could dare to speak in the name of all of the people of Israel? It was Rabbi Heschel, who began his famous article mentioned above, who demonstrated a way forward:

> I speak as a member of a congregation whose founder was Abraham, and the name of my rabbi is Moses. I speak as a person who was able to leave Warsaw, the city in which I was born, just six weeks before the disaster began. My destination was New York, it would have been Auschwitz or Treblinka. I am a

18. The Vatican took pains not to ask for forgiveness from Jews because it realized that the burden of deciding how to respond to such a plea would be overwhelming for many Jews, who could not speak on behalf of the dead, killed for example in the Crusades, in any case. The Vatican carefully directed prayers of remorse to God, the only One who could transcend the issues.

brand plucked from the fire, in which my people were burned
to death. I am a brand plucked from the fire of an altar of Satan
on which millions of human lives were exterminated to evil's
greater glory, and on which so much else was consumed: the
divine image of so many human beings, many people's faith
in the God of justice and compassion, and much of the secret
and power of attachment to the Bible bred and cherished in
the hearts of men for nearly two thousand years. I speak as a
person who is often afraid and terribly alarmed lest God has
turned away from us in disgust and even deprived us of the
power to understand His word.

He introduced himself as "a brand plucked from the fire," describing in this way his right to offer a Jewish answer to *Nostra Aetate*
and the following documents issued by the Vatican.

It was not until 2000 that there appeared, in *The New York Times*
edition of September 10, the declaration *Dabru Emet*, ("Speak
Truth"). This was composed by a group of Jewish thinkers and
signed by 220 intellectuals. The document was both well received
and criticized by Jewish commentators.

On December 3, 2015, a group of Orthodox rabbis released a
statement on Christianity entitled *To Do the Will of Our Father in
Heaven: Toward a Partnership between Jews and Christians*, which
has an extreme importance. Until that point there were encounters
between Orthodox rabbis and Christian leaders, but in almost all
these cases, with some very specific exceptions, they did not go any
deeper than polite and sympathetic expressions of political correct-
ness. The dialogue and its challenges were almost totally left in the
hands of Conservative and Reform rabbis. On this occasion a significant group of Orthodox rabbis are expressing their commitment to
a deep dialogical attitude toward Christians.

A second revolutionary aspect of the document is the title itself.
It is the will of God for Jews to be partners with Christians!

There is also an explicit statement that Christianity should not
be considered idolatry. The presence of graven images in medieval churches provoked discussions among rabbis about whether

Christianity is riddled with idolatry, and therefore whether Jews are prohibited from interacting with Christians. Such great twentieth-century sages as Itzhak Isaac HaLevi Herzog[19] and Hayim David HaLevi[20] saw the need to establish on clear *halakhic* grounds that Christianity is a non-idolatrous religion. *To Do the Will of Our Father in Heaven* would like to put an end, once and for all, to that discussion.

The starting point of the document is the affirmation of the turning point marked by the Shoah. It goes on to discuss the importance of *Nostra Aetate* and the teachings of Popes John Paul II and Benedict XVI that sought to implement the spirit of that declaration. *To Do the Will of Our Father in Heaven* recognizes the revolution in Catholic theology that is underway because of the affirmations in *Nostra Aetate* that God did not reject the Jews as the Almighty's beloved and covenanted people. These affirmations, as *To Do the Will of Our Father in Heaven* stresses in point 3, remove all doubts about concealed missionary purposes in contemporary Christian treatment of Jews. Therefore, the challenge from now on is to be sincere partners in the building of a better reality. Point 3 concludes by saying: "As stated by the Chief Rabbinate of Israel's Bilateral Commission with the Holy See under the leadership of Rabbi Shear Yashuv Cohen, 'We are no longer enemies, but unequivocal partners in articulating the essential moral values for the survival and welfare of humanity.' Neither of us can achieve God's mission in this world alone." The document takes – consciously or not – Heschel's prophetic vision in *No Religion Is an Island*, as a cornerstone for future behavior.

At the end of point 4, the document quotes the exegesis of Rabbi Naftali Zvi Yehuda Berlin (the Netziv of Volozhin), written at the end of the 19th century, on Genesis 33:4 in his famous *Ha'amek Davar*: "In the future when the children of Esau are moved by pure spirit to recognize the people of Israel and their virtues, then we will also be moved to recognize that Esau is our brother." This commen-

---

19. *Zekhuiot HaMiu'tim LeFi HaHalakhah, Tehumin* 2, 5741–1981, 169–179.
20. *Darkei Shalom, Tehumin* 9, 5748–1988, 71–81.

tary is undoubtedly a reaction to Rashi's gloss quoted above in the first paragraph of this essay. Rabbi Berlin concludes his commentary on the verse, saying: "in the way of a rabbi who was a real friend of Antoninus and so much more," which reveals that in Rabbi Berlin's view, during past generations there were genuine individual friendships and a common commitment between Jews and Christians; the problem was with collective attitudes.

Quoting different sources, the Statement affirms that Christianity has a function in God's plan for the spiritual enhancement of human beings. The most authoritative passage cited is the famous paragraph in Mishneh Torah, Laws of Kings 11:4 (uncensored edition), where Maimonides affirms:[21]

> It is beyond the human mind to fathom the designs of the Creator; for our ways are not His ways, neither are our thoughts His thoughts. All these matters relating to Jesus of Nazareth and the Ishmaelite [Mohammed] who came after him served to clear the way for King Messiah, to prepare the whole world to worship God with one accord, as it is written, "For then will I turn to the peoples a pure language, that they may all call upon the name of the Lord to serve Him with one consent" (Zephaniah 3:9). Thus the messianic hope, the Torah, and the commandments have become familiar topics – topics of conversation (among the inhabitants) of the far islands of many people.

The step taken by the Orthodox rabbis who composed or signed this Statement is very significant. In the Orthodox world, the possibility of interreligious dialogue is regarded with great hesitation, if not outright rejection. Spiritual audacity and courage is evident in this declaration, and the same qualities were demonstrated by all who have supported it with their signatures.

In 2017, I was invited by the very distinguished rabbis who authored the document to write an approbation of it. I did so with

---

21. Taken from Heschel's translation in "No Religion Is an Island."

pleasure, and my remarks were attached to the Statement in the month of May. I concluded those reflections by saying:

> Hence I append my full agreement to this document created by Orthodox Rabbis. Would that it be accepted by all Israel through an internal dialogue having the power to bring together all segments of our divided people so they can succeed in realizing the prophet Zechariah's and our Talmudic sages' challenge to us: "Love truth and peace."

In these sentences I tried to express the single point that displeased me in the document. This is the label of "Orthodoxy" that defines and limits the identities of the undersigned rabbis. In the Judaism of Talmudic times, different schools with different visions coexisted. The most famous of these were the Houses of Hillel and Shammai. There are sources in Talmudic literature that refer to their two attitudes in resolving the discussions between them. On certain occasions the controversies were resolved through knives and swords,[22] on others through respect, comprehension and dialogue.[23] In the second case the Talmud explains that they practiced affection and camaraderie between them to fulfill what was taught by the prophet Zechariah (8:19): "Love truth and peace" (Zechariah 8:19). As in the past, so today. The different Jewish movements have to find their way to affection and camaraderie through the search for truth and peace.

Truth and peace must come together. It is possible to have one without the other, but then the peace achieved is a deceptive peace.[24] Peace attained without complete sincerity is not a real peace. Reconciliation at large, and between Jews and Christians in particular, requires paving a path of truth. This was done in the past by all those

22. *Talmud Bavli Shabbat 17a; Talmud Yerushalmi, Shabbat Perek 1, Daf 3, Tur 3, Halakha 4; Tosefta Shabbat, Perek 1.*

23. *Bavli Yevamot 14b.*

24. This affirmation was inspired by the teachings of Rabbi Menachem Mendl of Kotzk. See: *Emet MeEretz Titzmah*, Ed. Netzah, Israel, 5721, 1962, paragraph no. 674.

who exerted their best efforts for mutual understanding and the development of interfaith dialogue. Such a path is expected by God, and undoubtedly will be blessed by Him, as in the stamp of His seal appears only one word: Truth[25] – the Truth that will lead to *Shalom*.

25. *Talmud Bavli Shabbat* 55b.

The Import of *To Do the Will* – a Catholic and a Jewish Perspective

PHILIP A. CUNNINGHAM AND ADAM GREGERMAN

INTRODUCTION: CHRISTIAN TRANSFORMATION, JEWISH DISINTEREST

The issuance in 2015 of the Statement *To Do the Will of Our Father in Heaven: Toward a Partnership between Jews and Christians* (hereafter *TDW*) with the approbation of dozens of Orthodox rabbis on three continents, is a historic benchmark in the post-Second World War "new relationship" developing between the two communities. As the authors admit, this became a possibility with the "promulgation of *Nostra Aetate* fifty years ago, [which] started the process of reconciliation between our two communities." That statement had dramatically burst upon the consciousness of the general public during the Second Vatican Council on October 28, 1965. Although preceded by statements from other Christian bodies[1], *Nostra Aetate* was released under the highest central authority of the world's largest Christian community. Its words, therefore, had enormous influence within and beyond the Catholic world, rippling like a seismic wave throughout the many varieties of Christianity. It was clear

---

1. The most prominent example is *An Address to the Churches* (*The Ten Points of Seelisberg*) from 1947, available at: http://www.ccjr.us/dialogika-resources/documents-and-statements/ecumenical-christian/567-seelisberg.

that its authors hoped *Nostra Aetate* could inspire reconciliation between Jews and Christians despite the antagonism and suspicion that had characterized their interactions for nearly two millennia.

In the following decades, many subsequent Catholic documents and similar declarations from other Christian communities echoed *Nostra Aetate*'s call. They urged friendship and dialogue between Christians and Jews. They also repudiated long-lived contemptuous teachings about Jews and Judaism.

Over time many Jews personally responded positively to these changes. However, the Jewish world at large remained mostly indifferent to or unaware of these unprecedented developments. Jewish religious and secular organizations apparently saw little need for any type of formal response. There are several reasons for this.[2]

First, unlike Christians, for whom serious consideration of Judaism is unavoidable (e.g., their biblical canon includes the story of ancient Israel in the Old Testament; at the center of Christian faith is Jesus, born a Jew; nearly all early writings were composed by his Jewish followers), Jewish theological self-understanding does not require religious engagement with Christianity. While Jews who became aware of *Nostra Aetate* and similar texts welcomed their novel, positive tone, they tended not to see any theological significance in them for their own religious life, hence they found no need for a communal religious response.

Second, contemporary Jews are aware of a long history of Christian hostility to Jews and Judaism, with Jews sometimes having been the victims of expulsions and murderous violence. It is to be expected that many would regard the apparently sudden shift in Christian views as unimpressive or insignificant, especially in the traumatic aftermath of the Nazi genocide of two-thirds of European Jews. There was no need to respond to what might amount to a temporary aberration from the inimical Christian norm.

---

2. See Deborah Weissman, "Has There Been a Jewish Response to *Nostra Aetate*?," in *Paths to Dialogue in Our Age: International Perspectives*, ed. Edmund Kee-Fook Chia and Fatih Erol Tuncer (Melbourne: Australian Catholic University, 2014), 33–49.

Third, there is no authoritative Jewish hierarchy or organization, and so no one to issue official, let alone binding declarations, unlike the Catholic Church. There are no recognized spokespersons ready to respond to Christian statements on behalf of the diverse and decentralized Jewish world.

Fourth, the Jewish culture of religious discourse as exemplified in rabbinic literature is quite different in presuppositions, methods, and categories from Christian theological procedures. Jews would therefore be disinclined to respond "in kind" to the types of theological formulations found in statements such as *Nostra Aetate*. As Deborah Weissman has concisely summarized: "Jews do not issue documents; they study texts, write commentaries on them, and then write commentaries upon the commentaries."[3]

For these reasons it is unsurprising that in the five decades since 1965, there have only been a handful of attempts to give some kind of organizational Jewish response to *Nostra Aetate* and similar Christian declarations.[4]

There is a further reason to call *TDW* a historic benchmark: it was the first text composed and endorsed by "Orthodox Rabbis who lead communities, institutions and seminaries in Israel, the United States and Europe." Orthodox Jews generally avoid theological engagement with Christians. This stance was encouraged by a leading Orthodox authority, Rabbi Joseph Soloveitchik, who in 1964 published an essay called "Confrontation."[5] He offered several reasons why Jews should not converse with Christians about

3. "Has There Been a Jewish Response to *Nostra Aetate*?," 47.
4. These include an unsuccessful effort in the 1970s by the French rabbinate to reply to a question from French Catholic bishops about "Christianity in Jewish Theology" (http://ccjr.us/dialogika-resources/documents-and-statements/jewish/765-fr-jewish-comm1973); the September 2000 American statement, *Dabru Emet: A Jewish Statement on Christians and Christianity*, which was composed by four Jewish scholars speaking only for themselves under the auspices of the Institute for Christian & Jewish Studies in Baltimore (https://icjs.org/sites/default/files/Dabru%20Emet%20-%20PDF%20copy.pdf); and a 2011 document from the Center for Jewish-Christian Understanding and Cooperation, *A Jewish Understanding of Christians and Christianity* (http://cjcuc.org/2011/05/24/cjcuc-statement-on-a-jewish-understanding-of-christians-and-christianity/).
5. Joseph B. Soloveitchik, "Confrontation," *Tradition* 6 (1964), 5–29.

their respective theologies and beliefs. One was the pressure that normal social interaction would place upon Jews to reciprocate friendly Christian overtures at the risk of compromising their own religious convictions: "we certainly have not been authorized by our history, sanctified by the martyrdom of millions … to trade favors [with Christians] pertaining to fundamental matters of faith, and to reconcile 'some' differences. Such a suggestion would be nothing but a betrayal of our great tradition and heritage."[6] The Rabbinical Council of America espoused Soloveitchik's views in a formal statement appended to his article.[7]

RESPONDING TO REAL REFORM

It is therefore significant that in 2015, the year of the fiftieth anniversary of *Nostra Aetate,* two groups of Orthodox Jews composed statements on the declaration.[8] In addition to *TDW,* other Orthodox Jews prepared an essay *Between Jerusalem and Rome: Reflections on 50 Years of Nostra Aetate* (hereinafter BJR). This was issued under the auspices of three major Orthodox organizations: The Conference of European Rabbis, the Rabbinical Council of America, and the Chief Rabbinate of Israel.[9]

6. "Confrontation," 25.
7. "Confrontation," 28–29.
8. We note publications by the American Jewish Committee, *In Our Time: AJC and Nostra Aetate: A Reflection after 50 Years* (https://www.ajc.org/sites/de fault/files/pdf/2017-09/AJC_and_Nostra_Aetate_IN_OUR_TIME.PDF) and the Anti-Defamation League, *50th Anniversary Nostra Aetate 1965–2015* (https:// www.adl.org/sites/default/files/documents/assets/pdf/education-outreach/inter faith-affairs/adl-nostra-aetate-50th-anniversary.pdf). Both texts focus on the history of the declaration but do not develop Jewish theological responses, although the ADL included the text of *Dabru Emet.*
9. It is available at http://files.constantcontact.com/6f28f4f9001/7ba1a585 -80c5-4ddb-b7ea-b2b36fbc8853.pdf. We also note the 2015 publication of a *Declaration for the Upcoming Jubilee of Brotherhood,* written by the French Jewish community and formally presented by the Chief Rabbi of France to the Cardinal Archbishop of Paris at a *Nostra Aetate* anniversary ceremony. For the French original, see https://www.ajcf.fr/Declaration-pour-le-jubile-de-fraternite-a-ven ir. For an unofficial English translation, see http://ccjr.us/dialogika-resources

Now, decades after *Nostra Aetate*, both Orthodox statements acknowledge genuine changes in Catholic teaching.[10] These include: the rejection of the notion of a divine curse on Jews for the crucifixion of Jesus; the condemnation of anti-Semitism; the affirmation that Jews are blessed with an eternal covenant with God; the Holy See's diplomatic recognition of the State of Israel; the abandonment of conversionary campaigns targeting Jews; and the hope that Jews and Christians could be partners in the service of God in the world. *TDW* and BJR thus reflect a transformed world. They speak in friendly tones, emphasize positive aspects of Christianity, and echo Christian hopes for cooperative endeavors.

After deciding to prepare statements for the fiftieth anniversary of *Nostra Aetate*, the authors faced the serious task of engaging with and being guided by Jewish tradition to address a topic raised only rarely in Jewish thought: the religious significance of Christianity for Jews and Judaism. Recognizing the dramatically changed situation after the Second Vatican Council, they sought to offer a positive assessment of Christians and Christianity, but as Orthodox Jews they were committed to working within the parameters of the received Jewish tradition. In this essay we ask whether the positive statements about Christianity made by these Orthodox Jews represent any departure from traditional Jewish thought and if so, in what ways?

/documents-and-statements/jewish/1356-declaration-for-the-upcoming-jubilee-of-brotherhood. Since this short text comes from the wider Jewish community, it is outside the scope of this essay which focuses primarily on the Orthodox statements *TDW* and BJR.

10. *TDW*: "We recognize that since the Second Vatican Council the official teachings of the Catholic Church about Judaism have changed fundamentally and irrevocably" (§2). BJR: "Over time, it has become clear that the transformations in the Church's attitudes and teachings are not only sincere but also increasingly profound, and that we are entering an era of growing tolerance, mutual respect, and solidarity between members of our respective faiths" (§Evaluation and Re-evaluation).

TRADITIONAL JEWISH MODELS

As background, it is necessary first to recall the traditional Jewish division of humanity into two categories, Jews / Israel and non-Jews / the nations. About the former category, there is of course much to be found in the Jewish tradition. About the latter category, there is far less. In traditional thought, the sharp divide between Jews and Gentiles is consistently maintained, and it is this division that is one primary marker of Jewish identity generally.[11]

Nonetheless, already in biblical times and then with greater sophistication in Second Temple and Rabbinic Judaism, Jews considered the theological status of those who are not Jews. Among the questions they asked were: What did God expect of them? Were they inherently evil, or could they be good without knowing the Torah? The rabbis did not assume that all non-Jews were forsaken by God. They suggested that God expected non-Jews to follow seven universal commandments. Appearing first in the *Tosefta* (late 2nd century CE), these were dated to the days of Noah as commands for all humanity to observe.[12] Non-Jews who observed them were judged to be "righteous among the Gentiles."[13]

In theory, when encountering or even thinking theologically about those from other religions, Jews need not examine their specific beliefs per se but their conformity to the Noahide principles. Did the teachings of the other religion prohibit idolatry, murder, theft, etc.? If the religion forbade such behavior and functioned with a reasonable legal system, then its followers could be considered righteous by Jews regardless of the other religion's specific theological claims. To bring more precision to what was stated above, humanity could thus be divided into two categories: Jews and non-

---

11. See Ruth Langer, "Jewish Understandings of the Religious Other," *Theological Studies* 64 (2003): 255–277, 263–264.

12. They are: no idol worship, no cursing the name of God, no murder, no sexual immorality, no theft, no eating the flesh of a living animal, and establishing a legal system of justice; see tAZ 8:4.

13. tSan 13:2.

Jews, with the latter judged righteous or unrighteous (according to their fidelity to the Noahide laws).

When later Jews interacted with Muslims and Christians, they recognized Muslims as strict monotheists. They could fulfill the Noahide stipulations and be considered righteous human beings. They might not possess the full knowledge of God's will that Jews in their covenantal life in the Torah had, but they rejected idolatry and could meet God's minimal ethical standards. Christianity, however, posed unique difficulties for medieval Jews regarding idolatry: did the doctrines of the Trinity and of the Incarnation and the production of "graven images" make Christians idolaters?

The trend into the medieval period was away from theological hostility toward Christianity and in favor of some interaction with Christians, for both economic and theological reasons.[14] Despite their Trinitarianism, prominent twelfth-century rabbis had somewhat tolerant views and refrained from denouncing Christianity as idolatry.[15] An exception was Maimonides (ca. 1138–1204), unquestionably the most influential medieval Jewish thinker, who praised the strict monotheism of Muslims but said "that this Christian nation, who advocate the messianic claim, in all their various sects, all of them are idolaters."[16] Nonetheless, in a text cited (but not quoted) in *TDW*, Maimonides saw a constructive purpose for Christianity:

> These words of Jesus of Nazareth and this Arab [Mohammed] who came after him were only to prepare the way for the Messiah-King and to order the whole world to serve the Lord altogether, as it says in Scripture: "For I shall unite all the peoples into a pure speech, all of them to call upon the name of the Lord and to serve Him with one shoulder [Zeph. 3:9]." ... How is this so? The whole world is already filled with the

14. Ruth Langer, "Jewish Understandings of the Religious Other," *Theological Studies* 64(2):May 2003, 269–270.

15. David Novak, *The Image of the Non-Jew in Judaism: An Historical Study and Constructive Study of the Noahide Laws* (New York and Toronto: Mellen, 1983), 84–86.

16. Commentary on the Mishnah: *Avodah Zarah* 1:3.

words of [their] messiah and the words of the commandments, and these words they have spread to the farthest islands and among many obstinate peoples, and they discuss these words and the commandments out of the Torah. They say, "These commandments were true, but are already invalid today, and are not meant to be perpetual.... But when the true Messiah arises and will triumph and be uplifted and exalted, all of them will immediately return and comprehend that their ancestors misled them."[17]

In this text, Maimonides, irrespective of his generally negative view of Christian faith, concludes that despite their supersessionist attitudes toward the Torah's commands, Christians (and Muslims) disseminate the commandments and knowledge of the God of Israel everywhere. When the true Messiah comes at the end of days, they will see the error of their past devaluing of the Torah as Jews understand it.[18]

Maimonides thus nuanced the previous categorization of Jews and non-Jews (righteous or unrighteous) by viewing certain non-Jews as agents in furthering God's intentions for the world. He could regard them positively, not on their own religious terms as Christians or Muslims, but by showing how their actions align with Jewish hopes. They respect Israel's scriptures and yearn for a genuine connection with the God of Israel. Because of particular features of their religion vis-à-vis Jewish belief they are not merely generic Noahides anymore.

A later theologian, Rabbi Samson Raphael Hirsch (1808–88), should be brought into this discussion, both because of his high sta-

---

17. Mishneh Torah, *Hilkhot Melakhim* 11:4 (uncensored version).

18. See Novak, *Image*, 200.

It should be pointed out that the Christian tradition had a similar view of the role of the Jews. Augustine of Hippo provides an anticipatory fifth-century mirror image of Maimonidean logic. He argued that Jews, "while they themselves are dispersed among all nations," prepare the way for the Church of Christ "in spite of themselves" by carrying the books of the "Old Testament" with them wherever they go [*City of God*, Book 15, Chapter 46]. Moreover, when Christ returns in glory and judgment, all Israel will turn to him.

tus in the Orthodox community to this day and because both *TDW* and BJR refer to his work.[19] A German Jew committed to traditional Judaism and also to integration into contemporary society, he describes quite favorably "the peoples in whose midst we live today." At the lowest level, he speaks of them as generic non-Jews who are expected to comply solely with the Noahide laws. He then raises his assessment, for he recognizes that he lives among Christians, who accept the divine origins of the Bible and the existence and sovereignty of God. This higher status, however, rests on their contribution to Jewish goals. It is because Christians "have accepted the Jewish Bible of the Old Testament as a book of Divine revelation" and "helped disseminate among the nations" its beliefs that they are set apart from pagans and idolaters.[20] He does not speak positively or negatively about their particular Christian views. In those he is uninterested; what prompts his praise are Christian claims that parallel Jewish claims.

JEWISH TRADITIONS ABOUT CHRISTIANITY AND TDW AND BJR

With this theological and historical context in mind, it is possible to more fully assess the claims made about Christianity in the contemporary statements *TDW* and BJR. There are relatively few resources in the Jewish tradition for them to draw upon in order to speak theologically about Christianity, for it is a topic that has been taken up by only a small number of thinkers. The Orthodox authors are influenced by, and indeed see as normative, the views of revered figures such as Maimonides, Hirsch, and a few others, and this limits how much their views of Christianity might be revised. Thus, in general they do not engage with Christianity on its own terms.[21]

---

19. They refer to the same passage, written in 1884; see Samson Raphael Hirsch, *Jewish Education, The Collected Writings* (New York and Jerusalem: Feldheim, 1996), 225–227.
20. He quotes here Rabbi Jacob Emden.
21. Though there are exceptions in *TDW*; see below.

Rather, like Maimonides and Hirsch, they attend to the particularity of Christianity when praising Christians for furthering Jewish or generic goals. Fifty years after *Nostra Aetate* and the emergence of profound changes in Christian theologies of Judaism, they are strongly influenced by earlier, pre-*Nostra Aetate* Jewish theologians. While they are far from indifferent to the changes that have taken place since the 1960s, they seek continuity with views established centuries ago.

In *TDW* these include "articulating the essential moral values for the survival and welfare of humanity" and "perfect[ing] the world under the sovereignty of the Almighty, so that all humanity will call on His name and abominations will be removed from the earth." Recalling traditional praise, the authors celebrate what Christians have in common with Jews, which besides moral values includes acceptance of "Jewish Sacred Scriptures" and "the ethical monotheism of Abraham." They go so far as to claim that Jesus "strengthened the Torah of Moses majestically," in essence recalling the Jewishness of the historical Jesus.[22] Like earlier writers, they cast these Christian beliefs as grounded in Christian faith but valuable according to a Jewish calculus.

Likewise, BJR includes similar reasons to praise Christians. On religious grounds, they "share common beliefs in the Divine origin of the Torah" (i.e., they believe what Jews believe). Using the ethical terminology of Noahides, Christians are asked to undertake "peaceful collaboration for the betterment of our shared world and the lives of the children of Noah." These are humanitarian goals, but indicate no engagement with the particularity of Christianity.

These excerpts illustrate the enduring influence of traditional approaches to Christianity and reflect the dominant perspectives of the Statements. However, there are three places where the authors of *TDW* tentatively move beyond the traditional model and affirm the religious legitimacy of Christianity in its own terms, as Christians might do for themselves. These hint at some possibilities for broader future reflection. For example, they write "We Jews and

22. They quote Emden here.

Christians have more in common than what divides us [including] *the relationship with the One Creator of Heaven and Earth*, Who loves and cares for all of us. . . ." The phrase italicized here (it is not italicized in the original) can be read to imply that Christians have a genuine, living connection with the God of Israel. This suggests a step beyond a one-way communication, of Christians praying to and yearning for God, and points toward something embracing two parties, Christians and God, interacting somehow. Surprisingly, the authors hint at the depth of that relationship by placing it in parallel with the Jewish relationship with God, about which they have no doubt. This is unexpected. While the authors otherwise speak almost entirely about the good that *Christians* do and can do, they hint here at a quality not just in Christian actions and beliefs but in *God's* involvement in the world *with* Christians. Notably, this relational aspect of Christianity is not valued because of its role in furthering Jewish goals. Rather, the authors suggest that it has an inherent value, akin to the Jewish relationship with God.

A second example from *TDW* is a guarded affirmation of a fundamental Christian claim upon which their relationship with God depends: "We believe that God employs many messengers to reveal His truth." Reading this as an oblique reference to Jesus (though not only Jesus), the authors appear open to the possibility that the God of Israel genuinely interacts with non-Jews.[23] This is no gentile delusion or fantasy, but a divine if indirect disclosure ("truth"). Christians of course see Jesus as the one sent by God, though the Jewish statement, in its vagueness, simply opens up this possibility. Nonetheless, this too is a bold claim and potentially far-reaching. It is categorically different from statements about what *Christians* "accept," "affirm," "believe," "remain dedicated to," etc., because it speaks about what *God* does ("employs messengers," that is, communicates) with Christians.

The third example is the use of the adjective "covenantal" when describing a responsibility shared by Jews and Christians: "Both

---

23. While in Jewish tradition God is shown interacting with non-Jews, in this context the interaction seems to be of a higher religious order.

Jews and Christians have a common covenantal mission to perfect the world under the sovereignty of the Almighty." The idea is repeated in *TDW*'s closing sentence: "Jews and Christians will remain dedicated to the Covenant by playing an active role together in redeeming the world." Covenantal language is of course central to Jewish identity. It captures the relationship between God and the people as well as the content or terms of the relationship, usually understood as commandments to be observed or responsibilities on both parties. Its usage in *TDW* is another hint of a special status for Christians, for in speaking of a Christian covenantal mission the authors introduce a striking parallel for Christians to the traditional Jewish notion of covenant. This Christian covenanting includes not just generic moral action ("to perfect the world under the sovereignty of the Almighty") but specific religious actions on behalf of the God of Israel ("all humanity will call on His name").

A comparison with BJR is instructive. Its authors also speak positively about what Christians do, and put it in Jewish terms: "... some of Judaism's highest authorities have asserted that Christians maintain a special status because they worship the Creator of Heaven and Earth Who liberated the people of Israel from Egyptian bondage and Who exercises providence over all creation." This favorable assessment assigns Christians a "special status" on account of their commitment to monotheism and more specifically to the God of Israel. The nature of this status is left unexplained, though it resembles the traditional claim (above) regarding Christians' religious faith. In contrast to *TDW*, there is no reflection of Christian self-understanding in BJR, nor any broader hint about God's being in a living relationship with Christians. BJR's authors give no sense that there are two "parties" involved with each other.

CATHOLICS ENGAGE THEIR OWN TRADITION IN THE LIGHT OF THE NEW RELATIONSHIP WITH JEWS

TDW occasionally and with caution alludes to some kind of covenantal relationship between the One God of Israel and Christians, which, of course, is how Christians understand themselves. Although most previous Orthodox writers were not prepared to consider this, in today's post-*Nostra Aetate* context the authors of *TDW* go further along the stream of traditional Jewish thought that viewed Christianity as having a role in the divine plan and hence having some kind of connection with the Holy One.

An equivalent dynamic is evident in the Vatican's reflections for the fiftieth anniversary of *Nostra Aetate, The Gifts and the Calling of God Are Irrevocable (Rom 11:29)* (hereafter G&C).[24] The theological horizons of the two statements are quite different. As noted above, the self-understanding of Jews does not need to take Christianity into account. Also, the Noahide tradition provided Jews with a conceptual framework to perceive righteousness among Gentiles. However, Catholic thought after *Nostra Aetate* must reckon both with a Judaism that is now engaged positively for the first time and with its own recurring tendency to restrict salvation to the baptized.[25] In grappling with the legacy of hostile Christian teaching about Jews, Catholics must sometimes directly contradict past claims, as when *Nostra Aetate* declared, "the Jews should not be presented as rejected or accursed by God, as if this followed from the Holy Scriptures," a view that had prevailed throughout Christian history.[26]

Nonetheless, with some similarities to the Orthodox authors of

---

24. Commission of the Holy See for Religious Relations with the Jews, *The Gifts and the Calling of God Are Irrevocable (Rom 11:29): A Reflection on Theological Questions Pertaining to Catholic-Jewish Relations on the Occasion of the 50th Anniversary of* Nostra Aetate *(No. 4)* http://www.vatican.va/roman_curia/ponti fical_councils/chrstuni/relations-jews-docs/rc_pc_chrstuni_doc_20151210_ebra ismo-nostra-aetate_en.html.

25. The most extreme expression of this soteriological exclusivism is probably in *Cantate Domino*, promulgated by Pope Eugene IV in 1441, during a period of intense competition for church leadership: The Church "firmly believes, professes, and proclaims that those not living within the Catholic Church, not only pagans, but also Jews and heretics and schismatics, cannot become participants in eternal life, but will depart 'into everlasting fire which was prepared for the devil and his angels,' unless before the end of life the same have been added to the flock . . ."

26. See for example John Pawlikowski, "Anti-Judaism," in *A Dictionary of Jewish-Christian Relations*, ed. Edward Kessler and Neil Wenborn (Cambridge: Cambridge University Press, 2005), 19–21.

TDW, the Catholic authors seek continuity with traditional teachings and so also begin gingerly to reinterpret received formulas. Out of many possible examples, space allows us to describe only one.

G&C declares, "Confessing the universal and therefore also exclusive mediation of salvation through Jesus Christ belongs to the core of Christian faith" (§35). As mentioned above, over the centuries many Christians understood this to mean that only Christ's followers were "saved." However, while reaffirming the centrality of Christ for human salvation, G&C repeatedly insists that "it does not in any way follow that the Jews are excluded from God's salvation because they do not believe in Jesus Christ as the Messiah of Israel and the Son of God" (§36).

Just as it could be said that *TDW* hints at a more-than-Noahide covenantal status for Christians, so here G&C affirms an ongoing covenantal status for Jews despite their rejecting Christian claims about God's revelation in Christ. The Vatican writers bluntly state the theological challenge they face: "That the Jews are participants in God's salvation is theologically unquestionable, but how that can be possible without confessing Christ explicitly, is and remains an unfathomable divine mystery" (ibid.).

Moreover, just as *TDW* showed signs of awareness of Christian self-understanding, G&C also has indications that Catholics have begun "to learn by what essential traits Jews define themselves in the light of their own religious experience."[27] Thus, it cites a rabbinic text in its own description of the Torah, while simultaneously evoking Christian soteriological language: "The Torah is the instruction for a successful life in *right relationship* with God. Whoever observes the Torah has *life in its fullness* (cf. *Pirkei Avot* II, 7).[28] By observing the Torah, the Jew receives a *share in communion* with God" (§24; italics added). Although Jews do not think of "salvation" as Christians do, the authors of G&C have learned from Jews and Jewish texts about

---

27. They here quote from the preamble to the Vatican's 1974 *Guidelines and Suggestions for Implementing the Conciliar Declaration* Nostra Aetate.

28. Cf. John 10:10b: "I came that they may have life, and have it abundantly."

their covenantal life with a God who saves, which therefore must (in Christian terms) somehow be "saving."

CONCLUSION

This analysis of an Orthodox Jewish text, *TDW*, and its comparison with a Catholic text, suggests that similar if not exactly parallel processes are unfolding in the two communities. Both sets of authors uphold the defining centers of their traditions – the Torah and Christ respectively. However, in our post-*Nostra Aetate* world both begin to reconceptualize traditional views of each other, although *TDW* does this much more tentatively. In different ways, this may prompt new understandings of their respective loci of revelation. The Orthodox writers can cautiously conceive of Christians as covenantal partners even though Christianity is not centered on the Torah, while the Catholic writers struggle with the paradox of Jews as "participants in God's salvation" even without receiving Christian revelation.

Although Jews and Catholics have different ways of doing theology, it is intriguing to see how both engage their respective traditions in response to their changed relationship. Perhaps by exploring together our respective ways of "traditioning,"[29] we can assist each other in being faithful to our particular religious identities while also enhancing our ability to learn of God from one another. *TDW* makes an important contribution to that prospect.

---

29. This term is defined by Mary Elizabeth Moore: "The concept of traditioning is based on the idea that the [faith] community lives in its tradition, passing on its past, living in its present, and moving toward its future.... [It affirms] the importance of passing on the community's beliefs, values, and practices and the importance of reflecting on and revising the community's actions." See Mary Elizabeth Moore, *Education for Continuity and Change: A New Model for Christian Religious Education* (Nashville: Abingdon, 1983), 17–18.

A Jewish Theology of Christianity

CHRISTIAN M RUTISHAUSER S.J.

PURSUING TRUTH

It is characteristic for Jews, as well as Christians of faith to constantly ask God's will regarding their lifestyle. This requires perceiving how times are changing and understanding that godly behavior does not merely mean abiding by never-changing rules. It is rather, acting appropriately to the situation in a way that corresponds with God's will. Therefore, religious education and a basic knowledge of the principles of one's own tradition, as well as a certain analytical perception of current affairs and a free self-confidence, are necessary to be able to recognize God's will on a particular matter. Errors may be made, but in the end, it is about searching for and finding practical truth before God, and then living it.

In fact, every dialogue is dedicated to the search for truth. Since its very beginning in the philosophical schools of Greece, dialogue means thinking, speaking, and trying out arguments in order to get to a deeper understanding and then be able to act accordingly. *Dia logos* is the motto: through words we get to dialogue. The philosophical tradition considers it essential for humans to continually review their own lives in a self-critical way, in constant interaction with others. This however, demands powers of judgment, freedom of expression, attentive listening, and respecting the other's arguments.

The dialogue document entitled *To Do the Will of Our Father in Heaven* testifies to the serious pursuit of truth before God. Any careless talking and acting "in the name of the father," if it is without a willingness to listen to the dialogue partner or appreciate the circumstances, will be revealed as vain self-promotion grasping for further authority. The document's subtitle *Toward a Partnership between Jews and Christians* refers to the dialogue as a process. The text aims to be a textual contribution to improving the relationship between Jews and Christians, nothing more and nothing less. Ambitiously, the text speaks of development from "hostility" to "partnership," since merely tolerated coexistence would not be enough before God.

CONTEXT OF THE DIALOGUE

Orthodox rabbis published the dialogue document on December 3, 2015, one week before the Holy See's publication of *The Gifts and the Calling of God are Irrevocable* concerning the relationship between the Roman Catholic Church and Judaism. Both documents explicitly commemorate the declaration published 50 years previously, *Nostra Aetate*, with which the Church officially initiated dialogue with Judaism at the Second Vatican Council in 1965. Though the Jewish document was published before the Vatican one, it has to be read as a response. Back in 2013, the development of the Vatican document had already begun, whereas a conference in Galilee in May 2015 initiated the Orthodox Rabbinic Statement on Christianity. This conference was organized by the movement *Neocatechumenal Way*. Vatican-related clergy as well as the initiators of our text were in attendance. Some of these Orthodox rabbis had also been direct contact persons for developing *The Gifts and the Calling of God are Irrevocable*. Thus, the authors of the Jewish document already knew its contents. Therefore, I will compare the Orthodox Rabbinic Statement with the Vatican document. Moreover, I will comment on it by also considering earlier Jewish responses to the Roman Catholic Church's offer of dialogue. In doing so I will refer to Rabbi Soloveitchik's essay "Confrontation," which has significantly characterized Jewish Orthodoxy regarding dialogue issues with the Roman Catholic Church. The essay was presented in part in a speech at the Rabbinical Council of America in 1964 on the development of *Nostra Aetate*. Another declaration that has influenced Jewish-Christian dialogue that I want to touch on is *Dabru Emet*, signed by Jewish academics from Conservative and Liberal circles in the year 2000.

RECOGNITION OF THE REPENTANCE OF THE CHURCH

To Do the Will of Our Father in Heaven coincides with the historic change that the Roman Catholic Church has been undergoing for half a century now. As was shown through numerous documents, conferences, and encounters, the Church has constantly trod a path of repentance towards Judaism. The Church's teaching of contempt, and the theology of replacement of the Jews by the Church in covenant with God, called supersessionism in specialist terminology, has been declared invalid. Furthermore, Jews are no longer accused of deicide. Most important for this Jewish document, however, is that the Church waives any institutional mission to the Jews. This was first phrased explicitly in the Vatican document *The Gifts and the Calling of God are Irrevocable* (paragraph 40). This is far from all. In publishing *Nostra Aetate* the Church set out a new theological framework to comprehend and do justice to Judaism. The old teachings of contempt and denial of existence were thus turned upside down. *Nostra Aetate* begins with a theology of religions. Religion means human pursuit of God, which is basically classified as positive by the Church (point 1). The Church recognizes what is true and holy in all religions, even though it is the Church's duty to proclaim Jesus as the Redeemer (point 2). In doing so, the Church represents religion theologically speaking as a so-called inclusivism, which regards Christianity as embodying the whole of truth, whereas other religious traditions realize parts of the truth.

Reading *Nostra Aetate* without deeper knowledge, one might think that the Roman Catholic Church puts Judaism on the same level as all other religions. This is explicitly noted in *The Gifts and the Calling of God are Irrevocable* (point 19). However, *Nostra Aetate* applies another kind of hermeneutics to Judaism in point 4: "As the sacred synod searches into the mystery of the Church, it remembers the bond that spiritually ties the people of the New Covenant to Abraham's stock." Thus, Judaism for Christianity is not simply another, separate religion. Rather, Christianity finds Judaism when reflecting on its own origins.

Therefore, the Roman Catholic Church does not consider dialogue with the Jews to be like other general interreligious dialogue. Instead, Jewish-Christian dialogue holds a unique position. *The Gifts and the Calling of God are Irrevocable* dedicates a separate chapter to the uniqueness of the Jewish-Christian dialogue (points 14–20). It traces the historical process by which Christianity has developed from a Jewish Messianic movement, inter alia. Judaism and Christianity formed through a process of mutual separation into different traditions of interpreting the same Hebrew Bible. As early as 2001, the Pontifical Biblical Commission honored the Rabbinic tradition in their document *The Jewish People and their Sacred Scriptures in the Christian Bible.* Although the Vatican explicitly refuses to speak of two equal and parallel covenantal traditions, one Jewish and one Christian (*The Gifts and the Calling of God are Irrevocable* point 35), it does, however, since the famous statements by Pope John Paul II in the 1980s, always speak positively of the "uncancelled" and "irrevocable" covenant between God and his people of Israel. "That the Jews are participants in God's salvation is theologically unquestionable" (*The Gifts and the Calling of God are Irrevocable* point 36).

Throughout the document *To Do the Will of Our Father in Heaven* the Orthodox rabbis acknowledge the repentance of the Catholic Church. Encounters and initiatives over the last 50 years have settled into new relationships. For the Roman Catholic Church, this document is very satisfying, since it confirms that its new orientation is recognized and accepted. What Rabbi Soloveitchik still doubted when *Nostra Aetate* was published, now seems to have become reality. Back then Soloveitchik still could not trust the Roman Catholic

Church's repentance. Proof of action was still missing. This is why he demanded that any dialogue had to take place on equal terms, under liberal, democratic conditions that guaranteed freedom of religion ("Confrontation," part II, section 3). He then imposed four conditions for dialogue:

(1) Judaism had to be recognized as an independent and autonomous religious community, and not named as Christianity's "older brother."

(2) The intimate faith relationship with God should neither be the subject of discussion nor subject to manipulation by the dialogue partner.

(3) Jews should not become involved in internal Church matters.

(4) Allegiance towards the sufferings that their ancestors endured under the Church's persecution should not be forgotten. Meaning there should be no careless forgiveness of injustices suffered.

INALIENABLE IDENTITIES IN DIALOGUE

The current Orthodox Rabbinic Statement *To Do the Will of Our Father in Heaven* seems faithful to Rabbi Soloveitchik's criteria. Individual articles of faith are not discussed in the text, and more than once, it is indicated that the partnership should aim to express itself in ethical improvements to the world. Remarkably, the approbative terms "brotherhood" or "brotherliness" that are often used by Christians when determining the relation between Jews and Christians are avoided. The negative brotherly relationship between Jacob and Esau does not come up either, which is traditionally used by Jews to depict the hostility of Jews and Christians, and dominates the last part of Rabbi Soloveitchik's essay "Confrontation." The three questions posed by Esau to Jacob's servants and their entourage: "To whom do you belong, and where are you going, and for whom are these before you?" in Gen 32:18 are interpreted by Soloveitchik in *midrashic* style: Jews do not discuss their faith or existence in any dialogue, but may contribute with the cultural part of their religion to political, scientific, or social projects. Always obeying the above-explained conditions for interreligious dialogues. Nowadays, in Jewish Orthodoxy, it is usual to interpret Soloveitchik's essay "Confrontation" to mean that theological dialogue is not possible with Christians, but collective social engagement can be. The new Orthodox Rabbinic Statement seems to point in the same direction, as it reads in the preface: "Jews and Christians must work together as partners to address the moral challenges of our era." The final paragraph, point 7, aims in the same direction, speaking of ethical responsibility in the world that the Jews are concerned with. This social and ethical collaboration of Jews and Christians has been one of the basic issues in Jewish-Christian dialogue for decades. It is emphasized in every document and is nothing new.

But reading the essay "Confrontation" carefully, one realizes that even here differentiation into "theologically unsuitable for dialogue" and "social collaboration as the target for dialogue" would be too simple. Soloveitchik presents anthropological, religious-philosophical, interpretive, and communicative lines of argument that are not always aligned. In any case, his reasons for determining what an Orthodox Jew may discuss or not in a dialogue, where free communication between equals is provided, are inconsistent. In his typology of different levels of man in the first part of "Confrontation," he speaks of an indescribable and mysterious part of every individual, which cannot be communicated to another individual, not even in the most intimate relationship. He is rooted in the humanistic tradition, like Montesquieu for example, who spoke of the ineffable human, saying: *individuum est ineffabile.*

For Soloveitchik, inexplicable faith as an existential decision and divine obligation is part of the human mystery. He distinguishes this from that part of religion and tradition that has become culture, which can be brought into dialogue with fellow humans and society. Obviously, Soloveitchik was influenced by the dialectical theology that distinguishes faith from religion. The existential and inexplicable decision to have faith is connected to the mystery of humankind. Religion and culture, however, are the communicable parts of religious existence – and one part of this is theology. According to Soloveitchik, in so far as there can be a theological dialogue, this dialogue must neither exert any pressure on the free decision to have faith, nor aim at formulating a common theology.

But this is exactly what Soloveitchik reproaches against Reform and Conservative Jews: together with Christians and secularists they subdue nature through technical and cultural achievements, but at the same time, they do not dare to confront them regarding religion. Soloveitchik views Liberal and Conservative Jews who do not strictly define themselves based on *halakhah* as structurally adapted to the Christian Western world even if they orientate themselves towards Jewish ideas. He demands a double confrontation, with nature as well as with Christian culture. This is not a blank refusal of Jewish-Christian dialogue. Rather, he aims at a structurally differentiated approach by Judaism and the *halakhah* that cannot simply be generally subsumed by religion and the Christian approach to the world. A dialogue, therefore, must not seek assimilation but express difference and otherness. This is because neither the Jewish decision to have faith as a response to the covenant at Sinai, nor the Christian decision to commit to the revelation of Jesus Christ, are negotiable.

In the same way, we should not read the Statement *To Do the Will of Our Father in Heaven* as "theological vs. social dialogue," since its substantial theological statements would then be overlooked. We need to bear in mind genuine Jewish-Orthodox strategy and argumentation. This can be read from Soloveitchik's perspective of distinguishing discussable belief and religion as cultural phenomena, which do in fact include a transfer of ethics, values, and social responsibility. The distinction between the theological and social, as well as between ritual and ethical areas, has become powerful in dialogue with the secular world, especially since Moses Mendelssohn. Theology in this case means the particular, and ethics means the universal, of Judaism. It is a distinction that the secular world has imposed on the believer, wanting the religious part to stay private, and accepting only the ethical part in public. The existence of faith must include both parts, from both a Jewish-Orthodox as well as from a Roman Catholic point of view. They cannot be separated as easily as it looks, and seems usual, today.

CHRISTIANITY FROM A JEWISH POINT OF VIEW

That said our view is that *To Do the Will of Our Father in Heaven* is not limited to the social collaboration and ethical challenges of Jews and Christians, even if this is the explicit objective of the Statement. More interesting, however, is what theological views are implicitly indicated. For the theological aspect always has priority for Roman Catholic dialogue partners, as they primarily deal with Judaism as a religion and culture, even knowing that Jewish identity can also be defined ethnically, nationally, politically, not to say irreligiously since the Age of Enlightenment, the Shoah, and the founding of the State of Israel. And not denying that the main ambition for dialogue on the Jewish side is often not religious. But even if the motives of Jews to have dialogue with the Roman Catholic Church may be strategic, like fighting against anti-Semitism, there are always theological contents involved. In particular, the present Statement is in its form and content traditionally rabbinic, and responds to *The Gifts and the Calling of God are Irrevocable*, which is the most theological document on Judaism put out by the Vatican so far.

Just as the Vatican document *The Gifts and the Calling of God are Irrevocable* summarizes a new theology of Judaism, the most interesting and new element in *To Do the Will of Our Father in Heaven* is its theological view of Christianity. The Jewish Statement not only acknowledges the moral reversal of the Church, now no longer despising Judaism but fighting anti-Semitism, it also considers how Christianity has reversed its view of Judaism positively, since the publication of *Nostra Aetate* as outlined above. As paragraph 2 points out, the Roman Catholic Church affirms the "eternal Covenant between God and the Jewish people." Further on it reads: "We appreciate the Church's affirmation of Israel's unique place in sacred history and the ultimate world redemption." Thus, the Statement shows understanding for the Church's theological concept of a salvation history that now allocates Judaism a positive position within the Christian overall interpretation of history.

This does not mean that the rabbis agree with this Christian inclusivism and share it. From the Jewish side there is instead an inverted inclusivism, locating Christianity in the Jewish interpretation of the world. Just as the Christian side has omitted the teaching of contempt, accusation of deicide, doctrine of privation, and mission to the Jews, so the Statement *To Do the Will of Our Father in Heaven* abolishes traditional Jewish judgments on Christianity: Christianity was mere idol worship because of the Trinity belief, Jesus was a bastard and a charlatan, and the Church resembled the hostile brother Esau. In particular, the whole of paragraph 5 is dedicated to the argument that Christians are not idol worshippers. They rather recognize God as the creator and redeemer of the Jewish people. Christianity is positively reinterpreted and embedded into the rabbinic worldview, which provides for all peoples to be led to the Noahide commandments and duty-bound to them.

To Do the Will of Our Father in Heaven manages its whole argumentation without a single unmediated quotation from the Hebrew Bible, although it is thematically present. In an Orthodox rabbinic style of argumentation, the text is rather based on traditional authorities. Medieval Maimonides and Yehudah Halevi are cited, as well as Rabbis Emden and Hirsch of modern times. There is, for instance, a statement that Christianity is faithful to monotheism and helped to spread the ethics of the Noahide commandments. It also acknowledges that Christians spread the belief in a Creator God and in the Torah as divine revelation. More problematic statements by the same rabbinic authorities concerning Christianity are overlooked, which is, in fact, legitimate according to the methodology of traditional arguments. Whereas the Church's mission to the Jews is a thing of the past, Christians and Jews have now to fulfill one mission: "Both Jews and Christians have a common covenantal mission to perfect the world under the sovereignty of the Almighty, so that all humanity will call on His name and abominations will be removed from the earth" (paragraph 4). This statement makes one sit up and take notice. What kind of covenant is meant here? A Christian might like to hear that Judaism recognizes the New Covenant in Jesus Christ as well, but I doubt this is meant here. Rather we have to consider the Noahide covenant that Christianity keeps according to the present document. Paragraph 6 proves that this interpretation is correct when speaking about different divine messengers who, according to the Jewish-Orthodox view, are sent out to spread the ethical and universal obligations of the Noahide covenant.

In this respect, it is notable that *To Do the Will of Our Father in Heaven* cites Rabbi Hirsch having taught that: "the Talmud puts Christians 'with regard to the duties between man and man on exactly the same level as Jews. They have a claim to the benefit of all the duties not only of justice but also of active human brotherly love'" (paragraph 4). Another citation of Naftali Zvi Berliner emphasizes this brotherly love once again, so that the demanded second judgment is present and the Jacob-Esau metaphor is explicitly turned positive at the same time: "In the future when the children of Esau are moved by pure spirit to recognize the people of Israel and their virtues, then we will also be moved to recognize that Esau is our brother" (paragraph 4).

In conclusion, the theology of Christianity contained in *To Do the Will of Our Father in Heaven* must be described as structurally and traditionally Orthodox, and is clearly associated with the Noahide covenant. This was repeatedly doubted, especially considering the historic dispute and Theory of God and Christology phrased in Greek and philosophically difficult to teach. Though recognizing the Christian self-image as a part of biblical monotheism, Christian's belief in Jesus as the Christ and in his New Covenant is not commented on. Thereby this dialogue document takes up a classical Jewish Orthodox position. There is no pluralistic religious theology in it as supported by some Jewish thinkers in recent decades. The text is not aiming at determining commonalities and differences between Jews and Christians. The dialogue here rather provides positive and appreciative room for the dialogue partner in its own faith perspective.

The same is true for *The Gifts and the Calling of God are Irrevocable*. The text does not address the dialogue partner but its own religious community, in order to share a positive view of Judaism. The rabbinic-inclusive perspective on Christianity is mirrored by an inclusive Christian view of Judaism. However the changes to the

Christian doctrinal system since *Nostra Aetate* are more complex, because the Church has incorporated the Jewish self-image of being in a special covenant with God into the teaching of the "unrevoked covenant" of Sinai, and has at the same time created a problem with the universal claim to salvation in Christ when it abandoned its mission to the Jews. How does the teaching of the universal claim to salvation in Christ and the teaching of the unrevoked covenant fit together? Despite discussing both statements using several theological arguments in the central chapter of *The Gifts and the Calling of God are Irrevocable,* this question is left unanswered, and left to be solved by God's wisdom: "That the Jews are participants in God's salvation is theologically unquestionable, but how that can be possible without confessing Christ explicitly, is and remains an unfathomable divine mystery" (point 36).

It should be appropriately appreciated that the Roman Catholic Church has decided to refer positively to real, existing Judaism of our days, and therefore to face an unsolvable question. For the Church could define itself without this kind of Judaism – and has long done so. The oft-heard statement in Jewish-Christian dialogue that Christians needed Judaism to define themselves, but Jews did not need Christianity, is therefore not correct. Rather the Church has decided to refer to Judaism and to others, and accordingly refused a self-definition as the one and only "true Israel." With this it has created a reference to Judaism whose significance has not yet fully come clear.

SIMILARITIES AND DIFFERENCES IN DIALOGUE

In comparing *To Do the Will of Our Father in Heaven* once again with Rabbi Soloveitchik's essay, a theology of Christianity can be noticed in the new document, whereas in "Confrontation" a general perception of religion is developed that distinguishes the non-negotiable existential core of religion from the cultural part of religion. Typologically Soloveitchik derives this from the relationship between two individuals. Only at the very end of the text is the Church indicated in terms of Jacob-Esau hostility. Furthermore, a secular and liberal society appears as a framework condition and model for Jewish-Christian dialogue on equal terms in "Confrontation." Soloveitchik reminds us that despite any cooperation, Judaism still needs to distance itself from other collective identities. In *To Do the Will of Our Father in Heaven* the secular, external world is first and foremost a field of ethical improvement and mission. It is measured by whether or not it has opened itself to the Noahide covenant.

This leaves us with comparing the Orthodox Rabbinic Statement with *Dabru Emet*, the declaration by Liberal and Conservative rabbis and Jewish scholars in the USA. Both documents are a positive response to the change in Christian theology. As in *To Do the Will of Our Father in Heaven, Dabru Emet* also begins with a description of the reversal process of Christians in the last decades, whereby not only the Roman Catholic Church but also the Protestant Church is explicitly referred to. "[W]e believe it is time for Jews to learn about the efforts of Christians to honor Judaism," it reads in the introduction. As the title of the text – *Dabru Emet* means to speak the truth – expresses quite clearly, it also has to do with a demanded situational and practical truth. Nothing less will deliver true dialogue.

It is not the target of *Dabru Emet*, however, to seek partnership for moral actions as phrased in *To Do the Will of Our Father in Heaven*. Rather it speaks of reflecting on what Judaism may now say about Christianity. "As a first step, we offer eight brief statements about how Jews and Christians may relate to one another." Reading these introductory phrases, one would expect that *Dabru Emet* has more to say to a theology of Christianity than *To Do the Will of Our Father in Heaven*. Surprisingly, it is the other way around. The reason, therefore, might be that *Dabru Emet* does not look at Christianity with a Jewish theological overall perspective, but intends to name the similarities and differences of both religious communities in single topics.

Dabru Emet begins with commonalities and similarities as per paragraph 1: "Jews and Christians worship the same God." What Christians will at once agree to might be unacceptable for Jews when thinking about the Christian Trinity. The next thesis reads as follows: "Jews and Christians seek authority from the same book – the Bible," meaning the Hebrew Bible called the *Tanakh* or Old Testament in their different forms, whereas the New Testament, which is the crucial Christian revelatory text, is not named at all. Thirdly, a highly controversial thesis is proclaimed: "Christians can respect the claim of the Jewish people upon the land of Israel." Paragraph 4 may obtain more approval: "Jews and Christians accept the moral principles of Torah."

Although these theses are differently commented on in *Dabru Emet*, they have aroused a lot of criticism, especially among Jews. Similarities were posited but had to be differentiated and taken back later. A dialogue between Jews and Christians that gives more priority to respecting the differences than seeking similarities seems more appropriate. In all fairness, it must be said that *Dabru Emet* does indeed name the differences in its main paragraphs. In this way, paragraph 6 states: "The humanly irreconcilable difference between Jews and Christians will not be settled until God redeems the entire world as promised in Scripture." And paragraph 7 starts with: "A new relationship between Jews and Christians will not weaken Jewish practice." This document does not miss the classical distinction and emphasis on autonomy either, even if great similarity or even commonality in theological contents is postulated.

Altogether, the eight paragraphs of the declaration seem additive, the last of them speaking of collaboration between Jews and Christians for justice and peace on earth. They do not make up a systematic theological overview of Christianity from a Jewish perspective. Compared with *To Do the Will of Our Father in Heaven*, however, this document's advantage is that it names some of the specific issues in Jewish-Christian dialogue, such as understanding of the Bible, the question of God, the theology of the nation of Israel, as well as the understanding of National Socialism. The short theses thus reflect current discussions in dialogue circles. Within the text, there is no reasoning with tradition, no citing of biblical texts, though biblical statements are mirrored all over. *Dabru Emet*, a short text in the form of assertions like *To Do the Will of Our Father in Heaven*, has been accompanied by a volume of essays presenting an academic discourse by Jewish and Christian scholars on the various topics. It is quite plain that these two documents are very different, each having its own value.

It needs to be said, however, that *Dabru Emet* has helped the dialogue between Jews and Christians to go a step further. Not only was the document quite widely noticed in Christian circles, but Christian theologians published a direct response to it in 2002: *A Sacred Obligation*. Its ten paragraphs cannot be discussed here, but they prove that Jewish-Christian dialogue has been in progress since World War II, and show that different Churches and different Jewish groups are involved in it. Jewish-Christian dialogue is alive.

Response to *To Do the Will of Our Father in Heaven*, 2015

PETER A. PETTIT

I.

The 2015 Orthodox Rabbinic Statement on Christianity[1] is a welcome voice from a community that has not typically been represented in the interfaith dialogue that has flourished over the past half-century and more. As many have recognized, the voice of Rabbi Joseph Soloveitchik (*z"l*) in his 1964 article, "Confrontation," seemed to speak a definitive "no" to any Orthodox inquiry about engaging Christians in theological dialogue.[2] Intrepid individual voices have ventured both another approach and a direct questioning of Soloveitchik's sufficiency in our more recent times. It is no accident that those voices are prominently represented in the leadership that crafted the 2015 statement and in the editing of this volume. At one

1. *To Do the Will of Our Father in Heaven: Toward a Partnership between Jews and Christians*, Orthodox Rabbinic Statement on Christianity, December 3, 2015, http://cjcuc.com/site/2015/03/orthodox-rabbinic-statement-on-christianity.

2. Jospeh B. Soloveitchik, "Confrontation," *Tradition: A Journal of Orthodox Thought* 6.2 (1964), 5–28. In the introduction of the article, the journal described Soloveitchik as "the acknowledged intellectual leader and spokesman for halakhic Judaism ..., formally recognized by the Rabbinical Council as its authority in all halakhic matters" (5). His authority was such that the community came to refer to him simply as "the Rav."

level, the only appropriate response to the Statement by a Christian reader must be, "Welcome! We're delighted that you're here."

Almost the entire project of Christian-Jewish dialogue for the past century, after all, has been initiated by the Christian community. Put simply, it was Christians who came to realize during that time – as Jews have long known – that our forebears did not give the Jewish community an honest opportunity to represent itself in public discourse. With James Parkes's research, the Rosenzweig-Rosenstock exchanges, and other initiatives on the continent and in the United States in the period between the world wars, the dignity of Jewish tradition and community came increasingly to public recognition. The pioneers documented the long Jewish struggle against misrepresentation by the voices of dominant Christian cultures. Decisively, the horror of realization that came in the wake of the Shoah – that Christian representation of Jews had played such a significant role in empowering the genocidal Nazi ideology and enterprise – spurred the re-assessment of Christian doctrine and ecclesial culture. This, in turn, led to a widespread call for dialogue, understanding, and rapprochement.

The dark stain of the Shoah on Western Christian culture made it evident that the main work to be done would be Christian repentance and renewal. The irony was not lost on many in the Jewish community that, in the call for dialogue, they were once again being asked to play a role in a story that is essentially Christian. More than once I have heard from a rabbi or Jewish communal leader some variant of the refrain, now current in the black, feminist, and other communities of subaltern experience: "Don't expect me now to do your work for you." Fair enough! Yet the encounter with living Judaism is the surest antidote to the various "hermeneutical Jews" of Christian projection. That encounter is best undertaken in a respectful and informed dialogue with contemporary Jews. So the invitations kept coming, and keep coming. Many Jews have been generous in their participation in the undertaking. Many others, understandably, have chosen to decline.

For Rabbi Soloveitchik, the principal motivation for declining was philosophical – not in the sense of a detached, unaffected rumination, but quite literally because of his understanding of religious epistemology. Jews and Christians know their religious insights in different ways and express them in different idioms, each one asserting the absolute truth value both of its knowing and of its way of knowing. These are "incommensurate," as he emphasized in italics in the 1967 addendum to his original 1964 article:

> There cannot be mutual understanding concerning these [doctrinal, dogmatic or ritual] topics, *for Jew and Christian will employ different categories and move within incommensurate frames of reference and evaluation.*[3] [emphasis added]

They cannot be negotiated, adjudicated, or compromised without surrendering the religious truth that they express. To ask a person to bring "individual and private"[4] religious truth into a dialogue is, for Soloveitchik, by (philosophical) definition to ask that one "question, defend, offer apologies, analyze or rationalize our faith."[5]

Yet, as Eugene Korn has pointed out, Soloveitchik devoted his life to speaking of religious truth both within and outside the Jewish community. His famous exposition on "The Lonely Man of Faith" was first delivered as a talk at a Catholic seminary.[6] In his discussion with Cardinal Willebrands in 1971, he observed, "All dialogue between Jews and Christians cannot but be religious and theological, for you are a priest and I am a rabbi."[7] For Korn, this does not render the Rav's position in "Confrontation" incoherent; rather, it clarifies the circumstance that prompted his counsel against engaging with

---

3. Joseph B. Soloveitchik, "Addendum," in *A Treasury of "Tradition,"* ed. By Norman Lamm and Walter S. Wurzburger (NY: Hebrew, 1967), 79, reprinted in *Bridges: Documents of the Christian-Jewish Dialogue, Volume One: The Road to Reconciliation (1945–1985)*, a Stimulus Book, ed. by Franklin Sherman (NY: Paulist, 2011), 417.

4. Ibid., 80.

5. Ibid., 79.

6. Eugene Korn, "The Man of Faith and Religious Dialogue: Revisiting 'Confrontation,'" *Modern Judaism* 25.3 (Oct., 2005) 294–295, and footnote 12 on 310–311.

7. Ibid., 297.

Christians. That, in turn, opens the door to asking whether the same circumstances still obtain in our time.

With the present statement, the collective response of the Orthodox leaders who signed it seems clearly to be, "No; the present circumstances are different." Korn identified the proselytizing impulse of Christianity as the key factor motivating Soloveitchik's strong caution against engaging in theological disputation. That impulse, he suggested, has been significantly interrupted by the promulgation of *Nostra Aetate* at the Second Vatican Council and by the succession of episcopal, curial, and papal pronouncements that have followed in its wake. With its repudiation of the "teaching of contempt" and its revocation of the deicide charge against the Jews collectively, *Nostra Aetate* "changed fundamentally and irrevocably" Roman Catholic teaching about Judaism and the Jews.[8]

The change thus perceived in the Roman Catholic Church is the circumstance that sets the stage for a Jewish response different from Soloveitchik's. As the Statement says *inter alia*, Jews no longer need to fear Christians as bent on missionary conversion, they need not expect disrespect, oppression, and rejection from the church, and they have other models than the adversarial relationship of Esau and Jacob to bring to encounters with Christians. Even more positively, "Jews have experienced sincere love and respect from many Christians" (paragraph 2), and "Jews and Christians are destined by God to be loving partners" (paragraph 4).[9] Not only, then, is this affirmation by the Orthodox community welcome because we have felt its absence as the era of dialogue has developed; it is inherently satisfying to have character and intention of one's own community

---

8. *To Do the Will*, paragraph 2.
9. Perhaps it is only my recent involvement in a Jewish wedding that alerts me to this, but the statement's translation of the Netziv's "our brother" as "loving partners" marvelously evokes the *re'im 'ahuvim* of the sixth benediction under the huppah. There the "bridegroom *and* bride" can be considered individually even in their emerging oneness, while the seventh benediction addresses the fuller unity of the "bridegroom *with his* bride." So here, the distinction of Jews and Christians described in paragraph 6 grants integrity and individuality to each, even as their commonalities and complementarity in a divine plan find expression in paragraphs 3–5.

recognized as salutary rather than malicious. And again, the irony runs deep as the shoe slips onto the other foot.

So the appropriate response is a heartfelt and enthusiastic welcome of the Statement and of the sentiment that it conveys. To have the Rav's cautions about Christian proselytizing and bad-faith engagement tempered by other voices from the rabbinic tradition, clearing the way for a more robust engagement between our communities, is a genuine blessing. We could not demand it; we could not expect it; we could not orchestrate it. We can only welcome it. And so, I trust, we do.

II.

From my own American Lutheran perspective, I would also suggest that there are relevant themes and values that have been nurtured in Christian communities other than the Roman Catholic. These are not necessarily central to *Nostra Aetate* or its developing legacy, yet they also can inform a broadened Jewish-Christian dialogue. Parkes and Rosenstock-Huessy, whom I have already referenced as among the earliest pioneers of Christian-Jewish encounter, were in the Anglican and Evangelical (Lutheran) communities, respectively. Evangelical churches in Germany took stock of their guilt and complicity in the Nazi regime already in the immediate post-war years and Protestant communions across Europe and North America, particularly, had developed a notable corpus of statements on Christian-Jewish rapprochement well before the Second Vatican Council.[10] Neither the Protestant nor the Roman Catholic developments emerged without awareness of and engagement with the other, but the Protestant developments are somewhat different in

10. Sherman, in *Bridges, vol. 1*, includes four German church statements, one from the Episcopal Church in the U.S., two from the World Council of Churches, and one from the Lutheran World Federation, all predating *Nostra Aetate*. Rolf Rendtorff and Hans Herman Henrix, eds., *Die Kirchen und das Judentum: Dokumente von 1945–1985* (Munich: Kaiser, 1988), include nearly two dozen pre-Vatican II Protestant texts from Germany, Hungary, the Netherlands, and Austria.

their emphases, complementing the Roman Catholic work in the churches' journeys toward their own transformation and toward reconciliation with the Jewish community.[11]

Two of the most significant Protestant contributors to new thinking about Jews and Judaism have been an American Episcopalian, Paul van Buren, and a German Evangelical, Friedrich-Wilhelm Marquardt. Both devoted major works to a comprehensive project of fashioning Christian theology in a different mold from the supersessionist/Augustinian one that has come to grief in the Shoah and every time a Christian denigrates Judaism. Their methods differ from the Roman Catholic in an important sense. Van Buren and Marquardt begin with the reality of biblical Israel and its witness, moving into the reality of Christian experience and witness from that framework. So Van Buren's multi-volume Theology of the Jewish-Christian Reality takes up *A Christian Theology of the People Israel* before moving on to considering *Christ in Context*.[12] *Nostra Aetate*, by contrast, begins with the church's self-understanding and looks back to biblical Israel and out to contemporary Judaism from the church's perspective. Thus, paragraph 4 of *Nostra Aetate*, which focuses on the church's relationship to Jews and Judaism, begins:

11. The predominantly North Atlantic context of these developments cannot be emphasized enough. Christian communities in Asia, Africa, the Middle East, and even South America to a certain extent, do not share the experience of the Shoah in the same way as the European churches and those closely related to them in North America and Australia. Their relationships to the Jewish community therefore take on different dynamics, grounded in different histories and hermeneutics. Even in North America, the Black church tradition relates to Judaism differently from the White church, due to a sense of shared identity with the Israelite slaves in Egypt and the persecution of the Jews in Europe. Those who now espouse a "new Christian Zionism" also point to singular figures along the whole history of Christian thought who might be understood to have stood apart from the dominant rejectionist hermeneutics of the Augustinian tradition. These complex dynamics require that a statement such as we are considering needs to invite response from different Christian communities, or needs to be explicit in directing its voice to the churches most affected by the Augustinian-European tradition of denigration relative to Jews and Judaism.

12. Paul van Buren, *A Christian Theology of the People Israel: A Theology of the Jewish-Christian Reality, Part II* (NY: Seabury 1983); idem, *A Theology of the Jewish-Christian Reality, Part 3: Christ in Context* (NY Harper & Row, 1988).

"As the sacred synod searches into the mystery of the Church, it remembers the bond that spiritually ties the people of the New Covenant to Abraham's stock."[13] It is because "the beginnings of her faith and her election are already found among the Patriarchs, Moses and the prophets"[14] that Israel's story is of interest and concern to the church.

The difference between these approaches can be striking, particularly when dealing with a theological topic such as covenant. Nurtured within a communion of communions that is shaped by challenges in the 16th-century and later to the exclusive claims of Roman Catholic (or any other) theology to control the divine word, Protestant theologians stood at the forefront of developments in biblical criticism and dialectical theology. Their historical perspectives and philosophical foundations opened up for them the multifaceted dimensions of reality and human engagement with it. In short, their scholarly methods led to theological insights about the limits of human claims to express truth fully and clearly. In that light, their questions about the nature of covenantal self-understanding and the relationship of a divine covenantal relationship with multiple communities fostered possibilities that are more difficult to imagine when one begins with a commitment to the unassailable truth of one covenantal model.

To be sure, on the central neuralgic issues of the deicide charge, anti-Jewish hermeneutics, and conversionary agendas, Protestants on both sides of the North Atlantic have also shared an appropriate opprobrium from the Jewish community. These are the elements that Korn identified as motivating Rabbi Soloveitchik's denial of dialogue as a productive course. They are also the elements that the present statement identifies as worthy of re-examination, in light of the changed circumstances within the churches. Korn goes farther, though, when he suggests that, Soloveitchik's caution notwithstanding, the changed circumstances can open doors to theological

13. http://www.vatican.va/archive/hist_councils/ii_vatican_council/documents/vat-ii_decl_19651028_nostra-aetate_en.html.
14. Ibid.

dialogue, as contrasted with the "disputation" that was the pattern of theological engagement in an earlier era.[15] While the present statement does not explicitly envision or endorse such theological dialogue, it does imply a number of theological issues that would be good candidates for the agenda.

III.

In paragraph 3, the Statement asserts that "God willed a separation between partners with significant theological differences, not a separation between enemies." Whether or not the "parting of the ways" was divinely willed is a question on which there would not be unanimity among Christians, as I would assume there also might not be among Jews. In light of the specific harm done to the Jewish community by Constantinian Christianity and the Christendom that it inaugurated, and the pagan heir to its anti-Judaism that became genocidal in Nazi ideology, the idea that the separation is divinely willed is at best challenging. Not only in regard to Jews, but – with the "superiority complex" that supersessionist hermeneutics bequeathed to the colonial powers of the modern era – in looking at the global impact of Christian missionary efforts on the material (and even spiritual) well-being of many peoples, it becomes nearly untenable. One need not attribute divine willing to the initial fact of the separation to affirm, with paragraph 3 of the Statement, that there have been positive outcomes from the separation and that "Jews can acknowledge the ongoing constructive validity of Christianity as our partner."

The Statement asserts in paragraph 5 that "we Jews and Christians have more in common than what divides us," and names Jewish Sacred Scriptures as one in the list. This is a confounding claim, particularly in an Orthodox rabbinic statement. From the standpoint of

15. Korn, "Revisiting," 295–296, 305–306. The simple fact of the Seelisberg Conference of the International Council of Christians and Jews in 1947 indicates that this era did not wait for *Nostra Aetate* to get underway.

Orthodox biblical study (it seems from the outside), the notion that Christians hold their Old Testament "in common" with the Jewish community is impossible. Rabbi Hirsch is quoted in paragraph 3 to the effect that "Christians 'have accepted the Jewish Bible of the Old Testament as a book of Divine revelation,'" but acknowledging a re-velatory character of the book and holding it in common as a source for the community's life are hardly the same.

The issue goes beyond the acceptance of norms of modern bib-lical scholarship within the Orthodox world, as TheTorah.com is promoting. It goes to the question of scripture itself – what con-stitutes it and whether the same words on a page in a synagogue and in a church can ever truly mean the same thing. As James A. Sanders has advanced in his canonical criticism, scripture is more than literature. It takes its character from the use to which it is put in a community.[16] It is shaped by the reading it is given and the theological context to which it bears a dialectical relationship. In an era of post-modern, post-structuralist biblical interpretation, it is difficult to sustain even the claim that two Christian communities hold a Bible in common. There is much to discuss if we are to affirm that Christians hold the "Jewish Sacred Scriptures" in common with the Jewish community.

Even in its vision of Jews and Christians joined as partners in *imi-tation Deo* in paragraph 7, the Statement challenges us to understand the relationship between the "models of service, unconditional love and holiness" that are mandated for Jews and for Christians. Each of these communal values is grounded in different scriptural sources and shaped by historical experiences that sometimes diverge widely for the communities. Servanthood in the Christian community is modeled on the Suffering Servant imagery from Isaiah that the gos-pel writers used to characterize Jesus's model for his followers. It

---

16. James A. Sanders, "Adaptable for Life," in *Magnalia* Dei, ed. by Frank Moore Cross, Werner E. Lemke, and Patrick D. Miller (NY: Doubleday, 1976), repr. in James A. Sanders, *From Saacred Story to Sacred Text* (Phildaelphia: For-tress, 1987), 30; and idem, *Canon and Community: A Guide to Canonical Criti-cism*, Guides to Biblical Scholarship: Old Testament Series, Gene M. Tucker, ed. (Philadelphia: Fortress, 1984), 19, 37–45.

is typically understood to include the voluntary acceptance of suffering in the interest of service, which is rarely if ever affirmed in
Jewish tradition. Unconditional love and holiness similarly emerge
within Jewish self-understanding and morality in different modes
and inflections from those among Christians. The statement, in recognizing that we use the same words and often the same scriptural
imagery to express our aspirations and sense of obligation, lays the
groundwork for a fascinating theological dialogue that can inform
and accompany our shared work "to address the moral challenges of
our era" (Preamble).

IV.

The call to moral solidarity is central to the Statement, climaxing
both its preamble, as just cited, and its final paragraph. There, it
appears as "Jews and Christians will remain dedicated to the Covenant by playing an active role together in redeeming the world." It is
echoed, too, in paragraph 3, which acknowledges "the ongoing constructive validity of Christianity as our partner in world redemption," and in paragraph 4, asserting that "both Jews and Christians
have a common covenantal mission to perfect the world under the
sovereignty of the Almighty." While this calling thus forms the back-
bone of the Statement's understanding of Christian-Jewish partnership in *imitatio Dei*, it is not clear that Christians will recognize
their own life with God in it. Here we may confront one of those
"ongoing differences" to which the Statement appropriately points,
without suggesting that the difference must continue to divide the
two communities.

To be sure, Christians highly esteem the virtues articulated in
paragraph 5 as shared between the two communities: ethical monotheism, the relationship with the One Creator, scriptural witness,
meaningful tradition, life, family, compassionate righteousness, justice, inalienable freedom, universal love, and ultimate world peace.
We have already noted that several of these deserve their own dialogue agenda. Beyond the particulars, however, the question arises

whether Christians understand themselves to be participants in the redemption of the world.

It is most often claimed that the world's redemption is the divine work of Jesus's death and resurrection, fully accomplished even if not yet fully evident in the world's history. To live in faith, which is itself a form and product of that redemption, brings sanctification both to the individual and to the wider community, even on a global scale. The matter of redemption itself, however, is not within human hands or on the human agenda; hearing and proclaiming the good news of redemption is. As Hans-Martin Barth has said in characterizing Martin Luther's theology, "the relationship God-human or God's glory-human salvation is so much in the foreground that the question of the 'destiny' of creation recedes."[17] Here, insomuch as Christians will themselves bring different nuances and understandings to a dialogue, but there is a general trend in the Christian community to rest redemption in the Christ event and to distinguish it from human endeavors toward improving worldly conditions.

Recognizing this distinction between the Statement's redemptive focus and Christian self-understanding evokes a further, fundamental question about the emerging relationship. It has to do with how we each construe the other. The statement, in paragraph 6, respects the differences between our two communities while also "affirm[ing] the fundamental ethical obligations that all people have before God that Judaism has always taught through the universal Noahide covenant." One of the virtues of Christianity named by Rabbi Jacob Emden and quoted by the Statement in paragraph 3 similarly reflects the role of Jesus in bringing the Noahide commandments to the nations. The statement, then, construes Christianity as an ethically enlightened and no-longer-threatening partner in an ethical task, something that presumably could be said of any non-Jewish community in the world that falls within the bounds of the Noahide profile. Christians themselves, of course, understand themselves as a community that is distinctive in the world.

---

17. Hans-Martin Marth, *The Theology of Martin Luther: A Critical Assessment* (Minneapolis: Fortress, 2013), 392.

Conversely, Christians even today construe biblical Israel as part of their own heritage and face the challenge, if they will not be supersessionists, of understanding Judaism in a framework that is coherent with their Christian identity. The categories of that understanding will be inherent to Christian theology and are likely to seem awkward, unnecessary, inadequate, or uncomfortable to Jews – perhaps even "all of the above." The Roman Catholic Church has taken as "obligatory a better mutual understanding and renewed mutual esteem," with the practical encouragement that Christians "strive to learn by what essential traits Jews define themselves in the light of their own religious experience."[18] Such an understanding will certainly inform, but does not constitute, a Christian theological account of Judaism. That will be framed as a Christian definition in light of Christian experience. It is the task that Van Buren and Marquardt, among the Protestants, and Philip A. Cunningham with his emerging "theology of shalom,"[19] among Roman Catholics, have undertaken.

The rabbinic statement places before us the issue of appropriate representation of another religious community in the language of one's own. It presses us back to Rabbi Soloveitchik's philosophical objection about the incommensurate nature of religious experience. Because Christians think of biblical Israel's witness as part of their own experience, they necessarily must construe in Christian terms something that Jews construe Jewishly. It is a daunting question for Christians, given the egregious offense that is our bequeathed heritage on this score. Those in the Christian-Jewish dialogue know that it is unavoidable for Christians, however.

This rabbinic statement and the historical work that lies behind it have begun to assemble the evidence of a Jewish heritage that con-

---

18. Johannes Cardinal Willebrands, Pres., Pontifical Commission for Religious Relations with the Jews, "Guidelines and Suggestions for Implementing the Conciliar Declaration *Nostra Aetate* (no. 4)" (1974), Preamble; http://www.vatic an.va/roman_curia/pontifical_councils/chrstuni/relations-jews-docs/rc_pc_chr stuni_doc_19741201_nostra-aetate_en.html.

19. Philip A. Cunningham, *Seeking Shalom: The Journey to Right Relationship between Catholics and Jews* (Grand Rapids: Eerdmans, 2015).

strues Christianity positively in Jewish terms. How that heritage will contribute to further formulations about Christianity within the Jewish community remains to be seen. In the continuing dialogue, each community will have to engage the other's new construals as a factor both in its self-understanding and in its view of the other. For that task, few markers yet exist. We shall have to discover them together.

What does now exist, in this Orthodox Rabbinic Statement on Christianity, is an overture to a stronger and more open relationship, with the possibility of engaging theological issues together. It is an overture that is worthy of note, laden with possibility, and heartily welcomed.

To Do the Will of Our Father in Heaven: Psychological and Spiritual Aspects

GABRIEL STRENGER, JERUSALEM

GENUINE ENCOUNTERS

True dialogue is based on the values and skills found in genuine encounter. This has been described by philosophers including Martin Buber, Hans-Georg Gadamer and Paul Ricoeur, and is today researched by contributors to relational psychoanalysis such as Jessica Benjamin. The values displayed in genuine encounters are honesty, modesty, compassion, and the acceptance of uncertainty (Benjamin, 2004). True dialogue goes beyond tolerance and pragmatism; it requires a pluralistic worldview that accords the dialogue partner a valuable point of view, and frees the individual from the existential blindness that naturally results from their own history and narrow humanity. These values are particularly significant for Jewish-Christian dialogue, which has suffered painful experiences in the past.

Participants in interreligious dialogue need certain mental abilities that cannot be taken for granted. So-called Intersubjectivity, "the process by which we become able to grasp the other as having a separate yet similar mind" (ibid.), is especially important. Although Intersubjectivity is considered an innate ability, being able to use it is a developmental achievement. It is human nature to be interested in the internal perception of one's vis-à-vis, but one must also be able to withstand and deal with the narcissistic insults inherent in these encounters.

Otherness is considered threatening to the self, occasionally causing fear and aggression. In interreligious encounters, the strain is particularly great, as the participants not only fear for their own identity, but for their religious tradition as well, with which they identify, consciously or unconsciously. The participants feel a psychological conflict between their need to approach representatives of other religions and their loyalty towards their own allies in faith through the generations.

The more complex one's own personal or religious identity, the better the prospects for genuine dialogue. Complexity here means a healthy balance between autonomy and bonding, without falling into the extremes of self-isolation or loss of identity. Mature eloquence is equally useful. It is speech that allows us to bear other viewpoints and interests, and protects interpersonal encounters from degenerating into a murderous power struggle." (Lacan, 1975). As with other abilities, skill in Intersubjectivity comes with practice. People experienced in interreligious dialogue can confirm that the ability to participate in dialogue is like a muscle that is strengthened through training.

Within dialogue, Intersubjectivity permits what Benjamin (1995) calls "mutual recognition." Participants perceive others as similar and different subjects at the same time. In other words, as human beings with their own psychic inner worlds that include faith, narrative, and feelings. The recognition of the other has to be worked on because it conflicts with inbuilt prejudices formed for psychological reasons. "Re-cognition" means "think again" and this is exactly what it is all about: reconsidering and correcting prejudices that one has formed about fellow human beings or other cultures and religions.

Jessica Benjamin points out the paradox that the satisfaction of our personal need to be recognized by another person depends on our ability to recognize that person as an independent subject. This is the reason why people who try to control and dominate others become entangled in a vicious circle within which they become more and more distrustful and fearful. The less a dictator allows his

entourage to have their own opinions, the lonelier and more para-
noid he becomes. Recognition feels real only when freely given. The
same applies to fundamentalists: the more they hide behind religious walls, the more threatening other religions appear to them.
Even when offered a hand in dialogue, they smell deceit and hostile
intent.

In the interreligious context, recognition means to respect the
other religion as a legitimate and independent form of belief – similar to and at the same time different from one's own form of belief.
If one side is able to take the initial step of recognition, it will be
easier for the other side to take a reciprocal step. The development
of the Orthodox Rabbinic Statement on Christianity (as described
by Rabbi Jehoschua Ahrens in this book) depicts this process very
well. Moreover, the preface of the Statement shows that the rabbis
recognize the conciliatory steps taken by the Christian side ("the
hand offered") as real. Based on this, they appreciate the Vatican
declaration *Nostra Aetate* in detail (paragraph 2). What the rabbis
say is more or less this: "Over the past 50 years you Christians have
turned around and revised your distorted image of Judaism. You
recognize our religion as an independent path to salvation. You have
let deeds follow your words and granted respect and love to our
people." This is followed by a reciprocal recognition of the salva-
tion-historical relevance of Christianity, which from a Jewish point
of view is rather revolutionary (paragraph 3).

The positive mention of Jesus in a quote by Rabbi Yakow Emden,
an important Jewish authority, is particularly moving. Jesus is extremely significant in the lives of numerous Christians, whereas for
many Jews, up to now Jesus has been a symbol of anti-Semitism and
the persecution of Jews, and is therefore like a red rag to a bull. In
each interreligious conversation, Christian participants will sooner
or later ask the anxious question: what do their interlocutors think
about Jesus? Mentioning him benevolently in the Statement shows
that the Jewish signatories have a thorough understanding of Christian concerns.

INNER IMAGES AND REAL ENCOUNTERS

Throughout their histories, all religions have developed ideas about and images of other denominations. These are usually pejorative and devalue "the alien" or "the heathen" in comparison with co-religionists. These images have not been developed for the sake of real encounters with others, but for internal discourse, and are mainly aimed at strengthening the religion's own identity. Daniel Boyarin (2004) impressively illustrated these processes through the parallel histories of early Christianity and Rabbinic Judaism in the first few centuries CE.

To actually meet the other means confessing the inadequacies of the images one has so far visualized. Within interreligious dialogue, traditional concepts do not necessarily need to be discarded. In the course of this new dialogue situation, a reinterpretation can often be reached. Idolatry and the biblical figure of Esau as the eternal opponent of Jacob/Israel are pejorative concepts traditionally connected in Judaism with Christianity. Both concepts are named in the Rabbinic Statement and put into a new hermeneutical framework (paragraphs 4 and 5), demonstrating that the aim of the Orthodox signatories is not to break away from Jewish categories of thinking, but to reconcile them with an improved relationship with Christianity, and to organically embed interreligious dialogue as a whole into Rabbinic Judaism. Mentioning familiar Jewish values, such as love, holiness, an intimate relationship with God, the image of God in humankind, and striving for the salvation of the world, serves the same goal, while deliberately including known verses or Jewish prayers (paragraph 4). Furthermore, six respected Jewish authorities from different epochs are cited, who have spoken benevolently about Christianity (paragraphs 3, 4 and 5). All these features indicate that reconciliation with Christianity does not mark a break in the signatories' identity, but complies with the true spirit of Rabbinic Judaism.

FEARS, DISTINCTION, AND AGGRESSION

The Statement mentions fears that have affected the relationship between Jews and Christians for generations. One central fear on the Jewish side is explicitly named: the possible misuse of interreligious dialogue for missionary purposes, which runs counter to the values of true dialogue. Furthermore, there is a call to overcome "understandable fears" on both sides (paragraph 3). Indeed, real dialogue must not ignore mutual fears. Being threatened by the other, and the aggression that results from this, is undeniably a basic human experience, as Sartre's well-known dictum *"L'Enfer c'est les autres"* (hell is other people) succinctly puts it. Intersubjective encounter, therefore, requires a continuous review of what is really happening between the participants. Ricoeur supports a "hermeneutics of suspicion" to critically question the motivations of the dialogue participants. Only after deep mutual trust has been established through dialogue over a long period can fears, defensive images, and even aggression be communicated. Telling each other about inner prejudices and fantasies during a personal discourse can be amusing and liberating. Switching to and fro, between inner images and the real presence of the other constitutes the essence of the intersubjective encounter and makes it possible to break free from the dead end of "mismeeting" (Martin Buber). Dialogue participants need to be willing to take responsibility for their own complexes and guilty entanglements, and whenever possible combine this with a good dose of humor.

Between the need for distinction and recognition, there is a natural tension that has a place in genuine dialogue. It is only when this tension breaks down, and self-assertion and mutual recognition are played off against each other, that the wish to dominate, to humiliate, or to eliminate the other arises (Benjamin, 1995). The Jewish-Christian relationship is strongly marked by the historical humiliation of the Jews, by the ritualized forced surrender of Synagogue to Ecclesia. Paradoxically, it is this devaluation of the other that makes recognition impossible for both sides. Once the other has lost their subjectivity and dignity, their recognition is no longer of any worth.

One's own aggression needs to be projected onto the other: it is they who do evil to me, poison my wells, etc. Or else fantasies of omnipotence are developed to avoid admitting any influence of the other on oneself. These solutions to the problem of otherness are based on fantasies that cannot withstand verification by reality, sometimes leading to difficult moments in dialogue when one person wants to tell the other: "You must be crazy – and if you're not, then I am!" (Benjamin, 2004). This is why honest dialogue requires that mutual fantasies, fears, and aggressions are admitted and worked through. As the pioneer of relational psychoanalysis Stephen Mitchell (1997) wrote: one becomes part of the solution by being willing to be part of the problem. This is why we need to accept feelings of loss, shame, and our own vulnerability (Benjamin, 2004), and be willing to accept the possibility that our religious tradition is not always beyond all doubt. Thus, outside criticism loses a lot of its threat. In this context, it is good to keep in mind the useful differentiation between surrender and submission that Emmanuel Ghent (1990) brought to the psychoanalytical discourse: surrender means being ready to loosen one's own need for control without submitting to the other. In other words: one does not submit to the other but to the relationship or dialogue and its values.

SPIRITUAL ASPECTS

"For by the light of Your face You have given us, Adonai our God, the Torah of life, and love of kindness, righteousness, blessing, mercy, life and peace" (*Sim Shalom*). In their Statement, it is obvious that the Orthodox rabbis are promoting values of love and peace. *Rahamim*, the Hebrew for compassion, originates from *rehem*, uterus, meaning to grant the other space within one's own spirit, so the other can be or become what they really are. *Rahamim* can therefore be understood as a biblical term for the intersubjective effort of mutual recognition.

As mentioned above, the Rabbinic Statement appreciates that the Christian side has let deeds follow their recognition of Judaism (paragraph 2). This is of special importance, since from a Jewish point of view, repentance (*teshuva*) is accomplished only when changes in specific behavior follow remorse and the begging of forgiveness (Maimonides, Mishneh Torah, *Hilkhot Teshuva*- Laws of Repentance 2:1). Though the Statement leaves out the term *teshuva*, the rabbis essentially acknowledge this process of repentance by many Christians, in contrast to earlier Christians' anti-Judaism. This in turn makes reconciliation with Christianity, as well as detachment from the traditional victim role towards Christians, now possible on the Jewish side. Moreover, Maimonides established the principle that begging for forgiveness should always be granted:

> It is forbidden [for the victim] to be cruel and unappeasable. He should instead be readily appeased and slow to anger. When the sinner comes before him to ask for forgiveness, he should offer it to him wholeheartedly and willingly. Even if the sinner caused that person a lot of trouble and sinned against him often, he should nonetheless not be vengeful or spiteful. For that is the way of the Children of Israel, whose hearts are fixed in this trait. (ibid. 2:14).

Spirituality means believing in humans and their goodwill, and not making it hard for them to repent. Reconciliation constitutes one of the most valuable celebrations of human freedom. It removes the power of the traumas of the past over the present and the future, and breaks down the roles of perpetrator and victim. All spiritual traditions support seizing the opportunities of the present moment. If it is at all possible to initiate peace between the religions now, the opportunity must not be missed.

Spiritual people are aware of being limited in their ability to think and understand. They revere God, seeing His immeasurability in contrast to their own limitedness. If this awareness is authentic, it will necessarily lead to a pluralistic worldview. Humans need one another to break free from the prisons of their own selves. Religions need one another to resist the temptation of fundamentalism. The revelation religions, as they appeared in history, could only bring mere fragments of a divine truth into the world. God's wisdom, reaching us through the Bible, has been condensed into language understandable by humans within a certain historical and social context. Even terms like "Judaism" and "Christianity" are generalizations that are often misused either apologetically or else as a battle cry. In these cases, the denigration of other religions often serves to cover up rivalries within a religion's own ranks. On the other hand, those who perceive pluralism within and between religions as a gift from God can overcome their fear of others and search for reconciliation.

In the Orthodox Rabbinic Statement, the remarks that no religion can fulfill God's mission in this world on its own (paragraph 3) and that God employs many messengers to reveal His truth (paragraph 6), bear testimony to this point of view. Surely these principles are true for those members of any religion who out of love of God and humility are willing to join the "Covenant of the Moderates" ("Bund der Gemäßigten" – Strenger, 2016). This applies also to Islam, the third Abrahamic religion, which from its very beginning has had much in common with Judaism both theologically and spiritually.

In conclusion, I want to remark on the daring sub-title of the Statement: *To Do the Will of Our Father in Heaven*. It is the right and duty of religious leaders to read the signs of the times in line with their beliefs, and draw consequences from them. But it was not political or pragmatic considerations that led the rabbis to make their Statement. Nor was it secular motives, or the values of the Age of Enlightenment alone, that led them to reconsider their beliefs. Rather, they were filled with trust in God and the wish to understand and fulfill the will of the God of Israel for this generation: the foundation of a partnership between religions for the sake of the whole of humankind.

But what does it mean when the rabbis call Christianity the "willed divine outcome" (paragraph 3)? Can we know what God wants? Can we speak of God's will in this particular sense? Possibly we can understand this phrase by looking at world developments over the past 50 years: the change in Jewish self-esteem following the Shoah and the foundation of the State of Israel, as well as the revolutionary theological changes in Christianity, and by seeing that the signatories have been convinced of the possibility of embracing Christians as partners in a joint mission to serve God. "God's will" is shown by human willingness to carry the divine values of love and righteousness into the world through the unity and coexistence of different religions. Their aims are the same, their paths different. The ability to happily accept the diversity of religions as a divine gift without fear of losing one's own hard-won identity and without wishing to convert the other, is vital for achieving true peace for our world.

Response to *To Do the Will of Our Father in Heaven:* Toward a Partnership between Jews and Christians

Gerald R. McDermott

As I was writing this chapter, the world was once more wringing its hands over Israel's attempts to defend itself. Hamas was cynically urging the people of Gaza to storm Israel's borders in the hope of breaking through to kill Jews, and the United Nations was censuring Israel for "disproportionate use of force." I wondered what Canadians would do if Americans were storming its borders to kill Canadians. Would we censure the Canadians for defending their borders?

The Orthodox Rabbinic Statement *To Do the Will of Our Father in Heaven* strikes me as exceedingly *generous*. When Christians for most of two millennia have stretched out their hands to kill Jews, the rabbis are now "accepting the hand offered to us by our Christian brothers and sisters." Millions of Christians still fail to recognize their spiritual kinship with Jews, but these brave rabbis want to accept the hand of Christians who are extending it in friendship and hope.

A second note of generosity is the rabbis' declaration that "the emergence of Christianity" is "neither an accident nor an error, but the willed divine outcome and gift to the nations." This is an extraordinary statement. After all the pogroms and other persecutions of Jews by Christians – not to mention the Holocaust in which some of its perpetrators were church-goers – and after eighteen hundred years during which many Christian theologians thought of their faith as inimically opposed to Judaism, it is remarkably magnanimous of Jewish leaders to acknowledge that God might have had something to do with the rise of Christianity.

A third sign of the rabbis' capacious thinking is their proposal that "God willed a separation between partners with significant theological differences, not a separation between enemies." The suggestion that Christians and Jews are not enemies, after centuries when Christians have treated Jews as enemies, is charitable indeed.

The rabbis present two reasons why Jews and Christians are not – and should not – be enemies. The first is that this is a special moment in the history of providence. This is, as they put it, a "historic opportunity." Finally, after two thousand years, many of us in both of our communities are realizing that we have been fighting needlessly. Of course we differ theologically, and there is a certain merit in frank but friendly theological argument. But the fighting that has predominated for far too long, the fighting that has led to cursing and harming and killing, has ended for the most part. It has been nothing less than sin, and momentous sin indeed. It has nearly ruined witness to the reality of the God of Israel, who has called both of our communities into existence. And truth be told, the vast majority of the sin has been committed by Christians against Jews. But now the Christian Churches have generally lamented their long history of anti-Judaism, and many have started to reach out to Jews in friendship, theological dialogue, and moral cooperation.

The other reason in this document for what should be the end of our enmity is the surprising range of our moral and theological agreements. The rabbis mention more than several: the monotheism of Abraham, the notion that this world was created and is not eternal, our common possession of Scriptures which both of our communities recognize as divine revelation (most Christians don't realize that the Hebrew Scriptures make up 77% of Protestant Bibles and that Jewish writings comprise close to 80% of the Catholic Bible), the conception of human beings as made in God's image, faith in the Exodus and other divine acts in Israel's history, confidence that God gave Israel his law, and shared understandings of the value of human life, family (I would add marriage), compassion, justice, freedom, and love. This is a remarkable set of agreements that are common to Jews and Christians, and that are not shared with other faith communities. Muslims, for example, do not share any Scriptures with Christians or Jews. Neither do Buddhists and Hindus, and none of these religions sees human beings as created in the image of the God of Abraham.

The rabbis apparently recognize what more Jews and Christians ought to recognize, that Orthodox Jews and Christians have common challenges – enemies if you will, and that they need to see that we have far more in common than our predecessors realized. We face militant secularists and relativists on the left, and radical Islam on the right. By militant secularism I mean the sort that will not permit Christians or Jews to speak as believers in public or to educate their young unless they agree with the latest cultural orthodoxies, on marriage for example. By radical Islam we mean the sort that kills those who disagree and opposes religious and political pluralism.

To Do the Will of Our Father in Heaven is about our shared vision, not our common enemies. Some may object, however, that our common vision is not so common, because it is belied by deeper differences. Jon Levenson, for example, has argued that Jewish and Christian perceptions of each of these commonalities are different because each comes within a different framework. For example, for Jews, Abraham is the father of faith in the oneness of God that excludes a Trinity, while for Christians, Abraham's willingness to sacrifice Isaac is a type of the Father's willingness to give up his divine Son Jesus. So Abraham for Jews is not quite the same as Abraham for Christians.[1] Levenson has a point. Each of our traditions sheds a different light at one level on what we share. But these differences do not negate what we share at another level. Both of our communities see Abraham as a model for faith in, and faithfulness to, the only

---

1. Jon D. Levenson, *Inheriting Abraham: The Legacy of the Patriarch in Judaism, Christianity, and Islam* (Princeton: Princeton University Press, 2012).

true God, the God of Israel. So yes, we have our differences. But let us not permit our differences to overshadow our agreements.

Among these agreements is the common conviction that Torah is the word of God. I appreciate the rabbis' recognition that Jesus "strengthened the Torah of Moses majestically" and taught "the immutability of Torah." He did indeed, but most Jews and most Christians are unaware of this. They have either forgotten or never heard that Jesus warned his Jewish followers, "Don't think that I came to do away with Torah or the prophets. I came not to do away with them but to fulfill them" (Matt 5:17).[2] The Greek word for "fulfill" is *plērōsai,* which means "to interpret the passage accurately and to live out the meaning of the text in practice."[3] To further reinforce the permanent validity of Torah, Jesus added that "until the heaven and the earth pass away, not an iota (the smallest Greek letter) or a horn (the smallest Hebrew stroke of the pen) will pass away from Torah until everything is accomplished" (Matt 5:18). He went even further to say that the lightest of Torah's *mitzvot* were binding on his disciples, "Whoever breaks one of the least of these commandments and teaches men to do likewise, will be called least in the Kingdom of Heaven. But whoever observes and teaches them, he will be called great in the Kingdom of Heaven" (Matt 5:19).

It was not only Jesus who taught Torah. So did the apostle Paul. In his last major epistle, which contains his most mature reflection on faith, Jesus, and Torah, Paul asked, "Are we then overthrowing Torah because of faith?" (Rom 3:31a). This was a rhetorical question. Paul was writing the Roman Christians that faith in the Messiah was more important than perfect compliance with every last *mitzvah.* Did this then mean Torah observance was not important? "By no means!" Paul thundered. "We affirm Torah!" Later in the epistle Paul said it another way, "Torah is holy, and the *mitzvah* is holy and righteous and good" (Rom 7:12).

---

2. I translate *nomos* as "Torah" in these verses because this was the usual translation for Hellenistic Jews of the Greek word in most uses, but especially in Matthew 5 and the Romans passages I quote.

3. Brad Young, *Meet the Rabbis: Rabbinic Thought and the Teachings of Jesus* (Grand Rapids: Baler Academic, 2007), 43.

Paul is sometimes called the founder of Christianity by those who think he opposed Jesus to Torah.[4] These scholars tend to say that Paul was the founder of replacement theology – the idea that God replaced his covenant with Jewish Israel with a new covenant with the gentile Church. But these scholars downplay or ignore another clear Pauline statement in the epistle to the Romans:

> In regard to the gospel, [my brother Jews who do not accept Jesus] are enemies, but by God's choice they are beloved [to Him] because of [their] Fathers. For the gifts and the calling of God are irrevocable. (Rom 11:28–29).

In other words, Paul was emphatic that God's covenant with Jewish Israel was not coming to an end. This is all the more remarkable when it is considered that Paul was writing at least twenty years after Jesus had left this world. It was dawning on Paul that the majority of his Jewish brethren were not accepting the gospel, and that he might die before the day when he predicted "all Israel" would be saved (Rom 11:26). Yet Paul was adamant that God still loved all of Jewish Israel, and their gifts and calling would not be revoked.

But Paul is intriguing for still another reason. In *To Do the Will of Our Father* the rabbis propose that God "willed a separation" between our two communities. Irving Greenberg has suggested one reason for this divine willing: that through the Gentiles the God of Israel's truth and morality would be disseminated to the world.[5] Paul agreed that this was the divine will but for another reason. Some of the rabbis had taught that when the Messiah came and all Israel accepted him, the world would end. Paul seems to have believed this, and to have concluded that this was why most Jews did not accept Jesus: God needed to open space and time for millions of Gentiles to find salvation. They would become adopted sons and daughters

---

4. For example, Gerd Ludemann, *Paul: The Founder of Christianity* (Amherst, NY: Prometheus Books, 2002).

5. Irving Greenberg, *For the Sake of Heaven and Earth: The New Encounter between Judaism and Christianity* (Philadelphia: Jewish Publication Society, 2004), 229.

of the God of Israel in the "commonwealth of Israel" (Rom 11:25–32; Gal 4:4–5; Eph 2:12–13).[6] Jesus seems to have taught something similar, that salvation comes from somehow joining Israel: "Salvation is from the Jews" (John 4:22).

But if all this is true, why have Jesus and Paul been seen by so many millions of Jews and Christians to have been against Torah and Jewish Israel? There are many answers to this question, but among the most important is the early history of the Church. Starting in the second century, Gentile leaders began to dominate the leadership of the Church, and they helped to spread a tradition that ignored Christianity's Jewish roots. I have written about this at some length.[7]

All Christians are either soft or hard supersessionists. Soft supersessionism is the idea that Jesus was the Messiah and therefore brought Judaism to a new stage. The Messianic Age superseded the age which waited for the Messiah. Hard supersessionism has two parts, one concerning the people of Israel and the other the land of Israel. The first part is the belief that God's covenant with the Jewish people of Israel was transferred to the (eventually) gentile Church after 33 CE because most Jews rejected Jesus as Messiah. The second part of hard supersessionism is the belief that while the land might be holy because of the history that transpired there, it is nevertheless unimportant theologically to God's present and future purposes.

All Christians therefore, by virtue of their faith in Jesus as Messiah, are soft supersessionists. The problem, according to this prescient Orthodox Rabbinic Statement, is with the hard supersessionists. They fail to see Paul's assertion and Jesus' suggestion that God's covenant with his Jewish people continues to this day. They also miss the ongoing theological significance of the land of Israel. These are enormously dangerous failures, and, as our Orthodox rabbis suggest, dangerous to far more than simply the Jewish community. *To Do the Will of Our Father in Heaven* implies that this

6. McDermott, *Israel Matters*, 124–26.
7. McDermott, ed. *The New Christian Zionism*, chap. 1; McDermott, *Israel Matters*, chap. 1.

view of Christianity's relationship to Judaism is a threat to the gentile Church itself and to the civilized world as well. Just as in the last century hard supersessionism "weakened resistance to evil forces of anti-Semitism that engulfed the world in murder and genocide" in the twentieth century, so too in this next century hard supersessionism could open the floodgates to new horrors.

Let me try to unpack the logic of this subtle warning. Without Nazism, communism could not have spread so easily to Eastern Europe and much of Asia. Stalin's communist regime was first strengthened by his pact with Hitler, and then by the Allies' need for Soviet help to defeat Hitler. The western Allies could not afford to hurt the Soviet cause for fear of losing their own. Stalin's massive army was needed on the Eastern Front to help destroy the Wehrmacht.

But after the Soviet victory in 1945, the Russians turned west to consolidate their gains in Eastern Europe and then east to spread their influence in Asia. Our debt to the Russians, contracted during our war against Germany, eliminated our moral ability to stop Stalin from enslaving Eastern Europe. The manifest success of his communism encouraged Mao to hope that a similar government could be imposed on China. It is doubtful that the Chinese Revolution of 1949 could have succeeded without the example and help of the Soviet regime.

Hitler therefore helped sow the seeds for totalitarianism far beyond Germany. But he could never have gained power in the first place without the Churches' hard supersessionist teaching that convinced Germans that the Jewish religion was fundamentally opposed to Christianity. To be sure, the Treaty of Versailles blaming and punishing Germany for the First World War created resentment and penury that Hitler's propaganda exploited. But Germans also heard him blame the Jews for their problems, and they were encouraged by his implicit promises to solve those problems by resolving "the Jewish question." The contingencies of history are ultimately mysterious, so it would be foolish to think that one factor was crucial to Hitler's triumph in the 1930s. But it would not be foolish to reflect that if German Christians had been convinced of

Christianity's Jewish roots, Hitler's rise to power would have been more difficult.

The Orthodox rabbis suggest, ever so subtly, that if hard supersessionism contributed to the catastrophe that was World War II, the rise of the new supersessionism could be just as perilous. By new supersessionism I mean two things. First there is the worldwide movement of Islamism that wants to destroy Israel and all Jews. It is hard supersessionism on steroids. If Christian hard supersessionists decry anti-Semitism, and most of them do, Islamist supersessionists embrace it. Therefore the two kinds of supersessionism are fundamentally different in character and intent. The first is merely theological, while the second is not only theological but political and military as well. Christian hard supersessionists disagree with Jews on God and covenant and land, but most wish Jews every earthly blessing. Islamist supersessionists, on the other hand, wish Jews a painful death.

Yet there is a strain in hard Christian supersessionism that resembles Islamist and even so-called moderate Muslim supersessionism. It is the strain that regards Judaism as retrograde and racist. This can be seen when Christians label Judaism, especially Zionist Judaism, as "ethnic" or "nationalist." These Christians speak of Jews as being a race of people, often claiming that Christians, in contrast, believe in God's calling "by grace not race." They think of Judaism as a religion of works and Christianity as a religion of grace. Jews, they say, think they are earning their way to heaven by their good works. Christians, they claim, realize that works won't save them, but God's unmerited grace will. Thus the two religions, it is claimed, have two different gods and radically different conceptions of how to get to that god. One god saves only those in the right race (who think their works make them deserving), while the other god saves because he loves all those who realize they are unworthy.[8]

This new supersessionism would not be so alarming if it were confined to polite theological debates in seminaries or Sunday

---

8. I use a lower case "g" in this case because neither the Jewish deity they describe nor the deity of hard supersessionism is the true God of Israel.

school classes. But it has broken out into the political and economic worlds. Think of the rise of the BDS movement on European and American university campuses, the proliferation of lethal attacks on Jews in Europe with little public protest, and the sustained attacks on Israel both at the United Nations and in most of the media. Of course, most of these cannot be blamed on bad Christian theology. Many in the BDS movement are not religious, and many Christians who criticize Israel do so because they have been led to believe that Israel's government has been unfair to Palestinians. Most attacks on Jews in Europe are perpetrated by Muslims. But what all these critics have in common is what most hard supersessionists agree on: the idea that Judaism is an old, racist, and unspiritual religion that has been superseded by newer religions that are spiritual and non-racial.

Yet even this crude supersessionism among Christians might be less dangerous than that of ethical universalists. These are Western elites whose religion is nominally Christian but formally Kantian. Reinhold Niebuhr called them "liberal universalists." They prize abstract principles divorced from the gritty realities of politics. As Robert Benne has described them, "They obsess about the iniquities of Israel and turn a blind eye to the depredations of Muslim groups and states." They are able to think that Israel is oppressive because they trivialize the existential dangers it faces. They "have an inflated idea about the room that Israel has to negotiate" and so hold it to "impossibly high standards of behavior."[9] They imagine that since Israel has survived, it can take chances. But they are blind to the visceral hatred of its enemies, and the tribal complexities of the region. When the world's media criticizes Israel for defending itself, liberal universalists are in high dudgeon.

Therefore we Christians have a twofold task. We must recognize, with Jesus and Paul, that God's covenant with his Jewish people is still in place. We must also see that the massive ingathering of Jews back to the land in the last one hundred and fifty years is a fulfill-

---

9. Robert Benne, "Theology and Politics: Reinhold's Niebuhr's Christian Zionism," in McDermott, *The New Christian Zionism*, 244–48.

ment of biblical prophecies, not only those of the prophets in the *Tanach* but also those of the writers of the New Testament. Peter, for example, used the word *apokatastasis* in Acts 3:21 for a future restoration that was still to come, the word used in the Septuagint for a future return of Jews to sovereignty in the land. Jesus told his disciples that the Father had fixed the time for a future restoration of Israel and that the time would be hidden from his disciples (Acts 1:6). This is the first task for Christians, to disabuse millions in the Churches of their hard supersessionism.

The second task is to join hands with our Jewish friends to heed the call of *To Do the Will of Our Father in Heaven.* We must follow the lead of these rabbis and join their efforts to teach the world about the God of Israel. We and they must proclaim without fear that there are moral absolutes written into the fabric of the cosmos, inscribed there by the Creator. Truth is real and outside of us, whether it is recognized by human beings or not. It is objective and not subjective. Of course our interpretations and applications of ultimate truth will vary depending on our cultural and historical contexts. But the basic lineaments of religious truth (that there is a Creator to Whom we are beholden) and moral truth (the second table of what we call the Ten Commandments) have been recognized by every great civilization for a reason – they are real. They reflect what is finally there, whether humans perceive them or not.

At this moment in the history of our planet, the truth of the creation is under attack by our intellectual and political elites. At the heart of creation are man and woman made in the divine image, and their procreative union in marriage and a family. This is the first institution. It comes both historically and ontologically before government, Church or synagogue. It is the basic building block of society. As the health of the family, so the health of society.

For the family to remain healthy, it must draw on truth about itself and the creation. That truth comes from divine revelation in the Hebrew Scriptures. This shows the connection between our two communities on the one hand, and society on the other. Only as we remain nourished by the revelation that we share, can families and society be sustained. This is why Christians must rid themselves of the hard supersessionism that has poisoned them and civilization.

This is also why Christian understanding of Judaism is the canary in the coal mine. When it has gone wrong, all hell has broken loose. Let us partner together to prevent a new breakout.

III.
FURTHER PERSPECTIVES

Interreligious Dialogue or *"Diaoukésis"*

DANIEL SPERBER

Interreligious dialogue today, the way I understand it, is very different from the phenomenon of the mediaeval Judeo-Christian disputations. Then, the purpose of the disputation was for one religion to discredit the other. It was generally an attack by a Christian representative against the Jewish faith, and the Jewish response was mainly defensive, and so that we are often cognizant to the undercurrent elements of self-justification in these responses.

Contemporary interreligious dialogue is of a wholly different nature. It is not an ideological fight between the sparring partners, and for this reason I would seek to coin a new term to define this new phenomenon. Rather than talk of a *dialogue*, which means an interpersonal discussion in which people "talk" to one another, I would suggest that it is a *diaoukésis*, a process of *listening* to one another. The purpose of this procedure is not for the one to *refute* the other, but rather that by listening to the other, one further clarifies one's own position, delineating the essential differences between the various positions. Consequently it can serve as a process of *self-clarification.* But in doing so one also learns of the strengths of position of the other, possibly highlighting one's own weaknesses, weaknesses which can benefit from adopting elements of the other. Thus both parties may benefit, enriching and strengthening their own faith, and not at the *expense* of the other.

Seen in this light, there can, in my opinion, be no objection to

interreligious dialogue, since it no way presupposes the delegitimization of the other, or the danger of the delegitimization of our own
faith. Conducted with respect and dignity, it can only be a "win-win"
exercise in which all parties enrich and enhance their own heritage.

Perhaps the philosophical basis for this attitude is well formulated (albeit vis-a-vis Christianity and Hinduism, etc.) by the great
Indian scholar and thinker Ananda K. Coomaraswamy, in his *Selected Papers 2, Metaphysics*, Princeton 1977, pp.39–41:

What is then, in the last analysis, the value of comparative religion, [and, hence, interreligious dialogue]? *Certainly not to convince
us* that one mode of belief is the preparation for another, or to lead
to a decision as to *which is "best."* One might as well regard ancient
or exotic styles of art as preparations for and aspirations towards
one's own. Nor can the value of this discipline be thought of as one
conducing to the development of a single universally acceptable
syncretic faith embodying all that is "best" in every faith; such a
"faith" as this would be a mechanical and lifeless monstrosity, by
no means a stream of living water, but a sort of *religious Esperanto*.
Comparative religion can demonstrate that all religions spring from
a common source; or, as Jeremias says, the "dialects of a single spiritual speech." We cannot, therefore, take the formulae of one religion
and insert them in another without incongruity. One can recognize
that many formulae are identical in different religions; confront, for
example, St. Thomas, "Creation, which is the emanation of all being
from the not-being, which is nothing" (*Sum. Theol.* 1.45.IC) with the
Vedic, "Being is engendered from nonbeing" (*asatah sad ajāyata*,
RV x.72.3), and such comparisons can be validly employed (even by
the most Orthodox) as, what St. Thomas calls, "extrinsic and proba-
ble proofs" of the validity of a given dogma.

But of greater value than this is the clarification that results when
the formulae of one tradition are collated with those of another. For,
as we have already seen, every tradition is necessarily a partial representation of the truth intended by tradition universally considered;
in each tradition something is suppressed, or reserved, or obscure
which in another may be found more extensively, more logically,
or more brilliantly developed. What then is clear and full in one

tradition can be used to develop the meaning of what may be hardly more than alluded to in another. Or even if in one tradition a given doctrine has been definitely named, a realization of the significance of this definition may lead to the recognition and correlation of a whole series of affirmations in another tradition, in all of which the same doctrine is implicit, but which had previously been overlooked in their relation to one another. It is thus a great advantage to be able to make use of the expression *Vedic exemplarism*; or conversely, to speak of Christian *yoga* immediately brings out the analogy between Bernard of Clairvaux's *consideration, contemplation,* and *raptus* with Sanskrit *dhāranā, dhyāna,* and *samādhi....*

As he stated,

> *Thus we may go so far as to assert on behalf of a true "comparative religion,"* that however a religion may be self-sufficient if it be followed to the very end to which it is directed, there can hardly be supposed a way so plain that it could not here and there be better illuminated by other lights than that of the pilgrim's private lantern; the light of any lantern being only a refraction of the Light of lights. A diversity of routes is not merely appropriate to a diversity of travelers, who are neither all alike, nor start from one and the same point, but may be of incalculable aid to any traveler who can rightly read the map; for where all roads converge, there can be none of them that does not help to clarify the true position ... [My emphasis, D.S.]

That, I would suggest, is the aim and the hope of our Judeo-Christian *diaoukésis,* "interfilial" clarification that may further tighten the bonds of amity between our respective faiths.

The Language Beyond Silence:
Reflections on the Statement by Orthodox Rabbis, *To Do the Will of Our Father in Heaven: Toward a Partnership between Jews and Christians*

Laurie Zoloth

We Jews and Christians have more in common than what divides us: the ethical monotheism of Abraham; the relationship with the One Creator of Heaven and Earth, Who loves and cares for all of us; Jewish Sacred Scriptures; a belief in a binding tradition; and the values of life, family, compassionate righteousness, justice, inalienable freedom, universal love and ultimate world peace.

I. INTRODUCTION

This sentence, made in *To Do the Will of Our Father in Heaven: Toward a Partnership between Jews and Christians,* by the Orthodox Rabbis in which they acknowledge that both Jews and Christians may live as equal in the world as persons of faith, is a remarkable one, both because of its extraordinarily innovative sprit, given the usual stance of Orthodoxy, and, paradoxically, because of its historical familiarity. The practice, if not the articulation of common project, and the willingness to reach out to Christians on the basis of a common religious sensibility has occurred with some frequency in Jewish history, for some communities. It occurs with regularity among other Jewish denominations, who have joined with Christians in the American Civil Rights movement, and projects for fair housing for the poor, against nuclear war, and in the support of Israel. Notably, Orthodox figures such as Rabbi Jonathan Sacks, and authors of this book, have worked with Christian leaders in support of joint causes. However, in our contemporary period, despite efforts at reconciliation by Christians, mainstream Orthodox rabbis have largely taken another path, one that has led away from a serious engagement with other faith communities. Few have publicly written in their capacity as leaders of Orthodox communities and institutions, about their commitment toward building a relationship with Christians, or understanding the theological claim such a relationship would make. It is this that makes the Statement "groundbreaking." It is fair to describe it as such.

Yet reflection on this statement as a scholar allows for a different assessment, and for this, I will turn to an important precedential moment in which Jews and Christians made a similar moral gesture, acting on the principles of common ground and finding a theological language on which to found their work. In this essay, I will describe this earlier effort, explain why the temporal, the geographical and the gendered response in this language was important and then spend some time illuminating the theology created by a social Christian minister and a feminist Jewish intellectual. Not tangentially, I will reintroduce a woman, Margarete Susman who despite being a leading thinker of the interwar period of Weimer Germany has been largely forgotten, and describe her work and her remarkable capacity for intellectual leadership and interfaith commitment. I will then return to a contemporary reflection on the claim made by the Orthodox rabbis with another example to set beside the logic of the argument made by their statement.

In considering a response to the current statement, let us now turn to that earlier moment in 1933, when German Jewish intellectuals, horrified at Hitler's election, began to seek refuge in Switzerland, leaving the Germany of their birth and the place of their most important hopes for Enlightenment and Jewish and German "*bildung.*" The salons and intellectual circles collapsed, the editors of publications suddenly found no room for Jewish essays, and the most presentient understood it was time to leave, fleeing to the Christian communities of Bern, Geneva, and Zurich. For in the most heavily freighted, tragic moment in modern Jewish history – during the mass murders of the Shoah, when Christians with guns killed the Jewish neighbors they had known for lifetimes, a similar, fragile recognition was made and statements similar to the one we consider in this book were written.

I will explore this moment in some detail, for such an historical narrative does two sorts of work: it allows us to understand the possibilities and limits of such a relationship, and it allows us to consider the leading role of women intellectuals in the interwar period and the immediate aftermath of the Shoah, thus reclaiming an argument from a participant in the development of modern Jewish thought that is often unknown to us, despite her considerable presence in her time.

II.   FROM ILLUSION TO DIALOGUE

Margarete Susman, arrives alone on the train to Zurich in 1933,[1] fleeing from an increasingly Nazified Germany; it is early in the demonic logic that will eventually destroy European Jewry, but she knows early that terror is ahead, for she is a close reader, and believes that the written word matters. She leaves behind her son, her sister, her beloved best friend, a circle of colleagues, and an extraordinary body of work, essays, five books of poetry, 3 volumes of literary criticism and modern cultural theory, a long history of friendship and joint work with a circle of assimilated, cultured, Jewish men and women, German born and educated in the finest Protestant

---

1. Susanne Hillman; "A Few Human Beings Walking Hand in Hand": Margarete Susman, Leonhard Ragaz, and the Origins of the Jewish-Christian Dialogue in Zurich, *The Leo Baeck Institute Year Book*, Volume 59, Issue 1, 1 January 2014, Pages 141–162, also at: https://doi.org/10.1093/leobaeck/ybu003

Enlightenment traditions. Some have long been active in interwar intellectual projects with Christian colleagues, hardly thinking of themselves as Jews, but, as anti-Semitism begins to extend into their circles, they find themselves turning toward their Jewishness with a sort of curiosity, born of a self-assertive certainty, as if one could simply choose a heritage, an interest and a discovered past.[2] George Lukas, mocked by his friends, studies "his ancestors and his race." Franz Rosenszweig turns to Hebrew translation, narrowly turning from conversion to Christianity. Walter Benjamin begins to read Jewish texts, philosopher Ernst Bloch begins to think of messianic redemption in Jewish terms. Martin Buber begins a "Bar Kokhba Circle." Karl Wolfskehl, leading German poet of the era, writes of his new Jewish insight: "All my patriarchs, you have awoken me/ I am son and heir to you all./ I am now aware of you. /Here I am, like you, the eternal exile, /Here I am, like you, the treasure of promises have accumulated within me. (42) He will begin to feel uncomfortable in the salons of Berlin: the "Cosmic Club" he founded, serious intellectuals splits because of the anti-Semitism he feels.

"Daughters" are "awakened" as well as sons: Margarete Susman, who, like Rosenszweig, turns from a Christian conversion the night before it is to be performed, begins to explore her own Jewish heritage. She is in her 20s when she decides to study Judaism, already a published poet, married to her non-Jewish husband, member of the German nobility, the painter and art historian Eduard von Bendemann.

Susman studies with Reform Rabbi Caeser Seilegman, and proves an eager student. She is particularly intrigued by textual studies and the Biblical literature that was Seiligman's forte. She writes a book about Rachel Varhagen, and develops what will be a lifelong friendship with Martin Buber.

She is an elegant writer – a lyrical poet, a master of the Ger-

---

2. Rabinbach, Anson, "In the Shadow of Catastrophe: German Intellectuals Between the Apocalypse and the Enlightenment," California Press, Berkeley, 1997, p.28. Here is cited George Lukas's friend, mocking Lukas's embrace of his Jewish heritage. "Gyuri has discovered in himself the Jew...."

man language and culture, she counts on her Christian friends as interlocutors and as editors, she has had a fine German university education, and knows the thriving world of German feminism. She has written about Varnhagen and Rosa Luxenberg in a book about Women and Romanticism. She is friends with everyone in the intellectual circles in Germany: George Simmel, Bernhard Groethuysen, George Lukas, with Gershom Scholem, and the dashing, charming Ernst Bloch. Karl Wolfskehl writes a poem dedicated to "M.S."[3] "*Why do you tremble? Why, possessor of my soul, is there fear in your eyes, and you fled weeping.*" Paul Celan writes to her, anxious that she should approve of his work, a relationship that will last into the 1960s.[4]

She is in the center of a circle of women intellectuals as well, all writers, artists, photographers or performers; and her best friends Gertrude Kantowitz and Elsa Lasker-Schuler. Cecile Frommer, Margarete "Gritli" Rosenstock-Huessy, Marianne Breslaur, Edith Landman, and poet Ilse Blumenthal-Weiss. They believed they were making a new sort of Jew: enlightened, creative and German.

It was an illusion, however, the notion that a new sort of Jew – a German-Jewish citizen, rational, yet steeped in Chassidic tales, cosmopolitan yet celebratory of Jewish thought, – could live in the German that turned increasingly anti-Semitic for the inescapable reality of Jewish birth, despite the university education, the service in Germany's war, the clever facility with the German language, the poetry, even the careful Christian education, deep friendships, and the intermarriages. None of it would turn out to matter. All of this world lies behind the dark Alps that circle her new home, and she arrives in the dark, "hating and fearing" even the German language in which all her work was written.[5] She will never leave Switzerland again.

3. Ben Pazi, Hanoch, "Four Faces of Hope following the Book of Job," *Moreshet: Journal for the Study of the Holocaust and Anti-Semitism*, 15: 2018, pps 68–102.
4. Hahn, Barbara, *The Jewess Pallas Athena: This Too a Theory of Modernity*, Princeton University Press, 2008.
5. Hillman,op cit

Alone in a Zurich winter, and poor (lying about her poverty so that she will be granted permission to enter the country,) she makes her way to a small, storefront project, the "Gardenhof" – an outreach and training center for workers established by Leonhard and Clara Ragaz in 1921. By 1933, in response to the increasing stream of immigrant Jews into Zurich, and in light of the hostile reception to them by the State, the *Gardenhof* also became a refugee center and hosted talks on religious and political topics, as well as offering food, clothing and support for Jewish refugees.[6] Ragaz had been on his own journey: a successful theologian and professor at the University of Zurich. WWI had turned him from the "guild theologians" to the work of socialist theorists. He quit his position to enact his ideas about a socialist Christianity, and while he had left the world of academic Protestantism, he found an intellectual interlocutor in the Jew, Margarete Susman. Susman and Ragaz studied together, read one another's work, turned to biblical texts, as well as social theories to understand and make sense of their present crisis. Susman had only managed to convince one friend – Elsa Lasker-Schuler, the renowned Expressionist poet – to leave when she did. Her sister and closest friend stayed until it was too late to escape. Captured at the French border, her sister killed herself and her captured friend Gertrude was sent to the concentration camps and died in Theresienstadt.

In the mid-thirties, writing about Franz Kafka, Susman had made the point that Kafka was the most profoundly Jewish of writers because his writings describe "the Jewish spirit," which she understood to be the realization of the absurdity of protest of the person who is innocent but is nonetheless enmeshed in suffering; suffering without meaning and without blame. Kafka's fiction is "modern" for Susman, because it gestures in this way to the Biblical figure of Job, who is, of course terribly punished in what amounts to a sinister game, and is reminded, when he protests, of the reality of God as an overwhelmingly powerful Creator, in whose cosmos Job's suffering cannot be understood, nor contained, nor ordered. Job's only

6. Hillman, op cit.

response, in the Biblical narrative, is prayer – of course a language of near silence. Job comes to understand his place in the vastness of a Creation that is utterly beyond his control, even of his understanding. For Kafka, she argues, already remote from his tradition, will need to seek a "language beyond silence," for in the utter chaos of modernity, prayer is not possible. She will return to this theme.

By 1935, Susman and Ragaz are deeply enmeshed in thinking about Biblical narratives, each the other's interlocutor, and as Susman will say, each the other's "mediator." She sees them as having a similar task. It is a difficult role. Initially warmly accepted by the Swiss Jewish community, Ragaz will be stung by their criticism of his supersessionism in his theological writings. Susman will reassure him that it is still possible that common ground can be found. As the war descended on the world she had left, and as Susman heard of the deaths, one by one, then in the millions, of her friends and family and the entirety of the Jewish world, she turned to another project, a radical, despairing account of the Book of Job, returning to her theme of innocent suffering; this time, with the lost Jews of Europe in the protagonist role. It would be the first book about the Shoah and the crisis of Jewish theology, published in 1946.

> After the violent rupture of the common ground which the world continues to break up with its strongest powers, every true bond between a Jew and a member of another people constitutes a little piece of creation, wrested from chaos, a gentle dawning of the messianic kingdom itself. 1946.[7]

It was difficult to find a publisher: the book was difficult, for Susman was making the claim that during the Shoah, as in the Book of Job, there was a *cesura* in ordinary human experience. In the Shoah,

---

7. Susman, *Das Buch Hiob*, 163–164: *"Jede wahrhaftige Verbindung zwischen einem Juden und einem Menschen eines anderen Volkes ist nach dem gewaltsamen Abbrechen des gemeinsamen Grundes, den die Welt mit ihren stärksten Kräften weiter abzubrechen bemüht ist, ein Stückchen dem Chaos abgerungener Schöpfung, ein leises Aufdämmern des messianischen Reiches selbst."* As noted in Hillman, op cit.

the world, humanity itself, was ruptured, morality shattered. As philosopher Hanoch Ben Pazi notes about Susman's work:

> The book of Job poses the following fundamental questions:
> From whence does profound human evil emerge? And what
> is the spasm that causes man to lose the image of God? In this
> way, the Holocaust is not only a political, ideological or histor-
> ical question; rather, it calls into question the very humanity of
> humankind.[8]

Susman suggests "turning to the old books" to seek a response
to the Shoah and returns to Job, noting that it is not a book about
Job, but rather about Satan, the Biblical name for the forces of nihilism and violence that gripped Europe. For Susman, the evil enters
the world of Job when Satan – in the words of the text – turns his
face away from God to leave to torture Job. This leave-taking, this
turning away from the face of God then allows him to turn away
from the face of Job, made as all humans, in God's image. The Nazi's
likewise had turned their face away, not seeing the image of God in
the faces of those they murdered. And this turning away from the
face of the other, this first rupture of relationships between human
friends, the first denial of the human face of the other, is the beginning of the Shoah. Modernity, totally dehumanizing and de-facing
ideologies are all based on this denial. She muses: when The Law is
not in the world, any atrocity is possible. Like Job, the Jews are innocent, yet suffer for the condition of humanity itself, at a time when
the critical moral moment demanded the encounter see the Jew as
bearing the image of God. It is brilliant reading of the text, and it is
also a deep recall of her own biography. Susman left Germany just at
the moment when the first boycott of Jewish business was ordered,
when Jewish participation in public education was limited, when
bonfires of Jewish books were lit on campuses across German uni-

---

8. Ben Pazi, op cit, 85. See also footnote 48 where Ben Pazi makes the point
that Susman was the first to understand the Shoah as a crisis for all humanity and
not only a Jewish problem.

versities and public squares, including, of course, the Hebrew Bible. The moral catastrophe that was the Shoah, she wrote, is about the inability to see the Divine in each human, a theological and ethical tragedy of horrible proportions.

The book was finally released to acclaim, and praised widely: "Herman Levin Goldschmidt compared the book's significance to Martin Buber's ground-breaking *Reden über das Judentum.*[85] Other Jewish readers were similarly enthusiastic. Gershom Scholem, for example, the noted scholar of the Kabbalah, was profoundly affected by the book, particularly its first part, and responded in a way that struck Susman as "very beautiful and positive." Susman's first teacher of Judaism, Rabbi Caesar Seligmann, professed to be "enraptured" by the book. He had read it three times, and each time he had been more moved.[88] Ilse Blumenthal-Weiss, Susman's poet friend who had recently been liberated from Theresienstadt, praised the book in similarly exalted terms. Susman had managed to grasp and depict "our Jewish existence in its entire compass, with all the visitations and grace [*Begnadungen*], with all death and eternal life" and with an "ardency *and* power" that was without example: "Splendid! Truly splendid!"[9]

And Susman plunged into the work of interfaith dialogue. The Jewish-Christian dialogue was immediately vivid directly after the war in Switzerland. Four months after the final armistice, a weeklong conference was organized by refugee Christian pastor Paul Vogt, who had steadfastly provided aid and support to Jews during the war. This first meeting was the inspiration for an organization Susman helped co-found – the *Arbeitsgemeinschaft für Christen und Juden* (The Working Group of Christians and Jews). By 1947, the organization released an official document, which was clear about the relationship between pre-war Christian theology and its deadly implications, writing thus:

Moved by the sufferings of the Jewish people, the Third Commission, in the course of a frank and cordial collaboration between Jewish and Christian members – both Roman Catholic and Prot-

9. Op cit, Hillman.

estant – were faced with the tragic fact that certain theologically inexact conceptions and certain misleading presentations of the Gospel of Love, while essentially opposed to the spirit of Christianity, contributed to the rise of anti-Semitism.

Ragaz did not live to see the State of Israel, but Vogt did, and he extended his support of the refugee Jews for their homeland. In the 1947 Seelisburg statement,[10] the "ten points" were explicitly theological – rejecting longstanding tropes of theological anti-Judaism, reminding "all teachers and pastors" to tell the story of the Passion without blaming the Jews or vilifying them. Here, the Statement makes clear the link between theology and ethical responses to actual human suffering. Interfaith dialogue begins after the Shoah, with the frank recognition that the theology of the Church must change. And over the next decades, it begins to do just that.

Susman continued to do interfaith work, living in Switzerland until her death in 1966, falling into relative obscurity, her work was not translated from German into Hebrew or English. Despite the Shoah, she remembered that she had been rescued by a Christian, her friend, Ragaz, a friendship when little else was possible. Susman wrote two more books, but what Susman ultimately believed in was a capacity for personal relationships, the face to face relationships, and for a private logic to take hold, the logic of shared scripture, and shared hope for a redemptive future, the logic of hope in a hopeless world. I narrate her story because it reminds us of the critical importance of that hope.

III. LIVING IN HISTORY

In her ongoing relationship with her Christian colleague, Ragaz, Susman stands as an example – although she is often missed – in the account of the Jewish Weimar period, of the relationships of German Jews such as Rosenszweig, Buber and Scholem to history, or rather, to the creation of a Jewish historical account that was both

10. https://www.prchiz.pl/pliki/Seelisberg_70.pdf.

within and without the tantalizing, seductive German culture of the interwar period. Susman wrote prolifically, always about the margins of this culture, women and German expressionism, Luxenberg, Kafka, and Freud. She was present, writing; the subject of everyone's correspondence, her work admired by the men who surrounded her and then largely forgotten.

Here, I will make the feminist note that of course, unlike Maimonides, Yehuda Halevi, Jacob Emden, and Samuel Raphael Hirsh, Susman wrote as a woman, albeit a highly intellectual and independent one. She had a family that was murdered, a scholarly community of Jewish writers and a community of women intellectuals which was scattered and slaughtered, and she was alone. Like many women scholars, her admittance to the intellectual circles, and of course, the remembrance of her participation in them, was fragile and easily erased. Her relationship to Ragaz began in her poverty, her vulnerability, in her escape from a Europe that was collapsing behind her – to this last place, where a Christian welcomed her into the project of hope in a darkened world.

It is a terrible thing to live, as a mortal being, in history, for it means you must inhabit the present. This decision, the take stock of the actual world, to attend to its complexity and the unknowing naiveté of every moment does not mean that one forgets the facticity of the long tethers to the past that is Jewish knowledge. But it does mean confronting the world as it is right now, imperfect, mutable, and dangerous. For a woman, it can be likened – literally and figuratively – to a divorce from her marriage, her country, and her language. Alone on the train, as Susman was in 1933, was to know the risks of trust. Yet there she was, trusting that the risk of interfaith relationships was necessary. Ragaz would die seven months after Armistice, and Susman was left in the middle of an argument with him, as is the trouble and the glory of all real talk. He was strung by the rejection of his Biblical commentary by the Jewish community of Zurich, and Susman's protestations – *who cares what the Federation thinks?* – were ultimately useless. But she did not stop, moving into the next four decades convinced that Jews and Christians must speak of the world between them.

IV. THE LEGACY AND THE REPAIR

Let me now return to some reflection on the Statement by the Orthodox Rabbis, which is made, I believe, in the spirit of that hope in which Susman so firmly believed. The Statement has two essential parts, the first makes three historical claims, and the second makes four theological claims. The Statement begins with an acknowledgement of the Shoah, and then asks the reader to move beyond that moment:

> The *Shoah* ended 70 years ago. It was the warped climax to centuries of disrespect, oppression and rejection of Jews and the consequent enmity that developed between Jews and Christians. In retrospect it is clear that the failure to break through this contempt and engage in constructive dialogue for the good of humankind weakened resistance to evil forces of anti-Semitism that engulfed the world in murder and genocide.

This is of course correct – we are now three generations past that rupture in history (though of course, not past all such ruptures – *pas* Yemen, for example, or Rwanda, Cambodia, or Syria.) However, one could argue – I would argue – that the Shoah is surely not ended. A reader of Susman, who believes that the rupture begins with the first act of human denial, does not insist that we believe that anti-Semitism is in the past, for that is not the basis of our dialogue, and, as the events between the 2015 and 2019 statement can remind us, anti-Semitism is clearly not concluded, not is it divorced from religious ideologies. But it is not necessary to live in a perfected world to conduct dialogue, and it is the failure to do so, that in part laid the ground for the collapse of European Christian morality, although it was not for lack of trying on the part of Jewish intellectuals, as discussed earlier, most of whom were only too eager with Christian colleagues. And because it is not necessary to live in a perfect world, it is surely correct to begin by understanding that nothing can possibly undo the Shoah, but that Christians have worked diligently to understand their failure. Here, where forgiveness is impossible, something else might take its place, as it did for Susman – the simple return to a relationship.

The Statement is also correct in its second historical point, noting that the official documents from the Church represent a serious change in Christian doctrine:

> *Nostra Aetate* and the later official Church documents it inspired unequivocally reject any form of anti-Semitism, affirm the eternal Covenant between God and the Jewish people, reject deicide and stress the unique relationship between Christians and Jews, who were called "our elder brothers" by Pope John Paul II and "our fathers in faith" by Pope Benedict XVI. On this basis, Catholics and other Christian officials started an honest dialogue with Jews that has grown during the last five decades. We appreciate the Church's affirmation of Israel's unique place in sacred history and the ultimate world redemption.

The rabbis in their statement endorse sincere support in word and deed to change key part of Church theology: they link the change to the recognition of the failure of the Church, and give credit for the actors in Church history that worked (in many cases, against opposition) to change.

The final historical point the Statement notes is that central figures in Jewish historical intellectual thought, claimed as part of the heritage of Orthodoxy – Maimonides, Yehudah HaLevi, Jacob Emden, and Samuel Raphael Hirsh – all established relationships with Christian scholars and all understood the Christian love of God as important and sincere.

The theological claim that is an inevitable part of that understanding is that the existence of Christianity cannot be a "mistake." Christians, thought Emden and Hirsh, are a part of a Divine plan. Further, they are a part of a "covenantal mission" to perfect the world; they feel subject to duties, especially to the duty of "active brotherly love." Moreover, notes the Statement, values that emerge from this common theology are shared.

Jewish Sacred Scriptures; a belief in a binding tradition; and the values of life, family, compassionate righteousness, justice, inalienable freedom, universal love and ultimate world peace. Rabbi Moses Rivkis (Be'er Hagoleh) confirms this and wrote that "the Sages made reference only to the idolator of their day who did not believe in the creation of the world, the Exodus, God's miraculous deeds and the divinely given law. In contrast, the people among whom we are scattered believe in all these essentials of religion."[6]

Christians and Jews have more in common than they have differences, adds the Statement. Jews have come to see that God has "many messengers" and that the ethical commands of the Noahide commandments bring order to the world.

Finally, the rabbis remind the reader that people of faith share a belief in the need to model their belief in actions. "In imitating God, Jews and Christians must offer models of service, unconditional love and holiness."

As straightforward as a statement that acknowledges that Christians and Jews have history, text, and some common theological premises – specifically, monotheism – in common, it has not been met with unqualified support. For some scholars, such as Jonathan Levenson, the concept is freighted with potential risks. Levenson's concern is that the theological differences between Christians and Jews might be ignored and or watered down, rendering such discourses meaningless. For Levenson, dialogue is only useful as a way of clarifying the validity of one's own theological claims, and since that is the case, each participant should assume competition and mutual prejudice as a starting point, not what is shared. Levinson describes Rabbi Joseph Soloveichik, as feeling that interfaith dialogue about theology is not possible, but friendly relationships based on mutually satisfying projects can be undertaken. Thus, working across faith communities to feed the hungry, help the poor, or provide social services is permissible, but not deep theological discussions such as that which the Statement wants to celebrate or that Susman and Ragaz, or Vogt's pastors thought possible.

What can one say about this critique? Similar opposition was raised in response to a statement called *Dabru Emet*. In this statement, Jewish scholars, leaders, and rabbis across the wider spectrum of Jewish life wrote to respond to decades of change in the Christian Church. It is understandable – for many, the accumulated trauma and hatred that culminated in the Shoah is still to recent. For others, the increasing anti-Semitism of the last period is too reminiscent of the impossibility of reconciliation. For others, the project itself is simply not feasible.

The writers of The Orthodox Rabbinical Statement write to disagree. They believe that the recognition of brothers (and ideally sisters) across religious barriers is possible. Their leadership focusses on the Orthodox community but it offers a strong justification for all Jews. It is important in particular because many Orthodox communities have largely rebuilt their structural and organizational forms after the destruction of the Shoah, at least in part, as a refuge from the larger social and political world – a world in which, as Susman said, the Law is absent. Modernity itself has presented itself as a challenge. And a modern Church that beckons toward collaborative discussions and partnerships, is seen as peripheral to the rebuilding effort, if noticed at all. Thus, the Statement represents a first order moral gesture. The critics are correct that it may lead to trouble, to the sort of confusions faced by the Jews of Susman's period, for example – instabilities, disorder and death. That is what this risky relationship is about. However, Susman might argue that only turning to the face of the Other will bring us back to normality, heal the rupture caused by the turning away, and allow us to see the image that is the face of God. The rabbis in this Statement tell us that if we turn back to Christians now, we will see them waiting for our gaze.

The Orthodox rabbis who made that moral gesture of hopefulness in their statement are motivated by an impulse similar to Margarete Susman, for we too live in history, in an historical era in which the power of the secular has so firmly established itself, made so monumental a claim on human interiority, inserted its justifying authority into every aspect of ethical and aesthetic elements of our lives, so that the only arguments against its logic are ones of religion, and the only communities, ones of faith. Why is it critically important for Jews to see Christians as allies? For many reasons, as listed above; a shared monotheism, a shared Text, a willingness to defend a tradition, and a shared set of values. It is also important because the community of believers is also a community of moral actors, who perform their theological commitments as they work to make a world in which their values – and not the values of the market-place – can be lived out, in particular, the value of the stranger and the outcast, the refugee and the vulnerable.

This statement is a beginning, a linguistic down payment on this promise, and as such, it is not only an abstract or trivial declaration. To work together means to see the position of the other as legitimate, defensible, and important. It is also important to those who think theologically. The theological ontology that sees an act of recognition as an act of faith is based on the encounter that sees the other as one's own sister or brother, the face we know and love, the bearer of the Divine.

Secularism and the Transmission of Faith and Action

Alon Meltzer

We live in a world and time of rapid change and transformation. How to effectively engage a generation where messaging is limited to Twitter and Facebook, where face to face communication has been replaced by short hand cryptic messages over portable devices, where the art of respectful dialogue has been replaced with an entrenchment of ideas and ideals, is the most pressing issue for communities of faith.

The 2015 statement, *To Do the Will of Our Father in Heaven,* signed by Orthodox Rabbis from around the world, speaks of a partnership between Jews and Christians following two millennia of tension, hostility, and dismissal. This partnership acknowledges that both religions are inherently different, yet connected to one another. More so, it acknowledges that we have a deep-seated united mission to engage the world in the ethical and moral teachings of the Almighty, to better the world and her inhabitants. The rise of secularism is a challenge that must be engaged with through such a partnership, and together we must act towards utilizing the tools of the modern world to better aid the transmission of faith and action.

Through this essay I am to engage with three key questions. First, what is the vantage point in which we should view secularism, secondly what can we learn regarding action and engagement from our key texts and liturgy, and finally, how do we effectively utilize the secular world to enhance the primary assignment of any faith-based community, namely, the transmission of faith and action.

Secularization can be viewed from two very distinct angles from the vantage point of religious practitioners; negative and positive. Those wanting to view and therefore react to secularism must only look at sociological theory that points to the process by which religions and their institutions, actions, and practices lose social significance (Bryan Wilson, Religion in Secular Society, 1966). Wilson breaks his argument into four key areas; statistical analysis, rationalism and disenchantment, the disengagement from and perhaps on the church within society, and finally religious pluralism.

As the world has transformed since the period of Enlightenment, there has been a gradual move to find purpose within and from the world that is divorced from the institution of organized religion. This has caused many, both within the Jewish world, but also from within the Catholic Church, to stand on the offensive, retreating into isolation of the self-imposed communal convent, decrying the perceived horrors of modernity. Insiders and outsiders alike might take the opinion that religion is dying.

Those wanting to take the view of positivism through secularization, need not only focus on the challenges that modernity has posed for faith-based communities, but also look to the new-found tools within the arsenal of religious practitioners simultaneously with the sacred and profane. Danièle Hervieu-Léger notes that secularization might merely be the reorganization of religion to meet the modern needs of its practitioners, in order to remain relevant (Religion as a Chain of Memory, 1993, 2000).

These challenges are experienced across faiths and communities around the world. Noting the incredible strength in the relationship between the Jewish and Catholic community, we must realize that we can be more effective, in transmitting our individual faith and spiritualism to our own next generations, if we continue that relationship and work together to collaborate on ideas and methodologies.

I would like to note here that from my vantage point, as a millennial Rabbi within the Modern Orthodox world, I can only see religion as a whole, and Modern Orthodoxy as a micro-community within the grander tapestry of faith and religion, in a period of growth and transformation.

First, we have seen a rise of fundamentalism, whilst founded in the stewing pot of reactionary policy. This must not be ignored in the discussion of the place of religion within the modern world, to discount it would be of grave disservice to both practitioners of fundamentalism, but also the very rise in moderate practice and belief of co-religionists.

Second, and this has become more noticeable because of the reaction to fundamentalism, there are, at least anecdotally, more people willing to discuss their religious beliefs, actions, and belonging, through social media, online communications, and other mediums, than even five years ago. For example, the response of mainstream Jewry, or Islam, who, within their faith-based communities, have rallied together to react with a moderate voice following a negative action of fundamentalism in their assault against modernity.

Third, the world has seen a rise in the search for spirituality. Rodney Stark and William Sims Bainbridge argued that secularism is likely a cyclical process, and that the modern rise of spiritualism, or the search for a greater spiritual purpose, could be the next phase of that cycle (*The Future of Religion: Secularization, Revival and Cult Formation*, University of California Press, 1985).

Finally, and to this I speak solely to the Modern Orthodox world, the community which I know best, we have seen a rise in institutions, publications, and conversations that would point to an unprecedented growth or transformation within our community. With this, it is important to perhaps recalibrate the argument. No longer should we be talking about whether religion has a place within the modern world, or the downfall of religion as a whole. Rather what we should be doing to inspire both the transmission of faith and action within the religious sphere.

David Voas and Abby Day note that religion in the UK is being used as a public marker of identity, not necessarily an affiliation to a faith, but a community.[1] Notably, Rabbi Mordechai Kaplan is said

---

1. David Voas and Abby Day, "Secularity in Great Britain," in *Secularism &*

to have understood religious identity to be broken down into three B's; belief, behavior, and belonging. The latter concept is automatic within the Jewish people, the notion of *klal Yisrael*, the Jewish nation, and even Rabbi Soloveitchik's discourse on *zera Yisrael*, the broader concept of the notion of Jewish peoplehood. This realization does not solve the imperative question of transmission of faith and action, rather it provides a guaranteed entry point that other faiths do not necessarily have.

The very idea of belonging is imperative within the modern secular world, and provides faith-based communities, the ability to interact with those wary, uninterested, or ignorant of behavior and action. By providing first and foremost a place in which to congregate, socialize, and connect, organized religion is one step closer to the ability to engage, educate, and encourage behaviors and belief of faith, religious teachings and practice.

This leads to the subsequent question of how to accurately, authentically, and inspirationally transmit behavior and belief, or perhaps more poignantly transmit faith and action to the next generation. Within Judaism, we are fortunate to have the ability to look back at a myriad of texts spanning two millennia, sitting alongside our primary written text of the Torah. We are able to draw from rich *halakhic*, legal, and *Midrashic*, exegetical texts that can inspire and engage both methodological, pedagogical, and historical tools to assist clergy, and more importantly parents, in their mission to transmit these fundamental elements of religious expression and connection.

A key example of such tradition is the Passover Seder and the accompanying text of the Haggadah. Central to the Haggadah is the notion of *b'chol dor v'dor*, that in each and every generation one must undertake a journey, through the texts and actions of the Seder night, to go from slavery through freedom. The Sages establish through a variety of explanations of different actions and statements from within the Seder night; a pedagogy and methodology as

Secularity: Contemporary International Perspectives, Barry A. Kosmin and Ariela Keysar, eds. (Hartford, CT: ISSSC, 2007).

to how to proceed through this transformation, and by association, how to transmit these key ideas to the next generation.

One such example might be found in the rabbinic explanations of the *charoset*. The Babylonian Talmud, Tractate Pesahim 116a (Koren Talmud Bavli, Pesahim Part Two, 2013), states:

> R. Eleazar son of R. Zadok said: It is a religious requirement. Why is it a religious requirement? R. Levi said: In memory of the apple-tree; R. Johanan said: In memory of the mortar. Abaye observed: Therefore one must make it acrid and thicken it: make it acrid, in memory of the apple-tree; and thicken it, in memory of the mortar.
>
> רבי אלעזר ברבי צדוק אומר מצוה וכו'. מאי מצוה? רבי לוי אומר: זכר לתפוח. ורבי יוחנן אומר: זכר לטיט, אמר אביי: הלכך צריך לקהוייה, וצריך לסמוכיה. לקהוייה – זכר לתפוח, וצריך לסמוכיה – זכר לטיט.

One side of the argument said the *charoset* is because of the mortar, yet the other side said it was because of the apple tree. The Talmudic tractate of Sotah, on 11b, explains that the Israelite women were optimistic of the future and therefore wanted to have more children despite the decrees of Pharaoh, unlike their husbands who thought the end was coming, and therefore abstained from marital relations. The women rightly won the argument, and had their children according to the Talmud in the apple orchards to hide from the watching spies of Pharaoh.

There is a further argument between the Pnei Moshe, the 12th Century Jerusalem Talmud Scholar, and the Korban Ha-Eidah, the 18th Century German Talmudist, where *charoset* is debated as being a symbol of the blood of the Jewish children that Pharaoh bathed in, or the plague of blood that began the process of redemption.

Charoset therefore becomes more than just a living memory of our slavery of bricks and mortar, rather it also gives us an emotional connection to the near demise of our people and our eventual salvation. We can also go one step forward, and associate the living memories of our recent history; the blood of our people in the Holocaust – a physical slavery paralleled with the blood of our soldiers in Israel who safeguarded our land and allowed for our salvation in the War of Independence in 1948.

These explanations provide valuable insight into the rich history of texts and discourse that can inspire the tools and methodology of the transmission of faith and action. Following from this we must understand how to utilize the secular world to enhance the sacred, building on Kaplan's mantra of belonging, behavior, and belief.

Rabbi Joseph Dov Soloveitchik was one of the most profound talmudic scholars of the 20th century, was seen as a serious intellectual not always engaged on the spiritual or the emotional side of Jewish thought; a doer, not an experiencer. Rabbi Soloveitchik writes in a eulogy at the passing of his son-in-law's mother, the Rebbetzin of Talne, declaring the importance to experiencing Judaism:

> I admit that I am not able to define precisely the Masoretic role of the Jewish mother. Only by circumscription I hope to be able to explain it. Permit me to draw upon my own experiences, I used to have long conversations with my mother. In fact, it was a monologue rather than a dialogue. She talked and I "happened" to overhear. What did she talk about? I must use a *halakhic* term in order to answer this question: she talked *me-inyana de-yoma*, [relating to everyday things]. I used to watch her arranging the house in honor of a holiday. I used to see her recite prayers; I used to watch her recite the *sidrah* [the *parashah*] every Friday night and I still remember the nostalgic tune. I learned from her very much. Most of all I learned that Judaism expresses itself not only in formal compliance with the law, but also in a living experience. She taught me that there is a flavor, a scent and warmth to mitzvoth. I learned from her the most important thing in life – to feel the presence of the Almighty and the gentle pressure of His hand resting upon my frail shoulders. Without her teachings which quite often were transmitted to me in silence, I would have grown up a soulless being, dry and insensitive. The laws of Shabbat, for instance, were passed on to me by my father; they are a part of *musar avikhah* [fatherly directives].

The Shabbat as a living entity, as a queen, was revealed to me
by my mother; it is part of the *torat imekhah* [motherly To-
rah]. The fathers knew much about the Shabbat; the mothers
lived the Shabbat, experienced her presence, and perceived
her beauty. The fathers taught generations how to observe the
Shabbat; mothers taught generations how to greet the Shabbat
and how to enjoy her twenty-four hour presence ("A Tribute to
the Rebbetzin of Talne," 1978).

Rabbi Soloveitchik explains that in his world view the father is
the law, the mother is the spirit. Ultimately the spirit is the love and
experience of the law. Judaism is not just formal compliance with
the law, rather it is the living experience.

In a world where secularism has seen an evolution in the pedagogy of parenting, of the quality of the home, and a change in the
reality of what constitutes a family in terms of both single parent
households as well as same-sex households who affiliate with faith-
based communities, we need to take the lesson of Rabbi Soloveitchik and reapply it to modern realities.

I would argue that we need to learn how to be both *mussar
avikhah*, the authority of the father, the discipline of both character
and transmission of law and text, as well as the *torat imekhah*, the
infusion of spirit and love, the experiential education.

Rabbi Dr. Norman Lamm writes that the goal of generation's past
was to aspire to one's ancestors, realizing that as we go further from
the source of divine revelation, we have a *yeridah hadorot*, a decline
of the generations. Today however, as he posits, we are no longer
to stand back and only aspire to their level without a fulfillment of
their greatness. In a world of modernity we have a responsibility to
aspire to surpass them. To only come close and then miss the mark,
and accept that we have theological reality that we cannot become
equals, is to put our entire future in jeopardy. Today, we must aspire
to become greater than our ancestors, we must utilize all the tools
of modernity to actualize that surpassing.

This leads to four practical applications of how we can equip
ourselves to aspire to greatness, and truly transmit both faith and

action. First, the use of technological tools to engage and inspire an educational growth and development of our people. Second, the use of technological tools to inspire both belief and behavior in terms of marketing, successful communication. Third, the change of mindset from being the gravitational center, to going out into the world and pulling people in through the use of, what is termed in the business world, Customer Relations Management (CRM). Finally, the sociological evolution of community through modern innovation to match the sensitivities of the modern world.

Rabbi Jeremy Wieder, Rosh Yeshiva of Rabbi Isaac Elchanan Theological Seminary of Yeshiva University once remarked that today we have access to more texts and information from our history than any of our previous sages, perhaps even the sum of all of them. We have databases and encyclopedias, reference guides, and indexes, digital archives of modern works as well as the collections of *genizah* documents. We must utilize this treasure trove of information to enhance our knowledge and to grow from it.

There are a myriad of discussion and information forums available for the modern practitioner of religion. Facebook is but one example, and the ability to engage with modern technological tools that equip our arsenal to engage and inspire active learning, communication and transmission of texts is incredibly important.

Among these discussions are topics such as whether DNA can be used to determine the status of a Cohen or Levi according to *halakhah* or what might be the *halakhic* objections of certain rabbi's against the *halakhic* prenuptial agreement which has a 100% success rate of preventing *agunot* – chained women unable to obtain a divorce. Others look at questions around text and nuance. For millennials, active Judaism is not inspired by what was taught or absorbed in hundreds of thousands of dollars of Jewish education. Flashy micro trips to Israel, like Birthright, might inspire, but the effects are short term, and the retention rate without follow up is lower than expected. Active Judaism is not inspired from within the synagogue, in the most part neither from the home.

All these things create, often at best, passive Jews who wander through their lives in a state of passivity, doing what they have done for their entire lives, never choosing or questioning, and we need to tackle this head on. We need to become inspirational and engaging in a medium that reaches them and engages with them and we need to continue to innovate.

Facebook is perhaps the medium for today, yet it might not be tomorrow. If rabbis and educators are not clued in on the lingo, and the technology that is being used, they are losing out on ways in which to engage.

In a world where my four-year-old can unlock my phone, remember a pin code for iTunes, and purchase things, I'd better hope that those who are going to dedicate their lives to inspiring her, can at the very least do the same, and even better, can actually innovate and create using the technological tools that we have been blessed with in our lifetimes.

Neither technology, nor computers, nor social media, can replace what we treasure most dear, our *sefarim,* our books and texts. But if we don't find a way to ensure that they inspire active engagement with said texts – whether for the sake of learning, for social issues, for religious growth – they will become irrelevant.

This to me is the greatest challenge we have today. We need to ensure that we are being innovative; we need to be connecting people, whether virtually or in person, in a safe environment that pushes people to question and challenge without the feelings of prejudice or fear, and with the ability to interact with, and *because* of, our texts and ideas.

Gone are the days where a day in school meant the only access to information was the words that were coming out of the teachers mouth, where even if the teacher had no skills, that was still the only thing that could be absorbed. We live in the digital age where kids can pick up a cell phone and pull down any piece of information they want, and any piece of information we, as parents and educators, do not want. If we don't utilize technological platforms successfully, we become white noise in the larger technological buzz.

We should be investing in technological advancements to engage members of our community to actively participate in the transmission and growth of information. The rise of the applications over a multitude of devices provides us with ways in which to engage on a new level. To utilize charismatic speakers to provide a steady and continuing level of relevant and inspirational content through video blogs and podcasts are easy enough to produce and disseminate. Maintaining relevancy and the ability to actively take part in serious issues through technological platforms must become a priority of our community – we cannot become mouthpieces nor soundbites – but we cannot remain silent, or afford to miss the mark and disappear into the eternal depths of the online world.

I hear from colleagues across the faith-based world that hours of time, money, and resources are put into the creation of programming and content only to find a half-filled room filled with the choir. We have to ask ourselves serious questions, make a *heshbon ha-nefesh*, to truly analyze what we are doing wrong.

Rabbis Joshua Stanton and Ben Spratt, penned an article in 2014 called "What Jewish Millennials Want," where they write, "We watch a Jewish world desperately trying to convince this rising demographic of the essential nature of Judaism. We try again and again to express to Millennials what they 'really' want and need, and why Jewish community is an answer to many of their struggles and support for their aspirations." Through this they created an in-person social network by utilizing the skills of the very people they wanted to engage and inspire.

Marketing and communications have become the key differential between success and failure of the modern world. The 2016 Neilsen Company report on digital screen time, examines large trends in penetration, users and usage across all platforms, showing how different demographics and race/ethnic groups spend their media time. They discovered that the average American spends on average ten hours thirty-eight minutes engaged in some sort of online technology or media engagement each and every day.

With this we must realize how we can effectively ensure marketing reach and effective communications of the services we offer. Whether it is programmatic and tactical, or something more ethereal, we must utilize the technological world to ensure that we are able to spread our message.

High quality micro productions of specific messaging from online faith-based interest groups, including that of Rabbi Lord Dr. Jonathan Sacks in his educational content, Chief Rabbi Ephraim Mirvis and the United Synagogues, have become more common within social media platforms. Content that is both disseminated through targeted advertising, as well as viral sharing, have become commonplace, generating conversation, relatability, and engagement. What their follow through success will result in is yet to be determined.

The ability to evolve and innovate within the online world is key to success, however we must also do this within the way that we engage with people. We live in a service-based, user pays world. The way in which we relate to the next generation of religious practitioners must be to adopt a level of customer relations management. The literal and original meaning of the expression "Customer Relationship Management" was simply, managing the relationship with your customer. Today it is used to describe IT systems and software designed to help you manage this relationship. Synagogue database software now includes full suites of CRM systems, and clergy must both update their skillsets to be able to manage such software and change their fundamental approaches to match such a shift in engagement processes.

We must be able to utilize well researched data to effectively engage with members of our "flocks," engage with them in their times of celebrations, remember their times of sorrow, be attuned to their greater contributions to society, and we must be able to recall the last conversations that we had with said person. We must engage with them much like a barista in a coffee shop can remember their name and order, whilst still offering them something new, or how a fine dining restaurant makes sure to record in a database the previous dining experience of any given customer so as not to repeat the experience. Of course, this cannot be trivial, rather we need to be able to recall significant moments of conversation and connections so that we can actualize the importance of the in-depth relationships that are so very important.

An example of this is the religious institution that solicits donations. If you want a continuation of funds from a given person –

an investment into the relationship – you must know who you are talking to and what they have previously committed, and you must have effectively and continually communicated how their investment has had a lasting effect within the project undertaken.

The same must be with our co-religionists. Clergy must know what the relationship is, they must know who they are talking to, they must acknowledge the investment committed by the person from past interactions and engagement, and they must be able to communicate the given conversation, instruction, or ritual in a way that engages and empowers. We must realize that in our modern world, these theories and software can be utilized to enhance the religious experience of those whom we are trying to transmit and engage into action.

All of these, the use of technology to enhance knowledge, to enhance marketing and communications, and the way in which we relate and engage, are forms of innovation. However, they are worthless unless the messages, teachings, and rituals themselves evolve and innovate as well.

I realize that innovation can be daunting, especially within issues of major debates around gender equality, the fluidity of gender, and the issues of LGBTQ rights. However, that does not mean that we must shy away from robust and authentic discussion, and through that an evolution of discourse and action.

We must utilize our sources, and deep roots of tradition to engage in debates, and through discussion and empathy, engage in areas where we can universally innovate. To practice isolationism is to threaten the very success of our transmission of faith and action within the modern world. We run the risk of discarding and forgetting the very people whom we need to enhance our faith and in turn transmit it to the next generation. We must utilize thinkers of the past, but also cultivate thinkers of the future, who can engage with our texts within the purview of modernity, as has been the role of Torah discourse in history.

Throughout this treatise I have maintained the view that religion is not dead, that religion in fact is thriving especially as it combines with modernity and secularism. However, we must accept the challenges that lie before us. Firstly, that we must acknowledge the importance of continuing to view secularism and modernity as a way in which we can enhance faith. Secondly, we must continue to engage with our texts in ways that inspire both fidelity and action. Thirdly we must utilize the various tools that modernity provides us with.

Rabbi Wieder made a statement that perhaps has had the greatest impact on my personal faith and engagement as a Modern Orthodox Jew. Modern Orthodoxy is about engaging and creating a synthesis between the modern world and the Orthodox world, between the evolution of values and ethics, and the deep homage to our texts and traditions. He continued, "The catch is where to place Orthodoxy." Our mission is how to do that while successfully transmitting faith and action to the next generation.

The Changing *Mesorah*: Orthodoxy on Interreligious Dialogue and Women's Leadership

MALKA Z. SIMKOVICH

Since the rabbinic legal system came into being almost two millennia ago, Jewish communities have entrusted male rabbis with guiding them in matters related to communal and religious life. At the same time, Jewish women within these communities and non-Jews living outside them have, in different ways, been kept at arm's length when it comes to active religious life and leadership, orbiting around or on the edges of the rabbinic system.

Substantial socio-religious changes, however, took place about fifty years ago that altered Jewish-Christian relations and intra-Jewish leadership dynamics. The first change came about following the publication and dissemination of *Nostra Aetate*, perhaps the most profound and radical document produced at the Second Vatican Council meeting in 1965. *Nostra Aetate* affirmed that Jews were not collectively responsible for the crucifixion of Jesus, and are not collectively rejected by God. The second change is a byproduct of Second Wave Feminism, which gained momentum in the early 1960s and offered a platform for challenging long-accepted norms regarding traditional women's roles in their families, communities, and professions. These changes led to an increase in formal Jewish-Christian dialogue, and increased debate regarding Jewish women's leadership. This essay will briefly consider how progressive change can be achieved by putting these developments into dialogue with one another.

EVOLVING RABBINIC ATTITUDES TOWARDS JEWISH–CHRISTIAN DIALOGUE

In the decades following *Nostra Aetate*, the Catholic Church produced a number of significant essays affirming the values of the Second Vatican Council and its commitment to Jewish-Christian dialogue. The most impactful of these are *Guidelines and Suggestions for Implementing Nostra Aetate* (1975), *Notes on the Correct Way to Present the Jews and Judaism in Preaching and Catechesis* (1985); *We Remember: A Reflection on the Shoah* (1998); *The Jewish People and Their Sacred Scriptures (2001);* and *The Gifts and Calling of God are Irrevocable* (2015).

While some Jewish leaders were quietly involved in dialogue with leaders of the Church, no major Jewish statement was publicly disseminated in the 20th century affirming the importance of dialogue in the same manner. Remarkably, the first widely circulated statement made by Jewish leaders on the topic of Jewish-Christian dialogue was not published until the year 2000. The effort to produce this statement was initiated not by clergy members or even community leaders, but by four academics working in the field of Jewish studies: Dr. Tikva Frymer-Kensky, Rabbi Dr. David Novak, Dr. Peter Ochs, and Rabbi Dr. Michael Signer. These scholars had been recruited by an interfaith organization in Baltimore, the Institute for Christian and Jewish Studies, to address foundational questions regarding Judaism and its relationship with Christianity. The document that they ultimately produced, which was called *Dabru Emet*, was published in The New York Times on September 10, 2000, and was ultimately signed by over two hundred rabbis and leaders working in a variety of denominational communities.

Dabru Emet comprised eight affirmations: Jews and Christians worship the same God, Jews and Christians seek authority from overlapping Scriptures, Christians can respect the Jewish claim

upon the land of Israel, Jews and Christians accept the moral principles of the Torah, Nazism was not a Christian phenomenon, the
differences between Jews and Christians will not be settled until
the end-time redemption, a new relationship between Jews and
Christians will not weaken Jewish practice, and finally, Jews and
Christians must work together for justice and peace. A number of
noted Jewish theologians and academics declined to sign *Dabru
Emet*, however. These leaders, including Dr. David Berger, Dr. Jon
Levenson, and Rabbi James Rudin, posited that the Statement ignored the relationship between Christian theology and the rise of
anti-Semitism in Germany that made space for the Nazis' attempted
genocide of the Jews.

Fifteen years after *Dabru Emet* was published and fifty years
following the *Nostra Aetate* declaration, a second major Jewish
document on Jewish-Christian dialogue was published: the Orthodox Rabbinic Statement on Christianity entitled *To Do the Will
of Our Father in Heaven: Toward a Partnership between Jews and
Christians* (henceforth *TDW*). This statement was spearheaded by
the Center for Jewish-Christian Understanding and Cooperation in
Israel, which was directed at the time by Rabbis Drs. Shlomo Riskin
and Eugene Korn, and David Nekrutman, all Orthodox Jews.[1] *TDW*
encouraged Jewish-Christian dialogue on the basis that the Church's
position towards Judaism had fundamentally changed.

Perhaps the most profound and innovative statement in the document is the declaration that "Now that the Catholic Church has acknowledged the eternal Covenant between God and Israel, we Jews
can acknowledge the ongoing constructive validity of Christianity
as our partner in world redemption, without any fear that this will
be exploited for missionary purposes."

Like the authors of *Dabru Emet*, the authors of *TDW* sought to
legitimize Jewish engagement with Christians in dialogue, despite
the long-damaged relationship between the two faith groups. To defend their position, the writers relied on historic precedent, citing

1. http://cjcuc.com/site/2015/12/03/orthodox-rabbinic-statement-on-christi
anity/.

Jewish authorities who lived in the medieval and modern periods and who expressed respect for Christianity, and whose writings are supposedly precursors to present-day Jewish-Christian dialogue: Maimonides, Judah ha-Levi, Jacob Emden, Samson Raphael Hirsch, and Shear Yashuv Cohen. The document was first signed by 25 high-profile rabbis in Israel, Switzerland, Germany, the United States, France, Serbia, and Finland. Soon, 46 rabbis would add their signatures, as well as two women, Rose Britton and Dina Najman.

Shortly after the publication of *TDW*, the Conference of European Rabbis and the Rabbinical Council of America produced another document that was officially presented to Pope Francis on August 31, 2017. This document, *Between Jerusalem and Rome: Reflections on 50 Years of Nostra Aetate*, was the product of collaboration between the Conference of European Rabbis (CER), the Rabbinical Council of America (RCA), and the Chief Rabbinate of Israel. It makes three references to Jewish tradition, emphasizing that "received tradition" lies at the core of Jewish survival:

The doctrinal differences are essential and cannot be debated or negotiated; their meaning and importance belong to the internal deliberations of the respective faith communities. Judaism, drawing its particularity from its received tradition, going back to the days of its glorious prophets and particularly to the Revelation at Sinai, will forever remain loyal to its principles, laws and eternal teachings.

While tradition is at the core of the Jewish religion, the writers clarify that such tradition cannot stand in the way of bettering the world:

[D]octrinal differences do not and may not stand in the way of our peaceful collaboration for the betterment of our shared world and the lives of the children of Noah. To further this end, it is crucial that our faith communities continue to encounter, grow acquainted with, and earn each other's trust.

The document argues for a rejection of the rabbinic status quo, which had officially rejected or ignored Jewish-Christian dialogue in favor of pursuing more public and formal dialogue.

While rabbinic literature shows little interest in engaging in dialogue for the sake of dialogue, and some rabbinic authorities had strongly come out against it in modern times, *Between Jerusalem and Rome* argues that the time has come for profound and systemic change.

Interestingly, both the Orthodox Union and the Rabbinic Council of America had been quietly involved in Jewish-Christian dialogue as members of the International Jewish Committee for Interreligious Consultations (IJCIC) since the 1960s. The IJCIC was established in the wake of the publication of *Nostra Aetate* as a means for Jewish representatives to interact directly with the Vatican. It took until 2017, however, for both the Orthodox Union and the RCA to advocate publicly for the work that they had long been doing, not on the basis of an official change of *mesorah* (religious tradition), but in response to the rapidly changing social and political climate.

Despite their differences in origin and tone, Jewish statements on Jewish-Christian dialogue share key themes. Each has contended explicitly with the Holocaust, focusing on the controversial matter of the degree to which the Church, and Christianity in general, played a role in the atrocities of the Holocaust. Interestingly, each of the three statements described above approaches the Church's role in fostering the anti-Semitism that led to the Holocaust in different ways. The authors of *Dabru Emet* make a hard separation between Nazi anti-Semitism and Christianity, noting that on the one hand, "Without the long history of Christian anti-Judaism and Christian violence against Jews, Nazi ideology could not have taken hold nor could it have been carried out." On the other hand, the authors also assert that "Nazism itself was not an inevitable outcome of Christianity. If the Nazi extermination of the Jews had been fully successful, it would have turned its murderous rage more directly to Christians."

TDW makes stronger accusations against the Church, blurring the lines between the anti-Semitism that led to the Holocaust and Christian theology. According to *TDW*, the Shoah, "was the warped climax to centuries of disrespect, oppression and rejection of Jews and the consequent enmity that developed between Jews and Christians. In retrospect it is clear that the failure to break through this contempt and engage in constructive dialogue for the good of humankind weakened resistance to evil forces of anti-Semitism that engulfed the world in murder and genocide." The authors of *TDW* also acknowledge the extraordinary turn-around made by Church leaders in the wake of the Holocaust more strongly than do the authors of *Dabru Emet*, noting that "since the Second Vatican Council the official teachings of the Catholic Church about Judaism have changed fundamentally and irrevocably."

The most recent Jewish document produced on Jewish-Christian dialogue, *Between Jerusalem and Rome*, speaks even more strongly about the inextricability of Christian anti-Semitism and the Nazi's project to exterminate the Jews. According to this document, "the Shoah constitutes the historical nadir of the relations between Jews and our non-Jewish neighbors in Europe. Out of the continent nurtured by Christianity for over a millennium, a bitter and evil shoot sprouted forth, murdering six million of our brethren with industrial precision, including one and a half million children. Many of those who participated in this most heinous crime, exterminating entire families and communities, had been nurtured in Christian families and communities." Like *TDW*, however, *Between Jerusalem and Rome* emphasizes the new page of history turned in the years following the Holocaust, noting that after World War II, "a new era of peaceful coexistence and acceptance began to emerge in Western European countries, and an era of bridge-building and tolerance took hold in many Christian denominations. Faith communities reevaluated their historical rejections of others, and decades of fruitful interaction and cooperation began."

The different statements regarding the Holocaust in these documents are representative of a broader difference between the three texts: while *Dabru Emet* seeks to underscore similarities between Jews and Christians, *TDW* and *Between Jerusalem and Rome* place more responsibility on the Church for the crimes of the Holocaust, but also give it greater credit for working to exorcise anti-Semitism from Church teachings in the years after the Holocaust. This indicates that Jewish and Christian interfaith leaders have become less inclined to focus solely on similarities between Judaism and Christianity based on the notion that dialogue is so fragile that it can dissolve in the face of foundational theological disagreement.

From *Dabru Emet* to *TDW* and finally to *Between Jerusalem and Rome* then, it is evident that Jewish leaders engaged in Jewish-Christian dialogue have become increasingly willing to face the theological and doctrinal differences that separate them. This suggests that Jewish-Christian dialogue has become a sturdy and more reliably independent entity whose members have the confidence to articulate their disagreements without worrying that they might be weakening the foundations upon which their dialogue has been built.

ORTHODOX RABBINIC PERSPECTIVES ON THE ORDINATION
OF WOMEN

In the wake of Second Wave Feminism, many Reform and Conservative Jewish communities began to actively promote an egalitarian view of religious life, which offered identical leadership opportunities to men and women. The Reform movement ordained its first woman rabbi, Sally Jane Priesand, in 1972 – a late date considering that the topic of women's ordination had been under discussion by Reform rabbis since the 1920s. The Conservative movement's flagship rabbinical school, the Jewish Theological Seminary, only began admitting women in the early 1980s. And perhaps not surprisingly, internal systemic changes in women's leadership did not occur in any substantive way in the Orthodox Jewish community until 1997, when an Israeli organization run by American-born scholar Rabbanit Chana Henkin founded a program to train women to provide legal rulings on the topic of family purity. Organizers and participants in this program made no claim to be training women for *semikhah*, rabbinic ordination. But since this program trained women who would be called *Yo'atzot Halakhah* (*halakhic* advisors), and these *yo'atzot* would issue legal recommendations that previously only ordained rabbis would have issued, many centrist and right-wing Orthodox rabbis opposed this program on the basis that these women were acting in the *capacity* of rabbis. Over time, the *Yo'atzot Halakhah* program became more mainstream, and today about 120 women have completed the training program, and over a dozen Orthodox communities in Israel, the UK, and the United States have hired *yo'atzot* in official capacities.

Perhaps the main reason that the *Yo'etzet Halakhah* program became more accepted by centrist Orthodox rabbis is that in the early 2000s, a core of Orthodox men and women began to openly support the ordination of women. A sharp backlash against this led to increased support for the *Yo'etzet* program: what was once considered controversial thus became mainstream in a relatively short period of time.

The most successful effort to ordain women within the Orthodox community has been spearheaded by Rabbi Avi Weiss, who founded the MAHARAT (an acronym for *Manhigah Hilkhatit, Ruhanit, v'Toranit* – legal, spiritual, and Torah-related advisor) program in 2009, and who ordained Rabba Sara Hurwitz in the same year. Much discussion regarding Weiss's rabbinical school focused on what women who completed the program's training would be called. While Hurwitz took the title Rabba, a feminized title of "Rabbi," others enrolled in the school would adopt its eponymous clerical title, "Maharat."

Weiss's project was initially ignored by the centrist and right-wing Haredi community, but Orthodox rabbinic organizations began to formally address the issue of female ordination in 2010 by issuing public statements opposing it. The Rabbinical Council of America, for instance, issued a press release of a statement at its 51st annual convention that explicitly opposed the ordination of women rabbis. The statement asserted that the question of what title a woman took on was irrelevant.[2] Women who called themselves "Maharat" and issued legal rulings would not be recognized by members of the RCA as rabbis or as *halakhically* authoritative community leaders, and RCA synagogues were not to hire these women.

2. http://www.rabbis.org/news/article.cfm?id=105554

The movement to offer women more opportunities to train as rabbinic legal experts continued apace, however, particularly in Israel. In 2013, Rabbi Shlomo Riskin founded a ten-year program at Jerusalem's Midreshet Lindenbaum, a school of higher education for women's Torah study, to train women to become judges for conversion and divorce. This program, called the Susi Bradfield Women's Institute of Halakhic Leadership (WIHL), was designed for women who had completed the Institute's initial five-year rabbinic ordination track. A year later, Rabbi Riskin published a defense of female ordination in his book, *The Living Tree: Studies in Modern Orthodoxy*. Another book, *Mah She'elatekh Esther V'te'as* ("What is your question, Esther, and it will be answered" – from the Scroll of Esther 7:2), was published the same year, and comprised the first set of *responsa* (rabbinic legal rulings in the context of case studies) published by ordained Orthodox women. Its editors were two women who had completed ordination programs, Rabbanit Idit Bartov and Rabbanit Anat Novoselsky. Other rabbis living in Israel such as Rabbi Herzl Hefter and Rabbi Daniel Sperber also began ordaining women, starting with Rahel Berkovitz and Meesh Hammer-Kossoy at Beit Midrash Har-El, and at the same time began to publish public defenses of their support for female ordination on social media.[3]

As word spread that Orthodox rabbis in Israel, along with Rabbi Avi Weiss in the United States, were actively training women for rabbinic ordination, conversations on social media outlets became increasingly heated. Intense refutations and counter-refutations increased on blogs and Facebook posts.[4] Rabbis including Rabbi Avraham Gordimer, Rabbi Shlomo Aviner, and Rabbi Gil Student wrote numerous articles and blog posts refuting Rabbi Weiss's, Rabbi Riskin's, and Rabbi Hefter's positions.

3. Among others, see https://library.yctorah.org/files/2016/07/02A-Sperber -On-Women-in-Rabbinic-positions-of-Leadership-10-20.pdf and http://blogs .timesofisrael.com/why-i-ordained-women/.

4. See, for instance, https://cross-currents.com/2015/03/15/rabbi-riskin-and -female-halachic-adjudicators-it-does-not-compute/ and http://haemtza.blogsp ot.com/2015/06/on-ordination-of-women-in-orthodoxy.html.

The year 2015 saw increased polarization between rabbinic camps supporting and opposing women's ordination. In the summer of 2015, Rabbi Riskin appointed Dr. Jennie Rosenfeld, a student at the Women's Institute of *Halakhic* Leadership (WIHL) at Midreshet Lindenbaum who had published widely on the topic of Orthodox Judaism and physical intimacy, to be *Manhigah Ruhanit* (spiritual leader) of the municipality of Efrat, a town just south of Jerusalem. Dr. Rosenfeld was hired to provide the community with *halakhic* rulings. While she was broadly welcomed in the Efrat community, the practice of hiring a *Manhigah Ruhanit* to provide religious leadership for a large community did not catch on elsewhere.

In the summer of 2016, another American rabbi living in Israel, Rabbi Daniel Landes, former head of the Pardes Institute, would ordain eight women and thirteen men in an Orthodox ceremony in Jerusalem. By this time, Rabbi Landes' move had some precedent in the Modern Orthodox world. But it also took a greater risk than earlier ordinations, since those that Rabbi Landes oversaw came on the heels of a statement published by the RCA in the fall of 2015, which expressed support for female educators, but affirmed the position that women cannot be ordained or take on rabbinic titles. This statement, which cites similar resolutions made in 2010 and 2013, reads:

> Whereas, after much deliberation and discussion among its membership and after consultation with *poseqim* [Orthodox rabbis who are qualified to administer legal rulings], the Rabbinical Council of America unanimously passed the following convention resolution at its April 2010 convention:
>
> 1. The flowering of Torah study and teaching by God-fearing Orthodox women in recent decades stands as a significant achievement. The Rabbinical Council of America is gratified that our members have played a prominent role in facilitating these accomplishments.
>
> 2. We members of the Rabbinical Council of America see as our sacred and joyful duty the practice and transmission of Judaism in all of its extraordinary, multifaceted depth and

richness – *halakhah* (Jewish law), *hashkafah* (Jewish thought), tradition and historical memory.

3. In light of the opportunity created by advanced women's learning, the Rabbinical Council of America encourages a diversity of *halakhically* and communally appropriate professional opportunities for learned, committed women, in the service of our collective mission to preserve and transmit our heritage. Due to our aforesaid commitment to sacred continuity, however, we cannot accept either the ordination of women or the recognition of women as members of the Orthodox rabbinate, regardless of the title.

4. Young Orthodox women are now being reared, educated, and inspired by mothers, teachers and mentors who are themselves beneficiaries of advanced women's Torah education. As members of the new generation rise to positions of influence and stature, we pray that they will contribute to an ever-broadening and ever-deepening wellspring of Talmud Torah (Torah study), *Yir'at Shamayim* (fear of Heaven), and *dikduk b'mitzvot* (scrupulous observance of commandments).

And whereas on May 7, 2013, the RCA announced:
In light of the recent announcement that Yeshivat Maharat will celebrate the "ordination as clergy" of its first three graduates, and in response to the institution's claim that it "is changing the communal landscape by actualizing the potential of Orthodox women as rabbinic leaders," the Rabbinical Council of America reasserts its position as articulated in its resolution of April 27, 2010.... The RCA views this event as a violation of our *mesorah* (tradition) and regrets that the leadership of the school has chosen a path that contradicts the norms of our community.

Therefore, the Rabbinical Council of America
Resolves to educate and inform our community that RCA members with positions in Orthodox institutions may not:
1. Ordain women into the Orthodox rabbinate, regardless of

the title used; or
2. Hire or ratify the hiring of a woman into a rabbinic position at an Orthodox institution; or
3. Allow a title implying rabbinic ordination to be used by a teacher of *Limudei Kodesh* (religious studies) in an Orthodox institution; and,
Commits to an educational effort to publicize its policy by:
4. Republishing its policies on this matter; and,
5. Clearly communicating and disseminating these policies to its members and the community.

This resolution does not concern or address non-rabbinic positions such as *yo'atzot halakhah*, community scholars, Yeshiva University's GPATS, and non-rabbinic school teachers. So long as no rabbinic or ordained title such as "Maharat" is used in these positions, and so long as there is no implication of ordination or a rabbinic status, this resolution is inapplicable.

Given that the RCA quotes its earlier statements made in 2010 and 2013 that opposed women's ordination, and that this 2015 statement does not offer a new position, it might seem curious that the RCA went to the trouble of producing another resolution. It is likely, however, that the continued efforts on the part of Modern Orthodox rabbis in 2013–2015 to ordain women, which ignored the RCA's earlier resolutions, compelled members of the RCA to reassert their opposition to women's ordination. This 2015 statement, then, was intended as a response to increased efforts to make systemic changes that undermined the stability of well-established rabbinical organizations.

It is also curious that the RCA's resolution provided no systemic legal or historical defense of the RCA's position to oppose female ordination. There is almost no explanation regarding the RCA's decision at all, which implies that the organization felt no need to substantively defend its stance. The only phrase that subtly points towards a justification of this position is that "the RCA views [the ordination of women] as a violation of our *mesorah* (tradition)."

While the RCA's resolution specified that *yo'atzot halakhah* may continue to train and work within the Orthodox community, it was nevertheless roundly condemned by advocates of women's ordination and made little or no difference to the yo'atzot program, which had been growing steadily since the early 2000s.[5]

As the RCA's statements provoked continued debate on social media, centrist Orthodox leaders continued to express concern for the growing move to ordain women within Orthodoxy. In early 2017, a cohort of Orthodox rabbis was selected by leaders of the Orthodox Union to draft a more systematic response to the matter of women's ordination. This cohort reached out to centrist and Modern Orthodox women leaders and collected data from them before coming together to compose a statement. In the fall of 2017, the Orthodox Union produced a lengthy statement that came out in opposition to women's ordination, but also called for increased action to hire women as paid educators in synagogues and Jewish community schools.[6] Like the RCA's 2015 statement, this 2017 statement expressed support for female educators, but clarified that these women cannot be ordained or take on rabbinic titles. It also made an appeal to precedent and *mesorah* in arguing that women must not be ordained. The committee of seven Orthodox rabbis who composed this statement argued that women's ordination cannot be accepted, based on the fact that it has never been accepted:

Religious practice must, rather, be the product of a *halakhic weltanschauung*, as elucidated by our *mesorah* and the careful, systematic explication of Torah and Torah values by renowned *halakhic* authorities, applying time honored methods of *halakhic* analysis developed over the millennia, and accepted over the millennia.

One intriguing commonality between the resolutions made by the RCA and the OU is that the writers emphasize their involvement in increasing female leadership, and in doing so, seek to legitimize their own role in the process of determining the capacities in which

5. See https://ots.org.il/tag/ordaining-women/.
6. https://www.ou.org/assets/OU-Statement.pdf.

women can function as congregational leaders. Note the following parallel comments:

> The Rabbinical Council of America is gratified that our members have played a prominent role in facilitating these accomplishments. (RCA, 2010)
>   It becomes our challenge – and responsibility – to help define the contours of professional synagogue roles that may be played by women that are permissible within the bounds of *Halakha* and our *mesorah* – and that conform to the norms of traditional *Halakhic* process. . . . On the professional side of the organization, the OU's recruitment, training, mentoring and promotion of talented women within our professional ranks has been a key organizational priority for the past several years. (OU, 2017)

Despite the OU's lengthy statement, most rabbis working to ordain women remained steadfast in their position, with one Modern Orthodox rabbi caustically commenting that "the OU should stick to tuna fish," referencing the OU's longstanding role in the certification of kosher foods.[7]

CONCLUSION: COMPARING THE ORTHODOX RABBINIC STATEMENTS ON CHRISTIANITY AND ON WOMEN'S ORDINATION

When comparing the 2015 and 2017 rabbinic documents that oppose women's ordination with rabbinic documents produced in these same years that argue for active dialogue with Christians, it is striking how substantially they differ from each other in methodology and terminology. When it comes to arguing against women's *halakhic* leadership, rabbinic statements employ the concept of

7. https://forward.com/news/362043/orthodox-union-adopts-policy-barring-women-clergy/.

mesorah as the foundation of their argument against women's ordination. Reliance on *mesorah* is the crux of the RCA's 2010 and 2013 statements about ordaining women:

- Due to our aforesaid commitment to sacred continuity, however, we cannot accept either the ordination of women or the recognition of women as members of the Orthodox rabbinate, regardless of the title.
- The RCA views this event [clarify which event] as a violation of our *mesorah* (tradition) and regrets that the leadership of the school has chosen a path that contradicts the norms of our community.

Yet *mesorah* is only vaguely alluded to in the most recent rabbinic documents on Jewish-Christian dialogue, and engagement with Christians is encouraged in recognition of the common integrity of all humankind, and in the interest of "peaceful collaboration." While documents regarding the ordination of women and Jewish-Christian dialogue are both implicitly concerned with the preservation of a stable and thriving internal Jewish community, it seems that the ordination of women is considered threatening to the stability of the Jewish community, whereas friendship and dialogue with Christians is no longer viewed as threatening or connected to a Christian desire to missionize, which would disrupt the stability of Orthodox Jewish communities.

Between Jerusalem and Rome, which in many ways builds on *To Do The Will of Our Father in Heaven*, argues that while it is true that many Christians demonized and marginalized Jews for centuries, the remarkable change in the Church's attitude towards the Jews reflected in *Nostra Aetate* calls for a formal rabbinic reevaluation of the Jewish people's relationship with Christians. In appealing to Jewish history, the writers of *Between Jerusalem and Rome* imply that while there is indeed a precedent that reflects a negative dynamic, this precedent can be changed. *Mesorah*, or the concept of an unbroken chain of Jewish tradition, is not contended with in a substantive way.

The RCA's statements regarding the ordination of women, on the other hand, make no appeal to historical patterns at all. This omission is striking since the authors of the RCA's statements would have had ample evidence to support their argument that the rabbis have historically opposed the ordination of women. But the RCA authors likely felt that they did not need to cite historical examples of rabbinic opposition to women's ordination; the appeal to *mesorah* alone was methodologically sufficient. The RCA's statements regarding women's ordination, therefore, are not as methodologically rigorous as the arguments supporting Jewish-Christian dialogue in *Between Jerusalem and Rome* and in *TDW*. In short, the authors of these latter two statements make an active historical argument to justify a dramatic change in rabbinic social policy concerning engagement in dialogue with Christians, whereas contemporaneous statements concerning the ordination of women do not engage in substantive arguments, but appeal to the importance of adhering to tradition in a broad sense.

One reason for the differences between the documents regarding women's ordination and Jewish-Christian dialogue has to do with the relationship dynamics of Orthodox rabbinic authorities and their interlocutors. In the case of Jewish-Christian dialogue, the rabbinic community is in a position of vulnerability. The Catholic Church has urged dialogue and reconciliation for decades, and many renowned Catholic leaders such as Pope John Paul II and Cardinal Bernardin have heeded the call to advocate for systemic changes within the Church when it comes to dialogue with Judaism and other faith communities. With a few exceptions of individuals who have been involved in projects such as the International Jewish Committee for Interreligious Consultations (IJCIC), the Orthodox Jewish community has only recently publicly acknowledged the changes made by Church leaders when it comes to its relationship with Judaism, and the changing dynamic between the Christian and Jewish leadership. Work done quietly for decades paved the way for rabbinic leaders to engage publicly in dialogue by drawing on the precedent quietly established almost fifty years ago. In this dynamic, the rabbinic community comprises the "community of the few," as

Rabbi Joseph B. Soloveitchik put it in his essay "Confrontation," published in 1964, whereas the Church comprises the "community of the many."[8] Engaging in dialogue and reconciliation as a minority requires entering into a room that has already been set aside, so to speak, for dialogue, and does not entail a concession of power.

The attitude of Orthodox rabbinic bodies towards women, however, reflects a dynamic in which the rabbis themselves are the "community of the many." Their attitude towards women remains largely stagnant, particularly in North American Jewish communities, where the Modern Orthodox and Haredi leadership are intermingled, and most Modern Orthodox rabbinic leaders hesitate to hire women clergy for fear of being isolated by their centrist and Haredi rabbinic colleagues.

Given the contemporaneous changes towards interreligious dialogue and towards women, and the common questions these changes have galvanized, it is not surprising that Orthodox rabbinic attitudes towards Jewish-Christian dialogue and towards the ordination of women are intrinsically intertwined with one another. The following anecdote illustrates this on a micro-level: I attempted to sign the Statement *TDW* in December 2015, but was told that the initial signatories were to be rabbis only, and the list would be opened to women in the future.[9] As noted above, the list did expand to include some women, and my own name was added about a year after the Statement was published.[10]

Given the methodological differences between statements that welcome dialogue and others that resist women's *halakhic* leadership, I suggest that we keep one issue in mind while we tackle the other. Orthodox Jewish leaders who seek to advance interfaith relationships based on the argument that all people are created in the divine image and are therefore entitled to a degree of dignity requires them to also consider conferring the potential for *halakhic*

---

8. Joseph B. Soloveitchik, "Confrontation," *Tradition* 6.2 (1964) 5–29.

9. http://www.jcrelations.net/To_Do_the_Will_of_Our_Father_in_Heaven: Toward_a_Partnership_between_Jews_and_Ch.5223.0.html.

10. http://cjcuc.org/2015/12/03/orthodox-rabbinic-statement-on-christia nity/.

expertise and leadership onto women, who would argue that the denial of such leadership deprives them of human dignity. Indeed, this tension is not exclusive to the Jewish community; Pope Francis recently affirmed his opposition to the ordination of women, while he has advocated for a universal approach to human dignity that requires the Church to focus on interreligious affairs.[11]

Finally, it should be optimistically noted that some of the individuals who have been most instrumental in moving Jewish-Christian dialogue forward at its early stages have advocated for integrating women into their communities and installing them in positions of leadership. Perhaps the best example of such an individual is Rabbi Irving (Yitz) Greenberg, a supporter of the Jewish Orthodox Feminist Alliance (JOFA), an organization founded by his wife, Blu, and a long-time advocate for Orthodox female leadership. More conversations should be had, however, regarding the interplay between advancing women's leadership and advancing interfaith relationships in the Orthodox Jewish community, as well as how to construct consistent methods designed to effect positive socio-religious changes in faith communities.

11. https://www.ncronline.org/news/vatican/pope-francis-confirms-finality-ban-ordaining-women; https://cruxnow.com/vatican/2017/08/31/shalom-alec hem-pope-francis-greets-rabbis-vatican-praises-fruitful-dialogue/.

Rabbi Joseph B. Soloveitchik, or "On What Jews and Christians Could and Should Talk with One Another About"

Andreas Verhülsdonk

When Rome's Chief Rabbi Riccardo Di Segni received Pope Francis on January 17, 2016, in the Great Synagogue of Rome, he acknowledged the path of reconciliation with Judaism that the Catholic Church had trodden during and after the Second Vatican Council and added, "We do not receive the Pope to discuss theology. Each system is autonomous; faith is not subject to communication and political negotiation."[1] The statement on Jewish-Christian dialogue by Rabbi Joseph B. Soloveitchik (1903–1993), the pioneer of Modern Orthodoxy, published more than 50 years previously, echoes in these sentences. In his essay "Confrontation," published in 1964, "the Rav," as his students reverently called him, distinguished a dialogue on social-ethical and political issues, which he supported, and a theological dialogue, which he rejected. This distinction quickly became normative in Orthodox Jewish circles. "Confrontation" not only served as the basis for the official statement of the Rabbinical Council of America (RCA) concerning interreligious dialogue. Until today, this essay is the leading reference text referred to by rabbis

---

1. *"Non accogliamo il papa per discutere di teologia. Ogni sistema è autonomo, la fede non è oggetto di scambio e di trattativa politica."* http://www.romaebraica.it/visita-papa-francesco-in-sinagoga/ (Dec 27, 2016).

who have taken part in dialogue with Christians of different denominations for many years, such as Eugene Korn,[2] Irving Greenberg,[3]
and Shlomo Riskin,[4] all of whom inspired and signed the Orthodox
Rabbinic Statement on Christianity.[5] Likewise, the RCA, the Conference of European Rabbis (CER) and the Chief Rabbinate of Israel
refer to "Confrontation" in their joint declaration *Between Jerusalem and Rome*, published in 2017.[6]

To distinguish what is special in Soloveitchik's argumentation, it
is useful to compare it with the Statement by a similarly significant
rabbinic authority, though he is not very well-known beyond Orthodox circles. In March 1967 – that is three years after the RCA's
statement and almost two years after the Council statement *Nostra
Aetate* – Rabbi Moshe Feinstein wrote two *responsa* on the occasion of a Jewish-Christian conference in Boston on the question of
whether a rabbi may take part in discourse with clergy.[7] In his letter
of March 1, 1967, to Rabbi Bernard Lander, later founder and head
of Touro College, Feinstein made it unambiguously clear that every
participation in discourses with clergy is "a grave violation of the
prohibition against appurtenances to idolatry."[8] Three weeks later
he confirmed this view in a letter to Soloveitchik and requested him
to adopt it. To no effect. Soloveitchik did not respond.

2. "The Man of Faith and Religious Dialogue: Revisiting 'Confrontation' after
Forty Years" (2003), https://www.bc.edu/content/dam/files/research_sites/cjl/te
xts/center/conferences/soloveitchik/Korn_23Nov03.htm (Dec 13, 2016).

3. *For the Sake of Heaven and Earth: The New Encounter between Judaism and
Christianity*, Philadelphia 2004, 13–16.

4. "Is Christian-Jewish Theological Dialogue Permitted? A Postscript to Rav
Joseph B. Soloveitchik's article, 'Confrontation'" (2012), http://cjcuc.com/site/20
12/08/30/is-christian-jewish-theological-dialogue-permitted-a-postscript-to
-rav-joseph-b-solovetichiks-article-confrontation/ (Dec 13, 2016).

5. *To Do the Will of Our Father in Heaven: Toward a Partnership between
Jews and Christians* (2015), http://cjcuc.com/site/2015/12/03/orthodox-rabbinic
-statement-on-christianity/ (Dec 13, 2016).

6. *Between Jerusalem and Rome. Reflections on 50 Years of Nostra Aetate*, New
York 2017, 12.

7. Cf. "A Jewish Legal Authority addresses Jewish-Christian-Dialogue: Two
Responsa of Rabbi Moshe Feinstein." Translated and annotated by David Ellen-
son, in American Jewish Archives Journal 52/2000, 113–128, cited 122–125.

8. Ibid., 122.

In his *halakhic* argumentation, Feinstein assumed that the "brotherly discourse" that the Council fathers call upon Catholics to do in *Nostra Aetate* only serves missionary goals: to move Jews to convert to Christian belief. Even though rabbis would not succumb to such missionary efforts, taking part in Jewish-Christian discourse would come within the proscription of seducing others to apostasy and idol worship (*Avodah Zarah*) (Cf. Dtn 13:7ff; Sanhedrin 63b). For it could not be precluded that religiously less firm Jews would follow the examples of rabbis and take part themselves in discourses with Christians, which would put them in danger of apostasy. Feinstein explicitly declined the differentiation between a dialogue about social-ethical and political items and a theological dialogue, as he reasoned that Christian representatives would discuss social-ethical items only as a pretext for addressing matters of faith.[9] Therefore he declared all meetings between rabbis and clergy to be forbidden without further ado.[10]

Whatever reflections may have led Feinstein to his judgment of Christian motives in dialogue with Jews, the experience of the last 50 years does not support his suspicions. Ever since the Catholic Church declared its "principled rejection of an institutional Jewish mission"[11] and confirmed that it did not support any missionary activities towards Jews, Feinstein's argumentation should be of historical interest only.

Unlike Feinstein, Soloveitchik did not write his statement as a *responsum* and he does not give any *halakhic* reasons for his point of view either.[12] There are neither any references to biblical or rabbinic commandments, post-*talmudic* authorities, comments, or

---

9. Cf. ibid., 123.

10. He speaks of "an absolute and clear prohibition against joint meetings of rabbis and priests" (ibid., 124f).

11. Commission of the Holy See for religious relations with Jews, *The Gifts and the Calling of God are Irrevocable (Rom 11:29). A reflection on theological questions pertaining to Catholic-Jewish relations on the occasion of the 50th anniversary of Nostra Aetate, (No. 4)*. http://www.vatican.va/roman_curia/pontifi cal_councils/chrstuni/relations-jews-docs/rc_pc_chrstuni_doc_20151210_ebrais mo-nostra-aetate_en.html, No. 40 (March 25, 2018).

12. As Eugene Korn points out (loc. cit.).

codes of laws in "Confrontation," nor any typical specialist *halakhic* terms like "permitted" (*mutar*) or "forbidden" (*assur*). He avoided the question of whether Christianity means idol worship[13] as well as the question of if it is permitted to lecture Christians on Torah and *halakhah*, which might indeed be interesting for a dialogue. It is due to the paradoxical history of the impact of this text that it has even been recited as a *halakhic* decision, as David Hartman observed.[14]

Instead of writing a *responsum*, Soloveitchik chose the literary genre of an essay, which he published in English (not in Hebrew) in *Tradition*, the magazine of Yeshiva University.[15] Obviously, he did not want to restrict his reflections to rabbis, but make them accessible to the wider public. The content statements of the essay are made accordingly, while he developed a philosophical argument. In this essay, as well as in other writings, he revealed himself as a religious philosopher perfectly familiar with epistemological questions. Unlike Feinstein, Soloveitchik was not only an outstanding Talmud scholar, but "a religious philosopher of consequence."[16] He had studied Philosophy, Mathematics, and Physics at Friedrich Wilhelm University in Berlin (today Humboldt University), and earned his Ph.D. with a philosophical work on Hermann Cohen, the founder of the so-called Marburg School of Neo-Kantianism. In "Confrontation," he tried to clarify the semantically indefinite and ambiguous talk about Jewish-Christian dialogue or a "brotherly discourse" (*Nostra Aetate*, No. 4) with the help of philosophical differentiation.

As opposed to Feinstein, Soloveitchik – and with him the RCA[17]

---

13. Concerning the question if Christianity is *avodah zarah*, cf. Frederek Mus-all "*Christentum ist Götzendienst (?): Einige Anmerkungen zu Moses Maimonides' Haltung zum Christentum in ihrem kulturgeschichtlichen Kontext*" in Ahrens et al. (ed.) *Hin zu einer Partnerschaft zwischen Juden und Christen: Die Erklärung orthodoxer Rabbiner zum Christentum*, Metropol, Berlin, 2016, 90–106.

14. Cf. *Love and Terror in the God Encounter. The Theological Legacy of Rabbi Joseph B. Soloveitchik*, Woodstock 2001, 132f.

15. *Tradition. A Journal of Orthodox Jewish Thought* 6/1964, 5–28. The essay is reprinted in: J. B. Soloveitchik, *Confrontation and Other Essays*, New Milford – Jerusalem 2015, 85–114. In the following, this edition is cited.

16. Cf. W. Kolbrener, *The Last Rabbi. Joseph Soloveitchik and Talmudic Tradition*, Indiana 2016, xii.

17. Cf. Statement adopted by the Rabbinical Council of America at the

– supported Jewish-Christian dialogue under the condition that the dialogue partners mutually recognize the autonomy and independence of their religious communities. This condition includes moral as well as epistemic implications. On the moral level, it means that Jews and Christians should face each other as equal partners in full religious freedom.[18] Nowadays this condition might sound obvious, if not trivial. In 1964, however, this was by no means the case, because it was still a year before the Catholic Church in its declaration *Dignitatis humanae* acknowledged religious freedom, which the Popes of the 19th century had vehemently fought against. For Soloveitchik, equality between both dialogue partners was even more important, as he was well aware of the social power imbalance between the "community of the many" and the "community of the few."[19] For him, mutual recognition as independent communities also meant not urging each other to change their liturgy or teaching.[20] Thereby he expressly did not rule out that the Churches will find such changes themselves in the course of a process of self-understanding.

On the theological level, Soloveitchik was equally eager to keep Judaism's autonomy and repel all Christian attempts at usurpation or supersession. He emphasized that Judaism does not define itself in relation to Christianity, let alone as a historic predecessor model, whose historical mission was fulfilled by paving the way for Christianity. Nor could Judaism be located within the Christian continuum of the old and new covenant.[21]

At the same time, he did not fail to see that the fundamental categories and premises of Christianity developed within Jewish culture.[22] Yet during the course of history, Christianity and Judaism separated not only institutionally; they differ in ritual and ethos, in

Mid-Winter Conference, February 3–5, 1964, in ibid., 114f.

18. Cf. *Confrontation*, loc. cit. 104f.

19. Cf. ibid., 110.

20. Cf. ibid., 109f. He may be thinking of the revision of the intercessory prayer for the Jews in the Catholic Good Friday liturgy.

21. Cf. ibid., 107f.

22. Cf. ibid., 106.

their doctrines, and in their eschatological hopes.[23] Christians and
Jews use different theological categories and move "within incommensurate frames of reference and evaluation."[24] They therefore
lack a shared language for a religious or theological dialogue. Thus,
he concluded, "The confrontation should occur not at a theological,
but at a mundane human level. There, all of us speak the universal
language of modern man."[25] The thesis of theological incommensurability of Judaism and Christianity represents the core of his argumentation and will be analyzed below.

Soloveitchik might have borrowed the term incommensurability
from contemporary philosophy. In 1962, Thomas Kuhn[26] and Paul
Feyerabend[27] had independently of one another introduced this
term into scientific theory, causing a controversial debate that also
engaged cultural and religious philosophy in the 1980s and 1990s.
In the course of the debate the term incommensurability experienced a semantic adjustment, not least by Kuhn and Feyerabend
themselves, before the controversy found its end at least for the
time being with Australian philosopher Howard Sankey's work.[28]
The starting point of the debate is the observation that scientific
progress in history does not proceed as an evolutionary process but
as a succession of theories under different conceptual conditions
using either new terms or similar terms with changed meaning, so
that the terms of one theory are not, or are only partly translatable
into the conceptual framework of another theory. Incommensurability means total or partial untranslatability of theories. The concept of the theory is defined broadly enough to subsume religions,
mythologies, or worldviews thereunder as well. Soloveitchik, too,

---

23. Cf. ibid., 102.
24. "On Interfaith Relationships" (1967), in id. *Confrontation and Other Essays*, loc. cit. 117–119, cited 119 (italicized in the original).
25. *Confrontation*, loc cit. 108.
26. *Die Struktur wissenschaftlicher Revolutionen*, 2. revised and updated edition, Frankfurt 1973.
27. "Explanation, Reduction and Empiricism," in H. Feigl/ G. Maxwell (Hg.),
Scientific Explanation, Space, and Time, Minneapolis 1962, 28–97.
28. *The Incommensurability Thesis*, Ashgate 1994; id., "Incommensurability:
The Current State of Play," in *Theoria* 12/1997, 425–445.

used the term incommensurability in the sense of untranslatability of religious terms and logic.

To understand why Soloveitchik introduced a term from the philosophy of science, it is reasonable to remember that as early as in his work *The Halakhic Man* (1944) he was already strongly reluctant to accept any attempts to discuss religion in terms of feelings, subjective perception, or mystical experience. He sharply distinguished *halakhic* man from *homo religiosus* and plead for a decidedly intellectual understanding of religion, which should be oriented towards science in its conceptual clarity and logical coherence.[29] Here the Talmud scholar is seen continuing the Lithuanian tradition of the rational Talmud approach (the "Brisker method"). In *The Halakhic Mind*, which was written in 1944 but not published until 1986, he embedded religious and particularly *halakhic* thinking in modern scientific history. In discussing the scientific and philosophical developments of the first half of the 20th century, he sought to show that the monistic understanding of reality based on natural sciences has collapsed, on the one hand because of recent developments in the sciences themselves (quantum mechanics) and on the other because of the emergence and establishment of humanities and cultural studies, giving way to an "epistemological pluralism."[30] The present age is characterized by the existence of different accesses to reality, which are not reducible to one another and not integrable into a philosophical synthesis. For the first time in history, this has opened up an opportunity to define a specifically Jewish approach to reality. For Soloveitchik, the Jewish approach to the world is a *halakhic* approach. He considered the *halakhah* not merely as a code of laws to secure the religious identity of a social community, but rather as an objective expression of the Jewish experience of God. It is not an esoteric teaching about God, but opens up an approach

29. Cf. *The Halakhic Man*, Philadelphia 1983, 141: "(...) religion should ally itself with the forces of clear, logical cognition, as uniquely exemplified in the scientific method, even though at times the two might clash with one another (...)." (footnote 4).
30. *The Halakhic Mind. An Essay on Jewish Tradition and Modern Thought*, New York 1986, 28 and beyond.

to reality under the condition of God's existence. *halakhic* thinking, with its own terms, rules of argumentation, and standards of evaluation, is the one source of a Jewish worldview that must be defined in the future.[31]

Reading *The Halakhic Mind* leaves an ambivalent impression. On the one hand, Soloveitchik succeeded in placing religious traditions in their own epistemic location within modern thinking and thereby preserves their unique character against possible scientific or philosophic totalitarian claims. On the other hand, he avoided the question of how to define the relationship of a *halakhic* approach to the world in contrast to, say, scientific approaches to the world, and how to face possible cognitive dissonances between different approaches to the world.[32] This is all the more disappointing as Soloveitchik particularly stressed the cognitive dimension of religion.

Against the background of *The Halakhic Mind*, it is intelligible why Soloveitchik welcomed the incommensurability thesis of Kuhn and Feyerabend and used it in the context of interreligious relations. It supports the theory of an epistemological pluralism and thereby the theological independence of Judaism, as well. As Jonathan Sacks correctly remarks, there is a direct path from *The Halakhic Mind* to the argumentation in "Confrontation."[33] The pluralism of religions cannot be traced back to a supposed universal religious experience, nor can philosophy take over the role of judge in a quarrel between religions. Rather, religions build different approaches to reality using their own terminologies, which are mutually incommensurable, that is, untranslatable. This does not exclude the fact that in Judaism and Christianity, similar terms are used, or that both religions

31. Cf. ibid., 102: "Out of the sources of *Halakhah*, a new worldview awaits formulation." Cf. also W. Kolbrener, "Towards a Genuine Jewish Philosophy. *Halakhic* Mind's New Philosophy of Religion," in M. Angel (ed.), *Exploring the Thought of Rabbi Joseph B. Soloveitchik*, Jersey City 1997, 179–206.

32. Cf. *The Lonely Man of Faith*, New York 2006, 7.

33. Cf. "Rabbi Joseph B. Soloveitchik's Early Epistemology," in id., *Tradition in an Untraditional Age. Essays on Modern Jewish Thought*, London 1990, 287–301, cited 297. Similarly, Daniel. Rynhold, "The Philosophical Foundations of Soloveitchik's Critique of Interfaith Dialogue," in *Harvard Theological Review* 96/2003, 101–120.

have mutually influenced each other throughout history. It can be assumed, however, that identical terms or terminological adoptions have different meanings due to their incorporation into different reference systems, therefore preventing equivalence.

If one takes the incommensurability thesis seriously, no dialogue at all is possible between Jews and Christians. Even on social-ethical or political issues, they could only communicate as members of the public, but not as Jews and Christians. That is definitely not Soloveitchik's position. If a Jewish-Christian dialogue on social-ethical and political issues is to be possible, then the Christian and Jewish traditions have to be translatable at least in parts. Indeed, Soloveitchik supports a partial or "local incommensurability" (Kuhn, Sankey) of religious traditions, which raises the question of what in religious traditions is translatable and what is untranslatable. He discusses this question in chapter 9 of his essay *The Lonely Man of Faith*, published in 1965, at the same time as "Confrontation," also in *Tradition* magazine.

The focus of this programmatic publication of Modern Orthodoxy, which can be compared with Samson Raphael Hirsch's *The Nineteen Letters* (1836), is on determining the relationship of the Jewish religion to modern culture. The style of argument and use of language (e.g. usage of the term *Kerygma*) indicates the influence of the debates on cultural Protestantism that Soloveitchik had experienced as a student in Berlin in the 1920s. It is remarkable that he developed the basic concepts of his programmatic publication in speeches he gave at the Catholic Seminary in Brighton (Mass.)[34] and the Institute of Mental Health, a joint cooperation by Yeshiva University, Harvard University, and Loyola Jesuit University[35] of Chicago. In this work, too, he addressed a broad rather than an exclusively Jewish audience.

---

34. Cf. W. Wurzburger, "Rabbi Joseph B. Soloveitchik as *Posek* of Post-Modern Orthodoxy," in M. Angel (ed.), *Exploring the Thought of Rabbi Joseph B. Soloveitchik*, loc. cit. 3–22, cited 17.

35. Cf. C. Rutishauser, "Doppelte Konfrontation." Rav Josef Dov Soloveitchik's controversial model for Jewish-Christian dialogue," in *Judaica* 59/2003, 12–23, cited 21.

With the aid of a religious-philosophical typology of man inspired by a genuine interpretation of the biblical Genesis, Soloveitchik elaborated on the differentiation of modern society into different spheres of action each with their own logic, especially the separation of culture and religion and subsequently religious and civic existence. There is a preview of this anthropology in the first part of "Confrontation," although it is terminologically less precise and logically less coherent. It provides a reference framework in which he locates the Jewish-Christian relationship as well as the relationship of religion to culture.

Soloveitchik interpreted both stories of creation in the book of Genesis in the light of experiences and issues of modern Western societies and identifies two dimensions of human existence that are dialectically connected with one another. In the first story, God creates man in his own image and commissions him to rule over nature (Cf. Gen 1:27f). According to Soloveitchik's interpretation, man is put facing the world and he enters into a technical-instrumental relationship with reality, which he explores in order to rule it. In his dominion over the earth, in the creation and development of culture, and in designing society, man unfolds his creative abilities and fulfills himself. That man was created in the divine image, Soloveitchik considers to be a commission to imitate the creativity of God in creating culture and society.[36]

In the second creation story, man, who is called Adam II by Soloveitchik in contrast to the Adam I of the first story, is put into a different relationship with reality, which essentially is not instrumental. He finds himself confronted by the secret of reality, asking "Why?" and "What for?" of the world and himself. But above all he finds himself facing God: "Adam the second lives in close union with God."[37] In the community with God, Adam II does not search for self-affirmation or self-realization, but for salvation. In using the Tetragrammaton for God, the second creation story prefigures the later covenant between God and Israel. Like Adam I, who founded a

---

36. Cf. *The Lonely Man of Faith*, loc. cit. 13–19.
37. Ibid., 22.

society based on shared interests, Adam II views himself appointed to a "covenantal community" that includes God as "leader, teacher, and shepherd" and is based on humility, willingness to make sacrifices, and self-dedication.[38]

Though Adam I and Adam II have different relationships to reality, pursue different goals, and follow different values, Soloveitchik did not represent a dualistic anthropology. Rather Adam I and Adam II build a dialectical union that is kept together by values and norms of the *halakhah*.[39] Humans have to complete both tasks in their lives. They are inhabitants of two worlds; their lives oscillate between civil society and the religious community.

Under this dialectical tension of Adam I and Adam II, Soloveitchik determines the relationship between religion and modern culture. With admiration he describes the scientific-technical progress and cultural achievements that modernity can be proud of. But modernity's successes seduce humankind to dissolve the dialectical union of Adam I and Adam II. Their cultural and social tasks govern them to such an extent that they neglect their relation to God.[40] The marginalization of religious belief, says Soloveitchik, has endangered the successes of modernity, at least in the long run. For humankind requires the "covenantal faith community" to establish a culture that not only applauds technical success but also satisfies human striving for a good life in both moral and esthetic respects.[41]

At this point Soloveitchik took up the incommensurability thesis again, modifying it at the same time. Though the logic of Adam I and Adam II are "not commensurate,"[42] it is possible, however, to translate religious terms, norms, and values into a cultural language that is understandable to all members of a society, the non-religious included. "Religious values, doctrines and concepts may be and have been translated into cultural categories enjoyed and cherished

38. Cf. ibid., 43.
39. Cf. ibid., 77–81.
40. Cf. ibid., 87.
41. Cf. ibid., 88f.
42. Ibid., 81.

even by secular man."[43] In this sense, Soloveitchik can speak of a Jewish-Christian culture, as Western culture is characterized by Jewish and Christian concepts.[44]

Translating into cultural terms, however, does not leave the semantic content of religious commandments and teachings untouched. In the process of translation they are inserted into a reference system that is oriented towards the self-realization of humankind (in the sense of Adam I) and are therefore interpreted functionally. Soloveitchik does not consider a functionalist perception of religion, which applies religious traditions to solving social or cultural problems, to be illegitimate, since the *Halakhah* is indeed useful for individual and social life.[45] But faith[46] does not merge into social functionality and is not revealed by social effects either. Soloveitchik described the experience of faith with emphatic words:

The man of faith is "insanely" committed to and "madly" in love with God."[47] This relationship with God is objectively expressed in the *Halakha*, whose commandments are observed by the faithful because of love of God, not for human purposes. Because the God-centered perspective of faith cannot be translated into the human-centered perspective of modern culture, there is a certain limit to the translatability of religious commandments and teachings into cultural categories. "If an all-embracing translation of the great mystery of revelation and its *kerygma* were possible, then the uniqueness of the faith experience and its commitments would be lost."[48]

43. *Confrontation*, loc. cit. 106. Cf. a. *The Lonely Man of Faith*, loc. cit. 91: "In short, the message of faith, if translated into cultural categories, fits into the axiological and philosophical frame of reference of the creative cultural consciousness and is pertinent even to secular man."
44. Cf. *Confrontation*, loc. cit. 106f.
45. Cf. *The Lonely Man of Faith*, loc. cit. 88.
46. Based on the language usage of the *kerygmatic* theology of the 20th century, Soloveitchik uses "religion" for the culturally translatable parts of religion and "faith" for the non-functional understanding of a relationship with God.
47. Ibid., 95.
48. Ibid.

An entirely culturally translated faith would not be faith anymore. With *The Lonely Man of Faith* Soloveitchik joined in the tradition of Modern Orthodoxy, the basic concepts of which were conceived by Samson Raphael Hirsch in the above-mentioned *The Nineteen Letters* (1836). Like Hirsch, Soloveitchik supports a perception of Jewish existence that is not reduced to synagogue and family but explicitly includes social, cultural, and political engagement, the accumulation of secular knowledge, facing the challenges of modernity, and collaboration with non-Jews. But while Hirsch warned his contemporaries that "a life of seclusion devoted only to meditation and prayer is not Judaism,"[49] Soloveitchik was faced with a Judaism that increasingly exhausts itself in political and humanitarian engagement, and in which a functionalist conception of its religious traditions is not uncommon. That is why he was particularly engaged in protecting and strengthening the love of God as the essence of Jewish identity. Which does not prevent him from representing and exemplifying to his students "a Judaism engaged with the world" (J. Sacks) with determination.

Perceiving Judaism in this way includes being ready for dialogue and cooperation with Christians on a social and cultural level. Such dialogue is "desirable and even essential"[50] according to Soloveitchik. And he considers it quite natural that the partners bring their religious beliefs into such a dialogue. The place for a Jewish-Christian dialogue is the shared public place, in which people holding different religious and ideological beliefs communicate on political, social, and cultural issues.[51] On issues concerning the relationship between humans and God, however, they cannot communicate reasonably nor come to an understanding, as the terms and standards they use are not translatable.[52] In other words, Soloveitchik called

---

49. Ben Usiel (Samson Raphael Hirsch), *Neunzehn Briefe über Judenthum*, Altona 1836, 73 (15. Brief). English translation available on https://www.sefaria .org/Nineteen_Letters?lang=bi, 15. Letter (March 27, 2018).

50. "On Interfaith Relationships," loc. cit. 119.

51. Cf. ibid.

52. Cf. ibid., 118f.

for a social togetherness of Jews and Christians and a respectful parallel existence of synagogue and Church in religious respects.

But is that to be the last word on Christian-Jewish dialogue? Looking back over the past 50 years, there are two developments that deserve particular attention but can only be touched on briefly here. The former naïve, because philosophically unreflected, dialogue rhetoric has given way to a clear awareness of the problems, obstacles, and boundaries of interreligious communication on the Christian side, as well. What's more, the incommensurability thesis has meanwhile been discussed theologically.[53] Currently the most sophisticated theory of interreligious relationships – "Comparative Theology"[54] – developed in the USA, is characterized by a willingness to reflect on one's own religious and epistemic conditions in dialogue with representatives of other religions, and the avoidance of religious theologies or hasty recourse to supposedly religious universals. Though they start out from the heuristic premise of a commensurability of religious traditions, their representatives admit to rather frequently coming across "partial incommensurability" in interreligious dialogue: "... with some texts we have to basically say that we ourselves do not know how they could be translated."[55] Those who take religious disagreements seriously and do not try to solve them hastily as varieties of similarities, will therefore not be able to avoid partial incommensurability.

53. Cf. N. Hintersteiner, *Traditionen überschreiten. Angloamerikanische Beiträge zur interkulturellen Traditionshermeneutik*, Wien 2001; A. Fetzer, *Tradition im Pluralismus. Alasdair MacIntyre und Karl Barth als Inspiration für christliches Selbstverständnis in der pluralen Gesellschaft*, Neukirchen-Vluyn 2002.

54. Cf. especially C. Cornille, *The Im-possibility of Interreligious Dialogue*, New York 2008.

55. "(...) bei manchen Texten kann man auch ganz grundsätzlich sagen, dass man selbst nicht weiß, wie sie übersetzt werden könnten." K. von Stosch, "*Zur Möglichkeit und Unmöglichkeit des interreligiösen Dialogs. Untersuchungen im Anschluss an Catherine Cornille,*" in *Ethik und Gesellschaft* 2/2011, 1–25, cited 7, http://www.ethik-und-gesellschaft.de/ojs/index.php/eug/article/view/2-2011-art -2 (Dec 30, 2016). Cf. C. Cornille, loc. cit. 167: "Even though one may be deeply familiar with all of the elements comprising the experience of devotion within another religion, the feeling of love for the *particular object of devotion* – that which is arguably the most important dimension of the experience for believers – remains inaccessible for anyone not belonging to the tradition."

By the end of the 1980s and beginning of the 1990s, the incommensurability debate had developed in a direction that led beyond Soloveitchik. In his late phase, Thomas Kuhn distinguished between "translate" and "understand." Regarding second language acquisition and bilingualism, he states that it is possible to understand and correctly interpret a certain term in a foreign language, although this term cannot be translated into the other language. Therefore, it is not translatability that is significant for understanding, but the ability to master the language of the other theory grammatically, semantically, and pragmatically.[56]

Differentiating between "understand" and "translate" is also the basic premise of the "second first language" concept, which the cultural philosopher Alasdair MacIntyre developed at the same time.[57] To understand another tradition, it is necessary, according to MacIntyre, to learn the language of a tradition as a second mother tongue "like a child,"[58] so not by means of translation into the mother tongue. Only bilingual competence allows a speaker to recognize which parts of another tradition can be translated into their own tradition, and which cannot. Cultural philosopher MacIntyre puts greater emphasis than science theorist Kuhn on the language connected with a lifestyle, so that learning a language demands at least a partial introduction to a lifestyle.[59]

The analogy of bilingualism can be useful for the comprehension of interreligious relationships.[60] The language analogy allows us to understand religions as a specific access to reality with their own grammar, semantics, and pragmatics connected to a corresponding lifestyle.[61] Understanding another religion is not based

56. Cf. Xiang Chen, "Thomas Kuhn's Latest Notion of Incommensurability," in *Journal for General Philosophy of Science/ Zeitschrift für allgemeine Wissenschaftstheorie* 28/1997, 257–273, cited 262–264. Similar reflections can be found with Paul Feyerabend, cf. N. Hintersteiner, loc. cit. 170.

57. Cf. "Whose Justice? Whose Rationality?" Notre Dame 1988, 370–388 (Tradition and Translation).

58. Ibid., 374.

59. Cf. ibid., 373f.

60. Cf. N. Hintersteiner, loc. cit. 316–320.

61. Cf. P. Ricœur, *Sur la traduction.* Préface de Marc Launay, Paris 2016, 29.

on comparing theological teachings, which are sorted according to similarities and differences, but on learning another religion as a second language. It is only such bilingual competence that makes a theologically substantial conversation possible at all, in which the theological autonomy of the partners – Soloveitchik's and the RCA's central concern – is maintained.

Learning another religious tradition, like learning a second language, is a challenging task that requires a strong motive embedded in one's own religious tradition, thus making it theologically justified. On the Christian side, such a motive is easily found since Christianity defines itself theologically not without reference to Judaism. Since the Catholic Church has significantly revised its view of and its relationship with Judaism in the last decades, and like Pope Francis, assumes that "God continues to work among the people of the Old Covenant,"[62] there is a strong theological motive for Christian engagement with Judaism. On the Jewish side, there has been no comparable motive discernable as yet. Soloveitchik knew the reasons for social and cultural collaboration between Jews and Christians, but not for a theological engagement with Christianity, though he himself had considerable knowledge of Christian literature from Tertullian to Karl Barth. That could now change with this new Orthodox Rabbinic Statement on Christianity. If Christianity is "the willed divine outcome and gift to the nations," and if both "Jews and Christians have a common covenantal mission to perfect the world under the sovereignty of the Almighty,"[63] then this serves as a reason for a theological engagement with Christianity. Time will tell if these statements will meet with universal approval in the Jewish community. The question of what Jews and Christians could and should talk with one another about, is left open.

---

62. *Apostolic Exhortation EVANGELII GAUDIUM of the Holy Father Francis to the Bishops, Clergy, Consecrated and the Lay Faithful Persons on the Proclamation of the Gospel in Today's World*, Nr. 249 on http://w2.vatican.va/content/fran cesco/en/apost_exhortations/documents/papa-francesco_esortazione-ap_20131 124_evangelii-gaudium.html (March 27, 2018).

63. *To Do the Will of Our Father in Heaven: Toward a Partnership between Jews and Christians* (2015), loc. cit. No. 4 and 5.

Rabbi Joseph B. Soloveitchik's Unexpected Contribution
Towards a Theology of Jewish-Christian Dialogue

Murray Johnston

In his 1990 *Dialogue with the Other: The Inter-Religious Dialogue*, the Roman Catholic theologian David Tracy proclaims that "[t]here is no more difficult or more pressing question on the present theological horizon than that of inter-religious dialogue."[1] One need only turn to the 2015 Orthodox Rabbinic Statement on Christianity, *To Do the Will of Our Father in Heaven: Toward a Partnership between Jews and Christians* to appreciate the urgency of Tracy's question. The Statement recognizes that the "enmity that developed between Jews and Christians" due to "centuries of disrespect, oppression and rejection of Jews" resulted in a failure "to engage in constructive dialogue for the good of humankind" during the 1930s and 1940s and a diminished capacity on the part of Christians to resist the "evil forces of anti-Semitism that engulfed the world in murder and genocide."[2]

Our own time, too, faces daunting challenges. The reality of democratic decline in a world awakening to the false alternative between

1. David Tracy, *Dialogue with the Other: The Inter-Religious Dialogue* (Louvain: Peeters Press, 1990), 27.
2. Orthodox Rabbinic Statement on Christianity, *To Do the Will of Our Father in Heaven: Towards a Partnership between Jews and Christians*, paragraph 1, http://cjcuc.org/2015/12/03/orthodox-rabbinic-statement-on-christianity/.

the moribund secularism of neoliberal globalism and the deformed faith of resurgent ethno-nationalism – in the midst of deepening ecological crisis – suggests in broad strokes the situation within which religious persons and communities practice their lives of faith.[3] To borrow from the twentieth century Jewish theologian and rabbinical scholar Joseph B. Soloveitchik, whose approach to Jewish-Christian dialogue is the focus of this paper, the "socio-cultural and moral problems" we share in common, direct our attention to the "spiritual aspects of our civilization."[4] Soloveitchik understands civilization as a "community effort through the millennia." It is dedicated to the "production, distribution, and consumption of goods, material as well as cultural."[5] Its purpose is to gain some measure of control over the conditions of existence in order to ensure a dignified life;[6] and issues such as war and peace, poverty, freedom, and civil rights point to its "spiritual aspects."[7] As Soloveitchik notes in "The Lonely Man of Faith" – an essay that began as a 1964 lecture to a Jewish and Christian audience at St. John's Seminary in Brighton Massachusetts[8] – the work of civilization must be related to "a

3. See David Hyatt, "The Redemption of Nature in the Philosophical Writings of Rabbi Joseph Dov Ber Soloveitchik" (PhD diss., Bar-Ilan University, 2015) for discussion of Soloveitchik's contribution to contemporary ecological thinking, especially chapter six, "*The Emergence of Ethical Man* – Rav Joseph B. Soloveitchik's Environmental Ethics in Context" (206–246).

4. Joseph B. Soloveitchik, "On Interfaith Relationships," in *Community, Covenant and Commitment: Selected Letters and Communications*, ed. Nathaniel Helfgot (Jersey City: Ktav Publishing House, 2005), 260–261.

5. Joseph B. Soloveitchik, "The Lonely Man of Faith," *Tradition* 7/2 (1965): 22.

6. Cf. Felipe Fernádez-Armesto, *Civilizations* (Toronto: Key Porter Books, 2000), 5. Civilization involves "a relationship to the natural environment, re-crafted by the civilizing impulse, to meet human demands.... One lesson of this book is that civilizations commonly over-exploit their environments, often to the point of self-destruction."

7. "On Interfaith Relationships," 261.

8. See Reuven Kimelman, "Rabbis Joseph B. Soloveitchik and Abraham Joshua Heschel on Jewish-Christian Relations," *The Edah Journal* 4/2 (2004): 8. In the accompanying note, Kimelman adds that Soloveitchik's daughter, Dr. Atarah Twersky, who attended the talk, indicated that it "comes under the rubric of general religious discourse" (19–20). The same can be said of "Confrontation," *Tradition* 6/2 (1964), Soloveitchik's essay on Jewish-Christian relations. Despite a very different audience – it began as a presentation at the 1964 midwinter conference

higher modus existentiae."[9] One of the responsibilities of contemporary theologians across faith traditions involves setting the successes and failures of our early 21st century way of life within "the framework of our religious outlooks."[10]

In "On Interfaith Relationships," a 1964 open letter that appeared in the *Rabbinical Council of America Record*, Soloveitchik approves of Jewish-Christian cooperation in addressing "socio-cultural and

---

of the Rabbinical Council of America – "Confrontation," too, counts as "general religious discourse." It responds to an issue that religious persons and communities have to face, namely, the reality of religious pluralism in our strangely secular age. To borrow from "On Interfaith Relationships," it focuses on "those universal aspects of man which are relevant to all of us" (259). The categories that Soloveitchik brings to bear on Jewish-Christian dialogue emerge from a *theologico-philosophical reading* of Genesis 2 and are thus intended to be universal in reach (5). The phrase "*theologico-philosophical reading*" alludes to the following passage in "The Lonely Man of Faith:" "Whatever I am about to say is to be seen only as a modest attempt on the part of a man of faith to interpret his spiritual perceptions and emotions in modern theologico-philosophical categories" (8). Soloveitchik's analysis of Jewish-Christian relations is set within a "theologico-Biblical ... frame of reference;" he situates the question of Jewish-Christian dialogue in relation to "the scheme of events and things willed and approved by God, when He ordered finitude to emerge out of infinity and the universe, including man, to unfold itself" (9). Further, Soloveitchik contrasts his approach to the kind of ecumenism that emerged from the Second Vatican Council. As he writes in a 1967 letter to Rabbi Pesah Levovitz, which appears as "On RCA Participation in an Interreligious Conference," in *Community, Covenant and Commitment*, 268, "Ecumenism as such is rooted in Christian theology and tradition and we as Jews, as a non-Christian community cannot and will not join this movement which is alien to us. Our concept of the brotherhood of man, solidarity of individuals, love and understanding of each other is rooted exclusively in our Judaic tradition which is basically a universal one." It should be emphasized that the preceding sentences were written following the promulgation of *Nostra Aetate* and thus suggest that Soloveitchik considered his approach an *alternative* to Christian ecumenism in general. On ecumenism from a Roman Catholic perspective, however, see Jerome-Michael Vereb, *"Because he was a German!" Cardinal Bei and the Origins of Roman Catholic Engagement in the Ecumenical Movement* (Grand Rapids: William B. Eerdmans Publishing Company, 2006); John Connelly, *From Enemy to Brother: The Revolution in Catholic Teaching on the Jews, 1933–1965* (Cambridge: Harvard University Press, 2012); and Charles Morerod, *Ecumenism and Philosophy: Philosophical Questions for a Renewal of Dialogue*, trans. Therese C. Scarpelli (Ann Arbor: Sapientia Press, 2006).

9. "The Lonely Man of Faith," 59.
10. "On Interfaith Relationships," 261.

moral problems."[11] Given his abiding commitment to democracy – his
contention in *Halakhic Man* that the "entire thrust of the *Halakhah*
is democratic from beginning to end," his insistence in "The Lonely
Man of Faith" that the "normative element in prophecy" ensures the
"democratization of the God-man confrontation," and his claim in
"Confrontation" that faith communities in the plural ought to act in
accordance with the principles of "religious democracy and liberal-
ism"[12] – one assumes that Soloveitchik would judge the erosion of
our democratic way of life a deeply troubling development. Indeed,
it would be precisely the sort of issue concerning which he would
encourage dialogue across faith traditions. According to the Cana-
dian philosopher Charles Taylor, "Democracy requires that each
citizen or group of citizens speaks the language in public debate that
is most meaningful to them."[13] Soloveitchik would agree with Taylor
on this point. Far from bracketing "theologically informed views on
the nature of the human person and society" from the public square
and perforce requiring persons of faith to adopt "secularist criteria,"[14] Soloveitchik stresses that Jews and Christians cannot address
issues of common concern using "agnostic or secularist categories"
but must avail themselves of a language that is "religious in nature
and Biblical in origin" – a language that represents the "universal
and public ... in religion" rather than the "individual and private."[15]
In "Confrontation" and "The Lonely Man of Faith," Soloveitchik's

---

11. Ibid., 261.

12. Joseph B. Soloveitchik, *Halakhic Man*, trans. Lawrence J. Kaplan (Philadelphia: Jewish Publication Society, 1983), 43; "The Lonely Man of Faith," 40; and
"Confrontation," 21 & 23.

13. Charles Taylor, *A Secular Age* (Cambridge: Harvard University Press,
2007), 532.

14. See David Novak, *Jewish-Christian Dialogue: A Jewish Justification*
(Oxford: University of Oxford Press, 1989), 6–9, for a critique of Soloveitchik's
approach to Jewish-Christian dialogue. Novak maintains that Soloveitchik's
position implies that "Jews are precluded from bringing into any discussions of
public morality with non-Jews their theologically informed views of the nature of
the human person and society;" consequently, they have no choice but to adopt
"secularist criteria of human nature and society" as the "basis of common discussion" (7).

15. "On Interfaith Relationships," 261.

treatment of the "universal and public in man" takes a decidedly practical turn. "Religious values, doctrines and concepts may be and have been translated into cultural categories," Soloveitchik writes in the former essay.[16] And in the latter, he states, "The idea that certain aspects of faith are translatable into pragmatic terms is not new.... Religious pragmatism has a place within the perspective of the man of faith."[17] At the same time, however, Soloveitchik adds that the "act of faith ... cannot be fully translated into cultural categories;" its projection onto "a cognitive pragmatic background" must remain incomplete.[18] It emerges, then, that the "theological *logos*" accomplishes two things. It reflects "the numinous character and the strangeness of the act of faith of a particular community;"[19] and it can be translated into the "cultural matrix."[20] In the background of Soloveitchik's twofold characterization of the kerygma of faith is his distinction between the "dimension of faith" and the "dimension of culture," one pointing to the "singular apocalyptic faith experience"

16. "Confrontation," 22.
17. "The Lonely Man of Faith," 60.
18. Ibid., 62.
19. "Confrontation," 23–24.
20. The term "cultural matrix" appears in Bernard Lonergan's classic formulation of the nature of the theological task in *Method in Theology*, Volume 14, *Collected Words of Bernard Lonergan*, ed. Robert M. Doran and John D. Dadosky (Toronto: University of Toronto Press, 2017), 2. "A theology mediates between a cultural matrix and the significance and role of religion in that matrix," where culture is understood as a "set of meanings and values that inform a way of life." The act of translation, so important in "Confrontation" and "The Lonely Man of Faith," holds a prominent place in Lonergan's theological method. Neil Ormerod and Christiaan Jacobs-Vandegeer, for instance, in *Foundational Theology: A New Approach to Catholic Fundamental Theology* (Minneapolis: Fortress Press, 2015), 314–315, note that the theological task culminates in the "transposition of meaning from the technical language of systematic theology into the *commonsense language* of a particular culture," that is, it culminates in the communication of "divine meanings and values into the concrete circumstances of people's lives, in all their social and cultural complexity" (emphasis supplied). We are not far from Soloveitchik on the translation of the kerygma of faith into "cultural categories," that is, the translation of the "theological *logos*" from the "dimension of faith" to the "dimension of culture." See *Insight*, Volume 3, *Collected Works of Bernard Lonergan*, ed. Frederick E. Crowe and Robert M. Doran (Toronto: University of Toronto Press, 1992), 196–269, for Lonergan's treatment of "common sense."

and the other to the "mundane cultural experience."[21] One of the claims that I want to make is that Soloveitchik's approach to Jewish-Christian dialogue takes both dimensions into account.

The purpose of this essay, then, is to provide a *preliminary sketch* of Soloveitchik's approach to Jewish-Christian dialogue, claiming that it represents an important theological mapping of what Tracy calls the *"terra incognita* of our present acknowledgment of religious pluralism."[22] In other words, Soloveitchik's distinction between permissible and impermissible approaches to Jewish-Christian dialogue and his opposition to Jewish involvement in theological discussions with Christians, especially during the Second Vatican Council,[23] do not exhaust the significance of his contribution. Still, it must be acknowledged that Soloveitchik's writings on Jewish-Christian relations are perhaps an unexpected source on which to draw for the development of a theology of Jewish-Christian dialogue. Indeed, the term "dialogue" does even not appear in "Confrontation." Instead,

21. "Confrontation," 22–23. It is not the aim of this essay to chart the development of themes across Soloveitchik's *oeuvre*. Still, it is worth noting that in his 1950–1951 lectures on the *Guide of the Perplexed*, Soloveitchik distinguishes between European and American theological emphases. One characterizes religion as a "non-cultural trend that is based on revelation" and the other as a "complex cultural experience." These two characterizations anticipate Soloveitchik's later distinction between the "dimension of faith" and the "dimension of culture," respectively. See Joseph B. Soloveitchik, *Maimonides – Between Philosophy and Halakhah: Rabbi Joseph B. Soloveitchik's Lectures on the* Guide of the Perplexed *at the Bernard Revel Graduate School (1950–1951): Based on the notes of Rabbi Gerald (Yaakov) Homnick*, ed. Lawrence J. Kaplan (New York: Ktav Publishing House, 2016), 114–115.

22. Tracy, *Dialogue with the Other*, 47.

23. For Soloveitchik's distinction between permissible and impermissible approaches to Jewish-Christian dialogue and his response to Vatican II, see the following: Lawrence Kaplan, "Revisionism and the Rav: The Struggle for the Soul of Modern Orthodoxy," *Judaism* 48 / 3 (Summer 1999): 290–311; Meir Soloveichik, "A Nation Under God: Jews, Christians, and the American Public Square," in *Yirat Shamayim: The Awe, Reverence, and Fear of God*, ed. Marc D. Stern (New York: Yeshiva University Press, 2008): 321–347; Kimelman, "Rabbis Joseph B. Soloveitchik and Abraham Joshua Heschel on Jewish-Christian Relations," 1–21; and Yigal Sklarin,"'Rushing in Where Angels Fear to Tread': Rabbi Joseph B. Soloveitchik, the Rabbinical Council of America, Modern Jewish Orthodoxy, and the Second Vatican Council," *Modern Judaism* 29/3 (October 2009): 359–360.

the guiding idea in Soloveitchik's essay is that of *confrontation*, a word that conveys something of the tension that persists in the *face-to-face* encounter between self and other.[24] Soloveitchik speaks of confrontation in three distinct contexts: the "covenantal confrontation" in which the the'finite "I"' meets the infinite He *"face to face;"*[25] the "cosmic confrontation" in which Jews and Christians participate

24. Cf. *Chambers Dictionary of Etymology*, ed. Robert K. Barnhart (New York: Chambers Harrap Publishers, 1988), 206. "**confront** *v.* About 1568, stand in front of, face, borrowed from Middle French *confronter*, learned borrowing from Medieval Latin *confrontare* assign limits, adjoin." "**confrontation** *n.* 1632, action of bringing persons face to face, borrowed from French *confrontation....* The sense of an encounter between hostile persons or groups is first recorded in English about 1955, in a context of international relations."

25. "The Lonely Man of Faith," 33 (emphasis supplied). "However, covenantal man of faith craving for a personal and intimate relation with God could not find it in the cosmic E-lohim encounter and had to shift his transcendental experience to a different level at which the finite 'I' meets the infinite He 'face to face." The term "covenantal confrontation" appears in "Confrontation," 17, and in "The Lonely Man of Faith," 30 & 67. In "Confrontation," Soloveitchik writes: "We believe we are the bearers of a double charismatic load, that of the dignity of man, and that of the sanctity of the covenantal community. In this difficult role, we are summoned by God, who revealed himself at both the level of universal creation and that of the private covenant, to undertake a double mission – the universal human and the exclusive *covenantal confrontation*" (emphasis supplied). Soloveitchik is critical of attempts to dissociate the meeting between the "finite I" and the "infinite He" from communication of the "divine normative summons." See, for instance, "The Lonely Man of Faith," 38–40, where Soloveitchik writes: "Any encounter with God, if it is to redeem man, must be crystallized and objectified in a normative ethico-moral message. If, however, the encounter is reduced to its non-kerygmatic and non-imperative aspects, no matter how great and magnificent an experience it is, it cannot be classified as a covenantal encounter since the very semantics of the term covenant implies freely assumed obligations and commitments." Soloveitchik's position can be contrasted with Gerald O'Collins's discussion of revelation in *Revelation: Towards a Christian Interpretation of God's Self-Revelation in Jesus Christ* (Oxford: Oxford University Press, 2016), 13. O'Collins writes: "Thus, revelation as a person-to-person, I-Thou encounter between God and human beings gives rise to true propositions.... *Dei Verbum* makes it abundantly clear that revelation means *primarily* God's personal self-revelation (*DV* 1–4). But that carries with it the conviction that, *secondarily*, the divine revelation discloses something *about* God and human beings." While both O'Collins and Soloveitchik offer a twofold account of revelation, the former emphasizes the communication of "true propositions," whereas the latter emphasizes the communication of the "divine imperative." The term "divine imperative" occurs in "Confrontation," 13, 18, & 22, and in "The Lonely Man of Faith," 39, 43–45, & 64.

in the "cultural enterprise of the rest of humanity," directing their attention to "the *secular orders with which men of faith come face to face;*"[26] and the "personal confrontation" in which Jews and Christians "*face each other* in the full knowledge of their distinctness and individuality."[27] But these three encounters do not occur in silence. At the heart of Soloveitchik's understanding of revelation – the face-to-face encounter between the 'finite "I"' and the "infinite He" – is the "divine normative *summons*" to which one is called to *respond* and which "forms the very core of [one's] new existential status as a confronted being."[28] Speech figures prominently in Soloveitchik's treatment of Jewish-Christian encounter. His characterization of the word as a "paradoxical instrument of communication" in Part I of "Confrontation" anticipates and parallels his distinction between the "cosmic confrontation" and the "personal confrontation" in Part II. The word serves both as a "medium of expressing agreement and concurrence, of reaching mutual understanding, organizing cooperative effort, and uniting action" and as a "means of manifesting distinctness, emphasizing incongruity, and underlining separateness."[29] It thus emerges that Jewish-Christian confrontation is a dialogical encounter that permits through the mediation of the spoken word both the organization of "cooperative effort" in response to common challenges and the manifestation of the "distinctiveness and individuality" of the Jewish and Christian faith traditions. In the remaining paragraphs, I want to look more closely at the following three items.

1. Soloveitchik's account of Jewish-Christian dialogue has two distinct aspects, one focusing on cooperation in response to "socio-cultural and moral problems" and the other on face-to-face encounters between persons of different faith traditions. This reading represents a departure from interpretations that limit a Jewish-Christian encounter to involvement in the "public world of

26. "Confrontation," 19 & 24 (emphasis supplied).
27. Ibid., 20 (emphasis supplied).
28. "Confrontation," 13. Cf. Novak, *Jewish-Christian Dialogue*, 145–148, for discussion on "The Primacy of Hearing in Scriptural Morality."
29. Ibid., 14–15.

humanitarian and cultural endeavors." Daniel Rynhold, for instance, argues that the "most important implication of Soloveitchik's approach is that dialogue between Jews and Christians can *only* take place at a level where we share common ethical or social concerns, i.e., where we can find common denominators."[30] Interpretations of this kind acknowledge Jewish-Christian involvement in what Soloveitchik calls the "cosmic confrontation" but neglect "the second personal confrontation of two faith communities, each aware of both what it shares with the other and what is singularly its own."[31]

2. Soloveitchik's twofold approach to Jewish-Christian dialogue reflects the argument and structure of "Confrontation;" and it is consistent with his guidelines on Jewish-Christian dialogue, according to which "discussion of social with moral problems" is encouraged but "debate ... on dogmatic and theological subjects" is discouraged.[32] It is important, of course, not to conflate so-called "theological dialogue" and "personal confrontation." The former transforms the "private" in religion into an *object* for discussion. It fails to appreciate that theological topics such as "Judaic monotheism and the Christian idea of Trinity" or "The concept of Covenant in Judaism and Christianity" reflect a faith community's "personal relationship" to God.[33] In contrast, the "personal confrontation" attends to the "singularity and otherness" of the faith traditions participating in the dialogue.[34] It recognizes that their respective theological *logoi* reflect "the strangeness of the act of faith of a particular community which is totally incomprehensible to the man of a different faith community."[35] In other words, it will emerge that the

---

30. Daniel Rynhold, "The Philosophical Foundations of Soloveitchik's Critique of Interfaith Dialogue," *Harvard Theological Review* 96 / 1 (2003): 105 (emphasis supplied).

31. "Confrontation," 20.

32. "On RCA Participation in an Interreligious Conference," 267.

33. "On Interfaith Relationships," 259–260.

34. "Confrontation," 18.

35. Ibid., 23–24. Soloveitchik's argument at this point in "Confrontation" implies a correlation between the "word of faith" and the underlying "apocalyptic experience." Soloveitchik's discussion of the "objectification process" and "reconstruction" or "retrospective analysis" in *The Halakhic Mind* (New York: Seth

incommensurability of the Jewish and Christian *words of faith* does not preclude dialogue but is integral to it.

3. In the opening paragraph, I turned to the Orthodox Rabbinic Statement on Christianity *To Do the Will of Our Father in Heaven* in order to draw attention to how much is at stake in Jewish-Christian dialogue – its failure during the Weimar period contributed to what Soloveitchik calls the "destruction of the world" and its reversion to "chaos and void."[36] The concluding paragraphs of this essay return to *To Do the Will of Our Father in Heaven.* Not only do I claim that Soloveitchik anticipates the Statement's call that "Jews and Christians must work together as partners to address the moral challenges of our era."[37] But I also argue that Soloveitchik provides an important perspective on the Statement's insistence that Jewish-Christian partnership "in no way minimizes the ongoing differences between

Press, 1986) provides the philosophical background. "Religion, which is perhaps more deeply rooted in subjectivity than any other manifestation of the spirit, is also *reflected* in externalized phenomena which are evolved in the objectification process of the religious consciousness. The aggregate of religious objective constructs is comprised of ethico-religious norms, rituals, dogmas, theoretical postulates, etc" (67, emphasis supplied). Cf. "The Lonely Man of Faith," 38, "Any encounter with God, if it is to redeem man, must be crystallized and *objectified* in a normative ethico-moral message" (emphasis supplied). Retrospective analysis is an interpretative approach that seeks to reconstruct the "underlying subjective aspects" proper to the aggregate of "religious objective constructs" under consideration. "Reconstruction," writes Soloveitchik in *The Halakhic Mind*, "a dominant methodological principle in philosophy, must be applied in the religious domain. There is no direct approach to pure religious subjectivity. Objective forms must he postulated as a point of departure, and by moving in the minus direction, one may gradually reconstruct underlying subjective aspects" (81).

36. See *Halakhic Man*, 141, 152, 153, 156–157, & 163–164, for Soloveitchik's use of the language of the "reversion of creation to chaos" to describe the terrible events of the 1930s and 1940s in Europe. The phrase "reversion of creation to chaos" comes from Jon D. Levenson, *Creation and the Persistence of Evil: The Jewish Drama of Divine Omnipotence* (Princeton: Princeton University Press, 1994), 26. Cf. Paul Mendes-Flohr, "The Ambivalent Dialogue: Jewish-Christian Theological Encounter in the Weimar Republic," in *Divided Passions: Jewish Intellectuals and the Experience of Modernity* (Detroit: Wayne State University Press, 1991), 133–167. An important task remains situating Soloveitchik's contribution in relation to the practice of Jewish-Christian dialogue that emerged during the Weimar period.

37. *To Do the Will of Our Father in Heaven*, preamble.

the two communities and two religions."[38] Specifically, Soloveitchik's approach permits Jews and Christians alike to appreciate the
significance of irreducible theological differences in the context of
Jewish-Christian encounter – differences that bring to the fore the
uniqueness of both Judaism and Christianity.

1.

Jewish-Christian dialogue has a twofold character – cooperation in
response to issues of shared concern and acknowledgment of the
"singularity and otherness" of one another's faith traditions. Soloveitchik does not make this point in an oblique manner. On the contrary, he emphasizes it. "Involvement with the rest of mankind in the
cosmic confrontation," he writes, "does not, we must repeat, rule out
the second personal confrontation of two faith communities, each
aware of both what it shares with the other and what is singularly
its own."[39] Jews and Christians ought to participate in both sorts of
encounter, the "cosmic confrontation" and the "personal confrontation." In another place, Soloveitchik distinguishes between the
Jew's "covenantal uniqueness and his *additional mandate* to face
another faith community as a member of a different community
of the committed" on the one hand, and his "readiness to and ca-
pability of joining the cultural enterprise of the rest of humanity"
on the other.[40] A fuller picture of the "cosmic confrontation" and
the "personal confrontation" thus begins to emerge. The former
sees Jews and Christians participating in the "cultural enterprise of
the rest of humanity," the purpose of which is "exercising control"
over their environment in order to attain human dignity.[41] And the
latter brings to the fore the face-to-face encounter in which Jews
and Christians are each aware of what they share in common and

38. Ibid., paragraph 6.
39. "Confrontation," 20.
40. Ibid., 19. (Emphasis supplied)
41. "The Lonely Man of Faith," 13.

what is singularly their own. When Soloveitchik speaks of the Jew's "additional mandate to face another faith community as a member of a different community of the committed," he acknowledges the integrity of the faith commitment of the Christian involved in the "personal confrontation" – even as he emphasizes in other places the incommensurability of Jewish and Christian theological *logoi* and the uniqueness of their respective apocalyptic experiences.[42]

In the early pages of "The Lonely Man of Faith" – an essay that provides in Leora Batnitzky's words "a fuller explication of Soloveitchik's theological position in connection with his view of interfaith dialogue"[43] – Soloveitchik considers the challenges that persons of faith face in contemporary society. He insists that these challenges be understood in relation to the "the scheme of events and things willed and approved by God, when He ordered finitude to emerge out of infinity and the Universe, including man, to unfold itself."[44] The contours of Soloveitchik's argument in "The Lonely Man of Faith" are well-known. Briefly, he educes from Genesis 1 the *practical* figure of Adam the first, who seeks "to harness and dominate elemental forces and put them at his disposal" in order to achieve a dignified life, which involves exercise of the "freedom of action" necessary to fulfill one's commitments and discharge one's responsibilities.[45] And he derives from Genesis 2 the *religious* figure of Adam the second. At the outset "The Lonely Man of Faith" emphasizes the "cosmic experience" – the "awesome dichotomy of God's involvement in the drama of creation, and His exaltedness above and remoteness from this very drama."[46] But this gives way to the "apocalyptic-covenantal encounter" between man and God. In the midst of crisis, the "finite 'I' meets the infinite He 'face to face;'" receives a "normative ethico-moral message;" becomes aware of "his

---

42. "Confrontation," 20 & 23.
43. Leora Batnitzky, in "Dialogue as Judgment, Not Mutual Affirmation: A New Look at Franz Rosenzweig's Dialogical Philosophy," *The Journal of Religion* 79/4 (October 1999): 539–540.
44. "The Lonely Man of Faith," 9.
45. Ibid., 12–14.
46. Ibid., 31.

exclusiveness and ontological incompatibility;" and finds redemption in the face-to-face dialogical encounter with the other, who is
"as unique and singular as he."[47] Of course, Adam the first and Adam
the second are not individuals *per se* but represent different aspects
of the human person.[48] Our modern world, according to Soloveitchik, evinces the diremption of these two orientations, privileging
the practical at the expense of the religious.[49]

Discussion of the convergences and divergences between "Confrontation" and "The Lonely Man of Faith" remains an important
task – one can see that the "cosmic confrontation" brings us into the
vicinity of Adam the first ("dimension of culture") and the "personal
confrontation" into the vicinity of Adam the second ("dimension of
faith"). But for our purposes, it is enough to note that Soloveitchik
situates the question of Jewish-Christian dialogue in relation to "the
scheme of events and things willed and approved by God." One of
the implications is that participating in the "cosmic confrontation"
and the "personal confrontation" is in keeping with the will of Our
Father in Heaven. Consider the following passage from Part II of
"Confrontation:"

> In the same manner as Adam and Eve confronted and at-
> tempted to subdue a malicious scoffing nature and yet nev-
> ertheless encountered each other as two separate individuals
> cognizant of their incommensurability and uniqueness, so also
> two faith communities which coordinate their efforts when
> confronted by the cosmic order may face each other in the full
> knowledge of their distinctness and individuality.[50]

47. Ibid., 25–26 & 33.
48. Ibid., 54. "In every one of us abide two *personae* – the creative majestic
Adam the first, and the submissive, humble Adam the second."
49. See, for instance, "The Lonely Man of Faith," 56. "Contemporary Adam
the first, extremely successful in his cosmic-majestic enterprise, refuses to pay
earnest heed to the duality in man and tries to deny the undeniable, that another
Adam exists beside or, rather, in him. By rejecting Adam the second, contemporary man, *eo ipso*, dismisses the covenantal faith community as something
superfluous and obsolete."
50. "Confrontation," 20.

This sentence accomplishes a number of things. It sets the question of Jewish-Christian dialogue within a biblical frame of reference. It establishes a parallelism between Adam and Eve's twofold confrontation – cooperation in subduing the environment and awareness of one another's "incommensurability and uniqueness" – and the twofold confrontation between Jews and Christians. It thus returns us to the distinction between the "cosmic confrontation" and the "personal confrontation," encouraging Jews and Christians to "coordinate their efforts when confronted by the cosmic order" and "to face each other in full knowledge of their distinctness and individuality." In his discussion of "Confrontation," Meir Soloveichik takes issue with the assumption that his uncle's work represents Christians not as members of a distinct faith community "engaged in singular normative gesture reflecting the numinous nature of the act of faith itself" but simply as "human beings, descendants of Adam, enjoined to work together [with Jews] for the welfare of the world."[51] In the passage from "Confrontation" that appeared earlier in this paragraph, Soloveitchik is explicit. He refers to "two faith communities" – Knesset Israel and the Church – both of which are *mandated* to participate in a twofold confrontation.[52]

2.

Soloveitchik's twofold approach to Jewish-Christian dialogue reflects the argument and structure of "Confrontation." Soloveitchik's essay is divided into two parts. Part I develops an anthropology through a theologico-philosophical reading of the second chapter of Genesis, claiming that the "[b]iblical account of the creation of

---

51. Ibid., 18–19, and Meir Soloveichik, "A Nation Under God," 324, respectively. At this point in "Confrontation," Soloveitchik insists that "Jewish identity ... can only be understood under the aspect of singularity and otherness;" then, in the next sentence, he states that there can be "no identity without uniqueness;" he goes on to speak of "two faith communities" as "individual entities" (18).

52. See "Confrontation," 13, 17, 19, & 20, for Soloveitchik's use of the language of mandate.

man portrays him at three progressive levels."[53] Part II situates the question of Jewish-Christian dialogue in relation to this tripartite anthropology. Jewish-Christian cooperation in the "cosmic confrontation" occurs at the second level, and the face-to-face "personal confrontation" at the third level.

Level one evinces a twofold deprivation: indistinction between oneself and the environment, whether cultural or natural, and irresponsiveness to the "divine normative summons."[54] One is not "existentially different" from the world within which one finds oneself.[55] Religious communities that fail to differentiate themselves from the reigning "cultural matrix" can be said to be non-confronted – communities whose members feel "no need to live a normative life and to find redemption in surrender to a higher moral will," craving instead "boundless aesthetic experience" and submergence in the "general order of things and events."[56] Such a life is neither dignified nor redeemed.

Level two has two distinct moments. On the one hand, no longer submerged within but now standing over against the "mysterious domain of things and events,"[57] one struggles to master the condi-

53. Ibid., 5.
54. Ibid., 18.
55. The phrase "existentially different" occurs in "Confrontation," 17.
56. "Confrontation," 5 & 7. Later in this same essay, 9, Soloveitchik writes: "Paradisical man, violating the divine commandment by eating from the tree of knowledge, suspended the ethical and replaced it with the aesthetic experience (*Guide of the Perplexed*, 1,2)." In "The Lonely Man of Faith," 63–64, one reads: "Western man is in a nostalgic mood, he is determined not to accept the dialectical burden of humanity. . . . He is desirous of an aesthetic experience rather than a covenantal one, of a social ethos rather than a divine imperative." See the sixth chapter, "The Tree of Knowledge and the Emergence of Sin," of *The Emergence of Ethical Man*, ed. Michael S. Berger (Jersey City: Ktav Publishing House, 2005), 95–128, where Soloveitchik discusses in more detail the theme of the destruction of the "ethical norm" in favor of aesthetic experience. Cf. *Halakhic Man*, 153, "The freedom of halakhic man refers not to the creation of the law itself, for it was given to him by the Almighty, but to the realization of the norm in the concrete world. The freedom which is rooted in the creation of the norm has brought chaos and disorder to the world. The freedom of realizing the norm brings holiness to the world."
57. "Confrontation," 9. "He discovers an awesome and mysterious domain of things and events which is independent of and disobedient to him, an objective

tions of one's existence in order to achieve a dignified life. On the other hand, "estranged from nature" and facing almost overwhelming challenges, one encounters God.[58] "'And the Lord God commanded the man.' The divine imperative burst forth out of infinity and overpowered finite man."[59] Agency and patiency find themselves conjoined at the second level of confrontation, which challenges humanity to lead a dignified-and-redeemed life. According to Soloveitchik, the emergence of I-awareness goes hand-in-hand with the experience of being "limited and opposed by a non-I outside," and awareness of one's singularity with the reception of the divine norm. "With the birth of the norm," writes Soloveitchik, "man becomes aware of his singularly human existence."[60] The implications of this statement are far-reaching, suggesting, for instance, that one moves towards one's proper humanity through responding to the "divine normative summons."[61] As Gilbert Meilaender observes, "Human beings have been created for covenant community with God."[62]

Turning to Jewish-Christian dialogue, cooperation in the "cosmic confrontation" represents the first moment of confrontation at the second level; and the second moment attends to the reality of revelation, without which one could not speak of the uniqueness of Judaism or Christianity. Soloveitchik would surely agree with David Novak that "one must recognize that Judaism is ... a singularity because of revelation," for it is "the Torah that makes Judaism stand out from anything else in the human background."[63] Similarly, one can also speak of the "singularity" of Christianity because of revelation – the incarnation, crucifixion, and resurrection of Christ Jesus. As the Roman Catholic philosopher and theologian Bernard Lonergan puts it, "What distinguishes the Christian ... is not God's

---

order limiting the exercise of his power and offering opposition to him."
  58. Ibid., 13.
  59. Ibid., 12–13.
  60. Ibid., 9.
  61. Ibid., 13.
  62. Gilbert Meilaender, *Neither Beast nor God: The Dignity of the Human Person* (New York: New Atlantis Books, 2009), 18.
  63. Novak, *Jewish-Christian Dialogue*, 129.

grace, which he shares with others, but the mediation of God's grace through Jesus Christ our Lord."⁶⁴ One of the questions that Soloveitchik's reflections on Jewish-Christian dialogue raise for both Jewish and Christian theologians concerns the significance of the *distinctiveness* of Judaism and Christianity within the context of dialogical encounter.

Throughout his writings, Soloveitchik considers the reality of revelation from a number of different angles. In the early pages of *And From There You Shall Seek*, for instance, he stresses that "God's revelation in times of crisis, from the depths of despair and distress, is a basic principle of Judaism." "God reveals himself to man," continues Soloveitchik, "to command him and to give him the responsibility for keeping laws and statutes, positive and negative commandments."⁶⁵ It is here that one locates Soloveitchik's phenomenology of revelation.⁶⁶ However, when Soloveitchik describes the "singular"

64. Bernard Lonergan, "Future of Christianity," in *Second Collection: Papers by Bernard J. F. Lonergan, S. J.*, ed. William F. J. Ryan and Bernard J. Tyrell (Toronto: University of Toronto Press, 1996), 156. See Frederick E. Crowe, *Christ and History: The Christology of Bernard Lonergan from 1935–1982* (Toronto: University of Toronto Press, 2015), 213–214, for discussion of this passage. Crowe insists that Lonergan's sentences do *not* imply that "Christ [is] the mediator of grace for Christians only," whereas I maintain that Lonergan's comments on Christian distinctiveness can be read otherwise, and this by bringing them into conversation with Soloveitchik on the uniqueness of faith communities in the plural and the significance of such uniqueness in the context of dialogical encounter.

65. Joseph B. Soloveitchik, *And From There You Shall Seek*, trans. Naomi Goldblum (Jersey City: Ktav Publishing House, 2008), 33 & 35.

66. Cf. David Novak, "Heschel and Revelation," in *Tradition in the Public Square: A David Novak Reader*, ed. Randi Rashkover and Martin Kavka (Grand Rapids: William B. Eerdmans Publishing Company, 2008), 39. "Soloveitchik's *Ish Ha-halakhah* is an ideal construction of the mind-set of the exemplary *ba'al ha-halakhah*, but it is not a phenomenology of the revelation that originally made such a mind-set possible." However, one finds such a phenomenology in Soloveitchik's treatment of the reception of the "divine normative summons" in the midst of "despair and distress." The phrase "divine normative summons" occurs in "Confrontation," 13. Note that Randi Rashkover, in "Jewish Responses to Jewish-Christian Dialogue: A Look Ahead to the Twenty-First Century," *Cross Currents* 50 / 1–2 (Spring 2000): 216–217, argues that "the conditions of the possibility of revelation for both Jews and Christians derives not from a secure sense of an ordered morality but rather from a common experience of crisis in our created order – a common sense of finitude or human limitation." Rashkover

ontological attitude of *halakhic* man, it is not the initial reception of the "divine normative summons" that receives emphasis but the "blending of the obligation with self-consciousness, a merging of the norm with the individual, and a union of an outside command with the inner will and conscience of man."[67] In "Confrontation" and "The Lonely Man of Faith," Soloveitchik's treatment of revelation moves in a somewhat different direction. Revelation occurs in the "depth of crisis and failure;" and human singularity emerges with the reception of the divine norm. But instead of examining the process according to which the union of commandment and conscience occurs, Soloveitchik emphasizes that awareness of one's uniqueness brings with it a mood of deep-seated loneliness and existential insecurity, which serves as the precondition for the face-to-face encounter between Adam and Eve. As one reads in "The Lonely Man of Faith," "if Adam is to bring his *quest for redemption* to full realization, he must initiate action leading to the discovery of a companion who, even though as unique and singular as he, will master the art of communicating and, with him, form a community."[68] This same theme of "communicating and communing" occurs in "Confrontation."[69] Soloveitchik describes the "personal confrontation" in terms of "the difficult dialectical art of [*ezer kenegdo*] – of being one with and, at the same time, different from his human confronter."[70] Given

concludes her essay with an examination of the "phenomenology of revelation" in Soloveitchik's "The Lonely Man of Faith" (218–219).

67. Soloveitchik, *Halakhic Man*, 40 & 65. Cf. *Maimonides – Between Philosophy and Halakhah*, 116, where Soloveitchik states that "[t]he Normative-Halakhic experience is a categorical imperative, while in the Mystical-Ecstatic experience, the normative and the intellectual blend; the norm is converted into part of my personality, into a principle of existence."

68. "The Lonely Man of Faith," 26. (emphasis supplied)

69. The phrase "communicating and communing" appears in "Confrontation," 16, and "The Lonely Man of Faith," 26.

70. "Confrontation," 16. The phrase "personal confrontation" appears three times in "Confrontation," twice in regard to the Adam-Eve encounter (16) and once in regard to the Jewish-Christian encounter (20). The earlier references contrast the Adam-Eve encounter with modern man's tendency "to dominate and subordinate" the other rather than communicate and commune with him or her. Soloveitchik uses similar language to describe the Christian tendency to view Judaism as "an object of observation, judgment and evaluation." Indeed, this is one

the parallelism that Soloveitchik establishes between the Adam-Eve encounter and the Jewish-Christian one, his treatment of the "art of communicating" raises the question of the redemptive character of Jewish-Christian dialogue. Eugene Korn moves the discussion in this very direction, commenting that the "third level [of confrontation] is redemptive existence" and then arguing that Part I of "Confrontation" can well be read as "a skillful attempt at inviting the Church to ascend to the third level of existence," indeed, as a demand that Christians no longer treat "Jews as objects of contempt" but recognize them as "fully dignified subjects."[71]

Level three turns to the face-to-face encounter. "This confrontation," writes Soloveitchik, "is reciprocal, not unilateral. This time the two confronters stand alongside each other, each admitting the existence of the other.... After gazing at each other in silence and defiance, the two individuals involved in a unique encounter begin to communicate with each other."[72] The "word" that the two individuals speak accomplishes two things. It serves as a "medium for organizing cooperative effort," so crucial to the "cosmic confrontation;" and it serves as a "means of manifesting distinctness, emphasizing incongruity, and underlining separateness." It "brings out not only what is common in two existences but the singularity and uniqueness of each existence as well."[73] This is precisely what happens during the "personal confrontation" in which Jews and

---

of the reasons Soloveitchik opposed Jewish involvement in Vatican II. "Such an encounter," writes Soloveitchik, "would convert the personal Adam-Eve meeting into a hostile confrontation between a subject-knower and a knowable object. We do not intend to play the part of the object encountered by dominating man" (21). One possible implication is that Soloveitchik could well meet with Christians if they showed themselves willing to practice the "dialectical art of [*ezer kenegdo*]," which occurs at the third level of confrontation. It is one thing for Christians to evaluate Judaism; it is another thing for Christians to evaluate their perception of Judaism, an exercise that brings the theme of repentance to the fore.

71. Eugene Korn, "The Man of Faith and Religious Dialogue: Revisiting 'Confrontation,'" *Modern Judaism* 25/2 (2005): 308. The question of the redemptive dimension of Jewish-Christian dialogue is one that I will leave for another time.

72. "Confrontation," 14.

73. Ibid., 14.

Christians become aware of what they share in common and what is singularly their own. The claim that Soloveitchik develops an account of Jewish-Christian dialogue that focuses on cooperation and face-to-face encounter is not meant to diminish the importance of his guidelines on permissible and impermissible approaches to such dialogue. One reads in "On Interfaith Relationships:"

> We are, therefore, opposed to any public debate, dialogue or symposium concerning the doctrinal, dogmatic or ritual aspects of our faith vis-à-vis "similar" aspects of another faith community.[74]
>
> We are ready to enter into dialogue on such topics as War and Peace, Poverty, Freedom, Man's Moral Values, the Threat of Secularism, Technology and Human Values, Civil Rights, etc., which revolve around the spiritual aspects of our civilization. Discussion of these areas will, of course, be within the framework of our religious outlooks and terminology.[75]

Soloveitchik's guidelines are clear. He discourages "public debate ... on the doctrinal, dogmatic or ritual aspects of [the Jewish] faith" because they reflect the "intimate relationship" that prevails between Israel and God – a relationship that cannot be understood across the abyss of religious difference.[76] But Soloveitchik encourages "dialogue on ... the spiritual aspects of our civilization" and believes that Jews and Christians should cooperate in addressing issues of common concern. Jürgen Habermas observes that human beings "enter into interpersonal relationships in order to cope, through cooperation, with the contingencies of the objective world." Such relationships have a "triadic" structure.[77] They focus on what

74. "On Interfaith Relationships," 259–260.
75. Ibid., 260–261.
76. Ibid., 259–260.
77. Jürgen Habermas, "A Philosophy of Dialogue," in *Dialogue as a Trans-disciplinary Concept: Martin Buber's Philosophy of Dialogue and Its Contemporary Reception*, ed. Paul Mendes-Flohr (Berlin: De Gruyter, 2015), 12–13.

the Protestant theologian H. Richard Niebuhr calls the "common third," that is, on "some object with which and about which we communicate."[78] When the "common third" is "socio-cultural and moral problems," Jewish-Christian dialogue is permitted. But when the "common third" is "dogmatic and theological subjects," which reflect "the numinous character and strangeness of the act of faith of a particular community," it is not permitted.[79] Jewish-Christian dialogue on "social and moral problems" is nothing other than participation in the "cosmic confrontation." It involves translating "aspects of the doctrinal and normative covenantal kerygma of faith" into cultural-pragmatic terms and bringing one's particular perspective and language to bear on "socio-cultural and moral problems."[80] It is important not to conflate "debate . . . on dogmatic and theological subjects" with the "personal confrontation." The former converts the "private" in religion into an *object* for discussion and thereby avoids the face-to-face encounter proper to the "personal confrontation."

Despite the clarity of Soloveitchik's guidelines, it is not always easy to determine when a topic is an appropriate object of Jewish-Christian dialogue and when it is not. In "On Interfaith Relationships," Soloveitchik lists a number of items concerning which it would be "improper" to enter into dialogue. One of them is "The Concept of the Covenant in Judaism and Christianity." Insofar as the Jewish or Christian conception of covenant reflects the "personal relationship to God" proper to one's faith community, it should not be the object of "public debate."[81] This does not mean, however, that Soloveitchik would discourage discussion of the "historico-cultural aspect" of the notion of covenant.[82] Consider Niebuhr's classic essay

---

78. H. Richard Niebuhr, *Faith on Earth: An Inquiry into the Structure of Human Faith*, ed. Richard R. Niebuhr (New Haven: Yale University Press, 1989), 46–47.

79. "On Interfaith Relationships," 260, and "Confrontation," 23.

80. "The Lonely Man of Faith," 57, and "On Interfaith Relationships," 261.

81. "On Interfaith Relationships," 259–260.

82. See "Confrontation," 21–22. "People confuse two concepts when they speak of a common tradition uniting two faith communities such as the Christian and the Judaic. This term may have relevance *if one looks upon a faith community under an historico-cultural aspect* and interprets its relationship to another faith

"The Idea of Covenant and American Democracy" and his claim that "a fundamental pattern in American minds in the seventeenth, eighteenth and early nineteenth centuries was the covenant idea."[83] From Soloveitchik's perspective, the idea of covenant in the early American social imaginary could well serve as an example of the translation of a theological topic into a particular cultural idiom. *Soloveitchik's guidelines do not preclude inter-religious dialogue on the "doctrinal and normative covenantal kerygma of faith" once it has been translated into the cultural vernacular.*[84] As Irving Greenberg puts it, while "Confrontation" may seem to prohibit Jewish-Christian dialogue, the essay in fact "opened the door to significant areas of joint learning and exchange."[85]

In addition to listing items that should be avoided, Soloveitchik provides examples of topics that should figure in Jewish-Christian dialogue. One of them concerns the meaning and value of freedom.[86] Niebuhr notes that "in the covenant conception the essence

community in sociological, human, categories describing the unfolding of the creative consciousness of man" (emphasis supplied). On the "historico-cultural aspect" of the idea of covenant, see Daniel J. Elazar's four volume work *The Covenant Tradition in Politics* (New Brunswick: Transaction Publishers, 1995, 1996, & 1998).

83. H. Richard Niebuhr, "The Idea of Covenant and American Democracy," *Church History* 23/2 (June 1954): 130.

84. Cf. Joseph B. Soloveitchik, *The Halakhic Mind*, 52. "Regardless of the shortcomings of pragmatism as a solution to our most perplexing epistemological problems, it is nevertheless advisable to apply, at times, the pragmatic principle to the appraisal of certain philosophical theories.... The ethical implications of any philosophical theory, as to its beneficence or detriment to the moral advancement of man, should many a time decide the worth of the doctrine." The same applies, I think, to the appraisal of the kerygma of faith that has been translated into the commonsense language of culture. The crucial question is the degree to which such translation contributes to the advancement of the cause of human dignity and the integrity of creation.

85. Irving Greenberg, "On the Road to Encounter between Judaism and Christianity: A Personal Journey," in *For the Sake of Heaven and Earth: The New Encounter between Judaism and Christianity* (Philadelphia: The Jewish Publication Society, 2004), 13–14. Provocatively, Greenberg adds that "Confrontation" ought to be viewed as a piece of "Marrano writing;" that is, "the surface words conveyed one message while the substantive depths expressed a very different meaning."

86. "On Interfaith Relations," 261.

of freedom does not lie in the liberty of choice among goods, but in the ability to commit oneself for the future to a cause."[87] Again, from Soloveitchik's perspective, Niebuhr's covenantal conception of freedom could well serve as an example of situating a topic pertaining to the "spiritual aspects of our civilization" within a particular religious framework. Niebuhr's outlook and terminology are decidedly Christian in character; but because they reflect the "universal and public ... in religion," they do not fall under Soloveitchik's prohibition. Indeed, according to Niebuhr, the capacity to commit oneself to a cause – for instance, to that of human dignity – is a sign of "mature selfhood" that goes to the heart of his Christian moral philosophy.[88] There is nothing in Soloveitchik's guidelines that would discourage engagement with Niebuhr's philosophy or with theologically informed approaches to the question of freedom that Christians may want to bring into the public square, for instance, during a time of democratic decline.[89]

Still, Jewish-Christian dialogue on "socio-cultural and moral problems," even when set within the "framework of our religious outlooks and terminology," should not become an occasion to lose sight of the significance of the "distinctness and individuality" of Judaism and Christianity. In his discussion of the genesis of *Nos-*

---

87. Niebuhr, "The Idea of Covenant," 133.

88. See H. Richard Niebuhr, *The Responsible Self: An Essay in Christian Moral Philosophy* (Louisville: Westminister John Knox Press, 1999).

89. It is worth noting that in the present context, Soloveitchik's distinction between Adam the first and Adam the second in "The Lonely Man of Faith" reflects sustained engagement with Karl Barth's treatment of covenant in *The Doctrine of Creation*, III.1, *Church Dogmatics*, trans. J. W. Edwards, O. Bussey, and H. Knight, ed. G. W. Bromiley and T. F. Torrance (London: T & T Clark International, 2004). See Gerald J. (Ya'akov) Blidstein, "Biblical Models," in *Society and Self: On the Writings of Rabbi Joseph. B. Soloveitchik* (New York: Orthodox Union Press, 2012), 73–75; and Alan Brill, "Elements of Dialectical Theology in Rabbi Soloveitchik's View of Torah Study," in *Study and Knowledge in Jewish Thought*, ed. Howard Kreisel (Beersheva: Ben-Gurion University of the Negev Press, 2006), 265–296. Commenting on "Confrontation" in "The Man of Faith and Religious Dialogue," 294, Korn remarks that "Alan Brill has demonstrated that [Soloveitchik's] *philosophic argument* is indebted to Karl Barth's dialectic theology as explicated in *Church Dogmatics. As such it would be resonant with a Christian theological audience*" (emphasis supplied).

tra Aetate, Thomas Stransky, a Paulist Father who served on the Secretariat for Christian Unity and contributed to the drafting of *Nostra Aetate,* summarizes Soloveitchik's guidelines, which were well-known to members of the Secretariat. Soloveitchik "opposed Jewish-Christian theological-religious dialogue," writes Stransky, and thus "the direct involvement and presence of Jews at a Catholic Council which would obviously highlight religion and theology;" but Soloveitchik "did *not* object to Jewish-Christian cooperation on societal issues of modernity."[90]

But Stransky does more than summarize Soloveitchik's position. He attends to Soloveitchik's reasons for discouraging "theological-religious dialogue." "Rabbi Soloveitchik," continues Stransky, "argued that the abyss between synagogue and church was too wide and too deep. Theological conversation encouraged false bridges, fake facades of supposed religious common ground foundations."[91] The phrase "abyss between synagogue and church" is especially striking. Initially, one might assume that it means that the distance between Knesset Israel and the Church itself is the problem; if this were the case, devising ways of bridging the gap would seem a fitting course of action. But such an approach – the construction of "false bridges" and "fake facades" – is not in keeping with acknowledgment of the "distinctness and individuality" of the Jewish and Christian faith communities. Gerald Blidstein suggests that Soloveitchik's comments on the distance between Judaism and Christianity are a form of veiled critique. He notes that Soloveitchik "discusses Christianity without touching on its status as a monotheistic religion" but then speculates that Soloveitchik's "emphasis on the unbridgeable gap" between Judaism and Christianity is "effectively equivalent

90. Thomas Stransky, "The Genesis of *Nostra Aetate*: An Insider's Story," in Nostra Aetate: *Origins, Promulgation, Impact on Jewish-Catholic Relations,* ed. Neville Landman and Alberto Melloni (Berlin: Verlag, 2007), 38.

91. Ibid., 38. Stransky continues: "Differences would be downplayed to underscore commonality and thus result in intellectual perversion. Even if Jews and Christians share some theological terms, they do not share their historically developed meanings." Nor do they share the apocalyptic experiences that are reflected in their respective theological *logoi*.

to tarring Christianity with the brush of idolatry." In other words, Blidstein is claiming that Soloveitchik is putting in question Christianity's "status as a monotheistic religion."[92] In contrast, however, I think something more salutary is at work. The image of distance is not meant to suggest the idolatrous nature of Christianity. It does not seek to transform Christianity into an object of evaluation, interpreting it against the "backdrop" of a non-Christian frame of reference.[93] Instead, the language of *metaphysical distance* is another way of acknowledging the "distinctness and individuality" of Judaism and Christianity. In other words, Stransky's reference to the "abyss between synagogue and church" needs to be read against the "backdrop" of Soloveitchik's treatment of confrontation at the third level.

"In each to whom I relate as a human being," writes Soloveitchik, "I find a friend, for we have many things in common, as well as a stranger, for each of us is unique and wholly other." Certainly, Jews and Christians relate to one another as human beings; but, in Paul Mendes-Flohr's words, "their humanity is refracted through the particularity of their community of faith."[94] It is precisely the revelation of the Torah and its embodiment in the life and words of one's Jewish dialogue partner that permits the Christian to acknowledge the uniqueness of the Jew's faith commitment. As Philip Cunningham puts it, there is a "deepening love for the distinctiveness of the Jewish or Christian other because of their edifying ways of walking with God."[95] The "irresolvable differences" between Judaism and

92. Blidstein, "Letters on Public Affairs," in *Society and Self*, 50.

93. Cf. "Confrontation," 21. "We are not ready for, a meeting with another faith community in which we shall become an object of observation, judgment and evaluation." Appended to "Confrontation," 28–29, is the 1964 Statement of the Rabbinical Council of America. It includes the following: "Any suggestion that the historical and meta-historical worth of a faith community be viewed against the backdrop of another faith" is "incongruous with the fundamentals of religious liberty and freedom of conscience."

94. Paul Mendes-Flohr, "Reflections on the Promise and Limitations of Interfaith Dialogue," *European Judaism* 46/1 (Spring 2013): 5.

95. Philip A. Cunningham, *Seeking Shalom: The Journey to Right Relationship between Catholics and Jews* (Grand Rapids: William B. Eerdmans Publishing, 2015), 249.

Christianity thus become an occasion for reconciliation.[96] Soloveitchik continues: "This otherness stands in the way of complete mutual understanding. *The gap of uniqueness is too wide to be bridged.
Indeed, it is not a gap, it is an abyss.*"[97] The ever-growing awareness
of the distance between Judaism and Christianity – the deepening
attentiveness to the "abyss between synagogue and church" – becomes, as it were, a measure of the health of the relationship between Jews and Christians. "In fact," continues Soloveitchik, "the
closer two individuals get to know each other, the more aware they
become of the metaphysical distance separating them."[98] The same
holds true for members of two different faith communities.

3.

In a recent collection commemorating the fiftieth anniversary of
Nostra Aetate, whose promulgation in October 1965 inaugurated a
"revolution" in Jewish-Christian relations, Soloveitchik's name appears only twice and in a far from favorable light. He is presented as
an impediment to Jewish-Christian dialogue that requires circum-
vention. As the book's editor Gilbert Rosenthal puts it, "Even the
Orthodox Jewish community, which for many years had shunned
inter-religious conversation or theological discussions, in great part
due to the admonition of Rabbi Joseph B. Soloveitchik, has been
drawn in."[99] One indication of this shift is the 2015 Orthodox Rab-

96. See Mendes-Flohr, "The Ambivalent Dialogue," 155–159, for discussion on
the connection between theological differences and reconciliation. Commenting
on the failed dialogue between Martin Buber and Karl Ludwig Schmidt, which
took place January 14, 1933, "two weeks before Hitler's appointment as chancellor," Mendes-Flohr writes: 'The certitude in the "uniqueness" of their knowledge
of God, which for millennia has constituted a "profoundly divisive factor" between the Church and Israel, [Buber] suggested, may also be the very source of
their ultimate reconciliation' (151 & 156). Schmidt proved unresponsive to Buber's
entreaties.
97. "Confrontation," 15 (emphasis supplied).
98. Ibid., 18.
99. Gilbert S. Rosenthal, "Introduction," in *A Jubilee for All Time: The Copernican Revolution in Jewish-Christian Relations,* ed. Gilbert S. Rosenthal (Eugene,

binic Statement on Christianity *To Do the Will of Our Father in Heaven.* The document recognizes that "since the Second Vatican Council the official teachings of the Catholic Church about Judaism have changed fundamentally and irrevocably;" and it calls for Jewish-Christian partnership in response to the "moral challenges of our era."[100] But contrary to Rosenthal, whose comments reflect less a close reading of "Confrontation" than repetition of a certain "rejectionist line" of interpretation that was in circulation even before Soloveitchik's essay appeared in print,[101] I think that Soloveitchik anticipates this turn towards dialogue in segments of the Orthodox Jewish Community. I have suggested in earlier paragraphs that Soloveitchik encourages Jews and Christians to understand their relationship "within the scheme of events and things willed and approved by God, when He ordered finitude to emerge out of infinity and the Universe, including man, to unfold itself;" and I have emphasized Soloveitchik's insistence that members of the Jewish and Christian faith communities are mandated to participate in both the "cosmic confrontation" and the "personal confrontation," cooperating with one another in response to "socio-cultural and moral problems" and turning to one another in a face-to-face encounter that discloses what each faith community "shares with the other and what is singularly its own."[102]

One can readily see in the Orthodox Rabbinic Statement the contours of the "cosmic confrontation." But one can also find passages that move in the direction of the "personal confrontation." Consider the Statement's insistence that Jewish-Christian partnership "in no

---

Oregon: Pickwick Publications, 2015), xxvii.

100. *To Do the Will of Our Father in Heaven*, paragraph 3.

101. See Edward K. Kaplan, *Spiritual Radical: Abraham Joshua Heschel in America, 1940–1972* (New Haven: Yale University Press, 2007), 260–261; and Alexander Even-Chen and Ephraim Meir, *Between Heschel and Buber: A Comparative Study* (Boston: Academic Studies Press, 2012), 276–278. Commenting on Soloveitchik's and Abraham Joshua Heschel's different responses to Vatican II, Even-Chen and Meir draw on Kaplan's discussion, noting that "Soloveitchik argued for barriers between Jews and Christians, spearheading the rejectionist line of the Rabbinical Council of America."

102. "Confrontation," 30.

way minimizes the ongoing differences between the two communities and two religions."[103] Certainly, these words want to ensure
that Jewish-Christian dialogue not occasion the blurring of theological differences. But something else is moving forward as well.
The document continues: "In separating Judaism and Christianity,
God willed a separation between partners with significant theological differences, not a separation between enemies."[104] This sentence
suggests that God approves of these very differences, which reflect,
to borrow from Novak, the reality that "Judaism and Christianity
are themselves grounded originally and irrevocably in revelatory
events."[105] The "metaphysical distance" separating Judaism and
Christianity does not work against dialogue but is its precondition.
As Martin Buber puts it, "entering into relation" presupposes a
"primal setting at a distance." "Genuine conversation," he continues,
"and therefore every actual fulfillment of relation between men,
means acceptance of otherness."[106] In the context of Jewish-Chris-

103. *To Do the Will of Our Father in Heaven*, paragraph 3.
104. *To Do the Will of Our Father in Heaven*, paragraph 3.
105. Novak, *Jewish-Christian Dialogue*, 124. Novak continues: "Jews and
Christians cannot step out of [their respective revelatory events] to assume a
simple humanity and still be intimately related to God and their own faith communities."
106. Martin Buber, "Distance and Relation," in *Martin Buber on Psychology
and Psychotherapy: Essays, Letters, and Dialogues*, ed. Judith Buber Agassi and
trans. Ronald Gregor Smith (Syracuse: Syracuse University Press, 1999), 4 & 13.
See Shai Held, "Terumah #1: Being Present While Making Space Or, Two Meanings of Tzimtzum," in *The Heart of the Torah*, Volume 1, *Essays on the Weekly
Portions: Genesis and Exodus* (Philadelphia: The Jewish Publications Society,
2017), 187–189, for a discussion of Buber's "Distance and Relation" in relation to
Kabbalistic and Rabbinic understandings of *tzimtzum* – both of which figure in
Soloveitchik's writings. See, for instance, *Halakhic Man*, 53–55 & 107–109, and
"Thou Shouldst Enter the Covenant of the Lord," in *On Repentance*, expanded
edition, ed. Pinchus H. Peli (Jerusalem: Maggid Books, 2017), 129–130, for different but complementary applications of the Rabbinic understanding of *tzimtzum*. And see Soloveitchik, "The Community," *Tradition* 17/2 (1978): 15–16, for
Soloveitchik's treatment of the Kabbalistic understanding of *tzimtzum* in relation
to interpersonal encounter. In a passage that recalls themes from Soloveitchik's
lectures on Maimonides' *Guide* and from "The Lonely Man of Faith," one reads:
"Thus, we may suggest the following equation: creation = recognition = withdrawal = an act of sacrifice.... The same is true of man. If lonely man is to rise
from existential exclusiveness to existential all-inclusiveness, then the first thing

tian dialogue, the "acceptance of otherness" cannot be dissociated from the "incommensurate" revelations that lie at the heart of the lived realities of these two faith communities.[107] Without such acceptance, the face-to-face encounter between Jews and Christians cannot occur.

In his study of Lonergan's universalist approach to religion, Frederick Crowe writes, "suppose that God loves a slow-learning people enough to allow them long ages to learn what they have to learn, suppose that the destiny of the world religions is contingent on what we all learn and do."[108] One of the lessons Jews and Christians have had to learn involves the recognition of the integrity of one another's incommensurable faith commitments; another concerns, in Lonergan's own words, the challenge of assuming *shared responsibility* for "the world in which they live."[109] The tragedy is

he has to do is to recognize another existence. Of course, this recognition is, *eo ipso*, a sacrificial act, since the mere admission that a thou exists in addition to the I, is tantamount to [*tzimtzum*], self-limitation and self-contraction. A community is established the very moment I recognize the thou and extend greetings to the thou" (15, emphasis supplied). See Lawrence J. Kaplan's "Editor's Introduction" to Soloveitchik's *Maimonides*, 20–68, for an illuminating and systematic presentation of the shift from "existential exclusiveness to existential all-inclusiveness" in the context of Soloveitchik's reconstruction of Maimonides' ethics. Similar language also appears in "Confrontation," 15, and in "The Lonely Man of Faith," 25. In the former essay – in a passage we have already looked at – one reads: "In fact, the closer two individuals get to know each other, the more aware they become of the metaphysical distance separating them. *Each one exists in a singular manner, completely absorbed in his individual awareness which is egocentric and exclusive*" (emphasis supplied). Of course, such exclusiveness is the final word in neither interpersonal nor Jewish-Christian encounter. The question of the significance of "existential all-inclusiveness" in the context of Jewish-Christian dialogue remains an important one.

107. Cf. "Confrontation," 23, "However, when we shift the focus from the dimension of culture to that of faith ... the whole idea of a tradition of faiths and the continuum of *revealed doctrines which are by their very nature incommensurate and related to different frames of reference* is utterly absurd, unless one is ready to acquiesce to the Christian theological claim that Christianity has superseded Judaism." (emphasis supplied)

108. Frederick E. Crowe, "Lonergan's Universalist View of Religion," in *Developing the Lonergan Legacy: Historical, Theoretical, and Existential Themes*, ed. Michael Vertin (Toronto: University of Toronto Press, 2004), 141.

109. Lonergan, *Method in Theology*, 332.

that these lessons began to be taken to heart only after the world was reduced to "chaos and disorder" during the 1930s and 1940s.[110] "The dark and terrible shadow of the Shoah over Europe during the Nazi period led the Church to reflect anew on her bond with the Jewish people."[111] From Soloveitchik's perspective, the first step in mending this "bond" involves, in Stransky's words, acknowledging the "abyss between synagogue and church." Without such acknowledgment, "singularity and otherness" go missing from the dialogue. In the present context, one notes that Soloveitchik speaks of hesed – over-abundant loving-kindness – as a relationship that preserves alterity. "God's hesed," writes Soloveitchik in his lectures on Maimonides' *Guide*, "means that He lets others share in His existence though there is an ontic gap between Him and them," thereby ensuring that the "otherness" of his creation not be negated.[112] Not the construction of "supposed religious common ground foundations,"[113] but the practice of the ethical norm of hesed recognizes and preserves the "gap" between Jews and Christians – sharing with loving-kindness in one another's existence without losing sight of the uniqueness of one another's incommensurable covenantal commitments.

It has not been the aim of this paper to venture even the beginning of a theological interpretation of Vatican II. [114] Still, I do not think that one is on controversial ground to note that the promulgation of *Nostra Aetate* represents a crucial moment of conversion in the life

110. See *Halakhic Man*, 153.
111. "'The Gifts and the Calling of God are Irrevocable" (Romans 11:29): A Reflection on Theological Questions Pertaining to Catholic-Jewish Relations on the Occasion of the 50th Anniversary of "Nostra Aetate,'" chapter 1.1, http://www .vatican.va/roman_curia/pontifical_councils/chrstuni/relations-jews-docs/rc _pc_chrstuni_doc_20151210_ebraismo-nostra-aetate_en.html.
112. Soloveitchik, *Maimonides*, 177–178.
113. Stransky, "The Genesis of *Nostra Aetate*," 38.
114. See Karl Rahner, "Towards a Fundamental Theological Interpretation of Vatican II," *Theological Studies* (1979): 716–727; and John D. Dadosky, "Towards a Fundamental *Re*-Interpretation of Vatican II," *The Heythrop Journal* 49 (2008): 742–763 and "Has Vatican II been *Hermeneutered*? Recovering its Theological Achievements following Rahner and Lonergan," *Irish Theological Quarterly* 79/4 (2014): 327–349.

of the Church. To borrow from Lonergan, the Second Ecumenical Council marks the emergence of a "new horizon," which "comes out of the old by repudiating characteristic features" – features such as supersessionism, the charge of deicide, the teaching of contempt, and anti-Semitism. It represents the beginning of "a new sequence that keeps revealing ever greater depth and breadth and wealth,"[115] at the heart of which is the affirmation that the covenant between God and Israel is "irrevocable."[116] In "Acquittal and Purification," Soloveitchik states that "[t]hrough repentance of purification man is reborn and he gains a new heart, a renewed spirit, another outlook on life and different horizons."[117]

Johannes Cardinal Willebrands, who served as the Secretary on the Secretariat for Christian Unity during Vatican II, draws on these very words from Soloveitchik when discussing the theological significance of *Nostra Aetate*. Not only does this document represent an expression of remorse for the terrible history of Christian anti-Judaism, *Nostra Aetate* also marks a departure from the "path of sin." It serves as a harbinger of a transformed Christianity. "[T] he act of the council," continues Willebrands, "was a communal act that must bear fruit in all the members of the church."[118] It exceeds the scope of the present effort to discuss Lonergan's and Soloveitchik's respective accounts of conversion and repentance. I suspect, though, that both would agree that without God's grace such personal and communal transformation cannot occur and that an im-

---

115. Lonergan, *Method in Theology*, 223–224.

116. See Gavin D'Costa, *Catholic Doctrines on the Jewish People after Vatican II* (Oxford: Oxford University Press, 2019) for a discussion of this issue. D'Costa emphasizes that this affirmation includes post-biblical Rabbinic Judaism. "The full authority of the magisterium stands behind the biblical teaching that the covenant with biblical Israel, God's people, is irrevocable (Romans 11:29).... The magisterium in the past and some important doctors of the church, in a limited and contextual fashion, support a further doctrinal implication. The cultic religious rituals of Rabbinic Judaism are alive and life giving, not dead and deadening. They come from God" (188).

117. See Joseph B. Soloveitchik, "Acquittal and Purification," in *On Repentance*, 9.

118. Johannes Cardinal Willebrands, "Introduction," in *Church and Jewish People: New Considerations* (New York: Paulist Press, 1992), 2.

portant theological task involves "translating" this teaching into the commonsense language of contemporary culture.[119]

The promulgation of *Nostra Aetate* has precipitated wide-ranging reflections on the theological significance of Jewish-Christian and inter-religious dialogue more generally. Soloveitchik's voice should be included in these conversations. Consider two recent developments. One highlights cooperation, and the other particularity and difference. Paul Knitter claims that the most enduring achievement of *Nostra Aetate* is its "exhortation to dialogue and collaboration;" and he observes that some fifty years after Vatican II, this "exhortation" has become an "obligation" in Pope Francis's 2013 *Evangelii Gaudium*.[120] And Jerusha Tanner Lamptey charts a movement from the theological inclusivism of *Nostra Aetate* towards a fuller "appreciation of differences and particularities" in Roman Catholic teachings on other religions. In addition to *Evangelii Gaudium*, she turns to Pope Francis's 2013 *Message to Muslims at the End of Ramadan*.[121] In the present context, I simply want to note that Knitter's and Lamptey's concerns are consonant with Soloveitchik's own emphases – on inter-religious cooperation in response to "socio-cultural and moral problems" and on the "distinctness and individuality" of faith communities in the plural.

It should be noted, though, that neither Knitter nor Lamptey attend to Jewish-Christian dialogue per se. An important trajectory

---

119. See, for instance, Soloveitchik, "Though Shouldst Enter the Covenant of the Lord," 130. "One dwelling place of the Eternal God is within the human heart. The second dwelling place of the Eternal God is inside the human brain. . . . When a person becomes a penitent it is because the Holy One, blessed be He, who is present within him has aroused and altered him to do so." Cf. Lonergan, *Method in Theology*, 251, "Foundational reality . . . is conversion: religious, moral, and intellectual. Normally it is intellectual conversion as the fruit of both religious and moral conversion; it is moral conversion as the fruit of religious conversion; it is religious conversion as the fruit of God's gift of his grace."

120. Paul F. Knitter, "*Nostra Aetate*: A Milestone in the History of Religions? From Competition to Cooperation," in *The Future of Interreligious Dialogue*, ed. Charles L. Cohen, Paul F. Knitter, and Ulrich Rosenhagen (Maryknoll: Orbis Books, 2017), 56–57.

121. Jerusha Tanner Lamptey, "Beyond the Rays of Truth: *Nostra Aetate*, Islam, and the Value of Difference," in *The Future of Interreligious Dialogue*, 214–217.

in post-Vatican II Roman Catholic teaching emphasizes the uniqueness of Jewish-Christian dialogue and questions whether such dialogue should even be called inter-religious. As one reads in "The
Gifts and the Calling of God are Irrevocable," a document that appeared in 2015, "Christianity is by its roots connected with Judaism
as with no other religion. Therefore the Jewish-Christian dialogue
can only with reservations be termed 'interreligious dialogue' in the
true sense of the expression; one could however speak of a kind of
'intra-religious' or 'intra–familial' dialogue sui generis."[122] Such an
approach recognizes, in Novak's words, that Judaism and Christianity share "common historical roots in the Old Testament and the
Pharisaic Judaism of the late Second Temple period;"[123] but it also
runs the risk of overlooking the significance of the "individuality
and distinctiveness" of Jewish and Christian faith commitments.
Gavin D'Costa raises an important issue in this regard. He cautions

---

122. "The Gifts and the Calling of God are Irrevocable," chapter 2.20. The
document continues:
    In his address in the Roman Synagogue on 13 April 1986 Saint Pope John Paul
II expressed this situation in these words: "The Jewish religion is not 'extrinsic' to
us but in a certain way is 'intrinsic' to our own religion. With Judaism therefore
we have a relationship which we do not have with any other religion. You are our
dearly beloved brothers and, in a certain way, it could be said that you are our
elder brothers."
    Cf. "Confrontation," 21–23, for Soloveitchik's comments on the language of
brotherhood to describe Jewish-Christian relations.
123. David Novak, "From Supersessionism to Parallelism in Jewish-Christian Dialogue," in *Talking with Christians: Musings of a Jewish Theologian*
(Grand Rapids: William B. Eerdmans Publishing Company, 2005), 23–24. Cf.
Jewish-Christian Dialogue, 114, where Novak writes: "No Jew, no matter how
well versed in Christianity, can ever understand the covenantal intimacy of the
Eucharist, without first literally becoming Christian;" in similar fashion, "No
Christian … can ever directly understand the covenantal intimacy of the Sab-
bath." In Soloveitchik's language, the "common historical roots" that Jews and
Christians share have to do with the "dimension of culture," whereas the lived
experience of "covenantal intimacy" directs our attention to the "dimension of
faith." See "Confrontation," 22–24, where Soloveitchik allows that one may speak
of "a common tradition uniting two faith communities such as the Christian and
the Judaic … if one looks upon a faith community under an historico-cultural
aspect;" but he emphasizes that when one turns to the "dimension of faith," the
incommensurability of the Jewish and Christian theological *logoi*, which reflect
different underlying apocalyptic experiences, comes to the fore.

that "this internalizing affirmation of 'Judaism' could well give rise to a 'new danger of failing to take seriously the otherness and diversity of Judaism?'"[124] Such a failure, from Soloveitchik's perspective, would obviate the possibility of dialogical encounter between Jews and Christians before it got underway.

It is striking that even before the conclusion of the Second Ecumenical Council, Soloveitchik, who decried Jewish involvement in theological discussions at Vatican II, articulated an approach to Jewish-Christian dialogue that represents an important mapping of the "new horizon" that the promulgation of *Nostra Aetate* inaugurated. As Korn puts it, "If R. Soloveitchik could not have predicted the revolution started by *Nostra Aetate*, perhaps he was able to dream of its possibility."[125] Not only do Soloveitchik's writings on Jewish-Christian relations recognize the possibility of a transformed relationship between Jews and Christians, they also provide a biblical and theological "frame of reference" within which later developments such as *To Do the Will of Our Father in Heaven* can find their proper place.[126] Further, they offer an important counterpoint to the "internalizing affirmation" of Judaism that one finds in some Christian theology – an approach that runs the risk of neglecting the "metaphysical distance" between Judaism and Christianity that the "incommensurate" revelations of the Torah from Sinai and the incarnation, crucifixion, and resurrection of Christ Jesus together establish.

---

124. Gavin D'Costa, "Between Doctrine and Discernment: The Question of the Jewish People and the Development of Doctrine Arising from Vatican II," in *The Past, Present, and Future of Interreligious Dialogue*, ed. Terrence Merrigan and John Friday (Oxford: Oxford University Press, 2017), 75.

125. Korn, "The Man of Faith and Religious Dialogue," 308.

126. See "The Lonely Man of Faith," 9. "Before beginning the analysis, we must determine within which frame of reference, psychologico-empirical or theologico-Biblical, should our dilemma be described."

Author Biographies

AHRENS, JEHOSCHUA

Rabbi Dr. Jehoschua Ahrens is Director Central Europe of the Center for Jewish-Christian Understanding in Jerusalem. He is a board member of the German Coordinating-Council for Christian-Jewish cooperation organizations and of the Muslim Jewish Leadership Council. In 2017 he was awarded the papal medal by Pope Francis personally for his work in Jewish-Catholic relations. Rabbi Ahrens is one of the initiators and authors of *To Do the Will of Our Father in Heaven.*

BLICKLE, KARL-HERMANN

Karl-Hermann Blickle is an entrepreneur and engaged in international business ethics and interreligious dialogue. He is chairman of the interreligious Stuttgart Lehrhaus Foundation and the S.H.A.R.E. Foundation for Microfinance, Fair Trade and Peacebuilding.

BOLLAG, DAVID

Rabbi Dr. David Bollag is a Modern-Orthodox Rabbi and lecturer in Jewish Studies at the Universities of Zurich and Lucerne. He has served as Rabbi in Switzerland, Germany and Israel, is the author of several books, and is actively involved in the Jewish-Christian dialogue. Rabbi Bollag was among the first rabbis to shape and sign the Orthodox Rabbinic Statement on Christianity and has co-published the German edition of a book about the Statement.

CUNNINGHAM, PHILIP

Philip A. Cunningham is Professor of Theology and Director of the Institute for Jewish-Catholic Relations of Saint Joseph's University in Philadelphia. He is also Immediate Past President of the International Council of Christians and Jews and webmaster for the Council of Centers on Jewish-Christian Relations (ccjr.us).

MCDERMOTT, GERALD
Gerald R. Mcdermott holds the Anglican Chair of Divinity at Beeson Divinity School in Birmingham, Alabama. He is editor of *The New Christian Zionism: Fresh Perspectives on Israel and the Land* (Inter-Varsity) and author of *Israel Matters: Why Christians Must Think Differently about the People and the Land* (Brazos).

DOLAN, TIMOTHY
Cardinal Timothy Dolan is Archbishop of New York. He was named Cardinal by Pope Benedict XVI in 2012, and previously was Archbishop of Milwaukee. Prior to that he served as secretary to the Apostolic Nuncio in DC, as a professor at Kenrick Seminary and St. Louis University, and as rector of the North American College in Rome. More recently he has served as President of the United States Conference of Catholic Bishops, Catholic Relief Services, and the co-chair of the National Jewish-Catholic Dialogue.

GREENBERG, IRVING
Rabbi Dr. Irving Greenberg served in the Orthodox Rabbinate and as Professor of Jewish Studies at City College of City University of New York. He served for 23 years as a Founding President of the educational organization CLAL: The National Jewish Center for Learning and Leadership and ten years as Founding President of the Jewish Life Network/ Steinhardt Foundation. Among his many writings are: *Living in the Image of God* and *For the Sake of Heaven and Earth: The New Encounter between Judaism and Christianity*. He is one of the initiators and authors of *To Do the Will of Our Father in Heaven*.

GREGERMAN, ADAM
Adam Gregerman is Associate Professor in the Department of Theology and Religious Studies and Associate Director of the Institute for Jewish-Catholic Relations of Saint Joseph's University in Philadelphia. He is vice-chair of the board of the Council of Centers on Jewish-Christian Relations and a member of the Committee on Ethics, Religion, and the Holocaust at the United States Holocaust Memorial Museum.

JOHNSTON, MURRAY
Professor Murray Johnston teaches philosophy and religion at Champlain College in Quebec. He wrote his Master's thesis on the epistemology of Rabbi Joseph Soloveitchik and is presently completing a

doctoral degree in Philosophical Theology in the field of Jewish-Christian dialogue. He is an associate of the Holy Cross Order, an Anglican Benedictine community in Canada and the United States.

KORN, EUGENE

Eugene Korn resides in Jerusalem and is the former Academic Director of the Center for Jewish-Christian Understanding in Jerusalem, which he helped found. He has served as Executive Director of the Center for Christian-Jewish Understanding at Sacred Heart University and National Director of Interfaith Affairs at the Anti-Defamation League. His writings on Jewish ethics and theology have been translated into Hebrew, Italian, German and Spanish. He holds a doctorate in philosophy from Columbia University and was ordained as Rabbi by Pirchei Shoshanim program of the Israeli Rabbinate. He was one of the first rabbis to support and shape *To Do the Will of Our Father in Heaven.*

LENK, MARCIE

Dr. Marcie Lenk has devoted her intellectual life and career to organizing educational programs and teaching Jews and Christians (and people of other faiths) to appreciate the basic texts, ideas, history and faith of the other. She earned a doctorate at Harvard University in 2010 with a dissertation entitled, *The Apostolic Constitutions: Judaism and Anti-Judaism in the Construction of Christianity.* She also holds degrees from Harvard Divinity School and Yeshiva University.

MELTZER, ALON

Rabbi Alon Meltzer currently lives in Sydney, Australia, where he is the Rabbi of Or Chadash Synagogue and Director of Programs at Shalom. He earned Masters degrees from the University of Auckland in Sociology, from Bernard Revel Graduate School in Medieval Jewish History, and Rabbinic Ordination from Rabbi Isaac Elchanan Theological Seminary of Yeshiva University. He is now pursuing a doctorate at Victoria University, and has represented the Australian Jewish Community at local, national and international interfaith gatherings.

PETTIT, PETER

Peter A. Pettit is Director Emeritus of the Institute for Jewish-Christian Understanding of Muhlenberg College, in Allentown, Pennsylvania, USA. He currently serves as Teaching Pastor at St. Paul Lutheran Church in Davenport, Iowa and Vice-President of the Friends and Sponsors of the Martin Buber House in Heppenheim, Germany. He is on the North American faculty of the Shalom Hartman Institute and the Evangelical Lutheran Church in America's Consultative Panel on Lutheran-Jewish Relations.

RISKIN, SHLOMO

Rabbi Shlomo Riskin is Founder, Chancellor Emeritus and Rosh HaYeshiva of Ohr Torah Stone. He also serves as the Chief Rabbi of Efrat. His contributions to Israel and world Jewry over the course of the past five decades have been instrumental in shaping today's Modern Orthodox society. He earned a doctorate in Jewish Studies from New York University, and is one of the initiators and authors of *To Do the Will of Our Father in Heaven.*

ROSEN, DAVID

David Rosen, KSG CBE, is the International Director of Interreligious Affairs of the American Jewish Committee and a member of the Israel Chief Rabbinate's Commission for Interreligious Relations. He is President of the world interfaith body Religions for Peace, Honorary President of the International Council of Christians and Jews, and a past chairman of the International Jewish Committee for Interreligious Consultations. He is the former Chief Rabbi of Ireland. Rabbi Rosen is one of the initator and authors of *To Do the Will of Our Father in Heaven.*

RUTISHAUSER, CHRISTIAN

Dr. Christian M. Rutishauser, SJ is Provincial of the Jesuits in Switzerland. He studied Philosophy and Theology in Fribourg, Lyon, Lucerne and Jerusalem. He is the former Program Director of the Lassalle-Haus Bad Schönbrunn, Center for Spirituality, Interreligious Dialogue and Social Responsibility in Switzerland. He was previously Lecturer in Jewish Studies in Munich, Fribourg, Rome and Jerusalem, member of the Swiss and German Episcopal Conference Commissions for the Dialogue with Judaism, and has been Permanent Councilor of the Pope for Dialogue with Judaism since 2014.

SIMKOVITCH, MALKA

Dr. Malka Z. Simkovich holds the Crown-Ryan Chair of Jewish Studies and Director of the Catholic-Jewish Studies Program at Catholic Theological Union in Chicago. She is the author of *The Making of Jewish Universalism: From Exile to Alexandria,* and *Discovering Second*

Temple Literature: The Scriptures and Stories That Shaped Early Judaism, which received the 2019 AJL Judaica Reference Honor Award.

SKORKA, ABRAHAM

Rabbi Dr. Abraham (Armando) Skorka was ordained by the Latin-American Rabbinical Seminary in Buenos Aires. Currently he is University Professor at the Saint Joseph's University in Philadelphia. He was Honorary Professor of Jewish Law, Salvador's University of Argentina, and has been awarded the Doctor of Hebrew Letters, *honoris causa*, by both The Jewish Theological Seminary of America and the Pontifical Catholic University of Argentina, as well as Doctor of Theology, *honoris causa*, by Sacred Heart University in Fairfield, Connecticut. He is Rabbi Emeritus of the Benei Tikva Congregation and Rector Emeritus of the Latin-American Rabbinical Seminary. Rabbi Skorka is the author of many books and articles, and co-author with Pope Francis of *On Heaven and Earth*.

SPERBER, DANIEL

Daniel Sperber is a leading scholar of Jewish law, customs and ethics. He was Dean of the Faculty of Jewish Studies at Bar Ilan University, where he was also President of the Jesselson Institute for Advance Torah Studies. In 1992 he was awarded the Israel Prize for Jewish Studies. He has published more than 30 books and 400 articles on Talmudic culture, Jewish law, and Jewish tradition facing modern problems. Rabbi Sperber holds a Ph.D. in Classics and Hebrew Studies from University College in London. Today he is Rabbi of Menachem Zion Synagogue in the Old City of Jerusalem.

STRENGER, GABRIEL

Gabriel Strenger was born in Basel, Switzerland, and today lives and works in Jerusalem as a clinical psychologist. He is a lecturer in Psychoanalytical Psychotherapy at the Magid Institute of the Hebrew University of Jerusalem. Gabriel Strenger is active in the German-speaking world teaching Torah, lecturing and singing at different institutes, and engaging in interreligious dialogue. His books *Jüdische Spiritualität* ("Jewish Spirituality," 2016) and *Die Kunst des Betens* ("The Art of Prayer," 2019) were published by Morascha Press in Basel.

VERHÜLSDONK, ANDREAS

Andreas Verhülsdonk is a student of French literature and theology. He earned a doctorate in this field, with a thesis on the French intellectual, Félicité Lamennais. Since 2000 he has worked in the Secretariat of the German Bishops' Conference. His tasks include the relationship with the Jewish community in Germany.

WILLIAMS, ROWAN

Dr. Rowan Douglas Williams, Baron Williams of Oystermouth, Doctor of Philosophy and Doctor of Divinity, is a Welsh Anglican bishop and theologian. He was archbishop of Canterbury from 2002 to 2012 and spent much of his earlier career as an academic at the universities of Cambridge and Oxford. He is currently Master of Magdalene College. In addition to writing over thirty theological and historical texts, Dr. Williams is a poet, and his collection *The Poems of Rowan Williams* was long-listed for the Wales Book of the Year award in 2004. Some of the eleven languages he speaks and/or reads are English, Welsh, Spanish, French, German, Russian, Greek, and Biblical Hebrew. He is considered one of the foremost Christian philosophers of our day.

ZOLOTH, LAURIE

Laurie Zoloth, Ph.D., is the Margaret E. Burton Professor of Religion and Ethics, and Senior Advisor to the Provost for Programs in Social Ethics at the University of Chicago.